THE SOUND OF LAUGHTER

THE SOUND OF LAUGHTER

PETER KAY

C
Century · London

Published by Century 2006

2 4 6 8 10 9 7 5 3

Copyright © Peter Kay 2006

Peter Kay has asserted his right under the Copyright, Designs
and Patents Act 1988 to be identified as the author of this work

This book is a work of non-fiction based on the life, experiences and
recollections of the author. In some cases names of people, places, and details of
events have been changed and characters created for artistic purposes and to
protect the privacy of others.

First published in Great Britain in 2006 by
Century
Random House, 20 Vauxhall Bridge Road,
London SW1V 2SA

www.randomhouse.co.uk

Addresses for companies within The Random House Group Limited can be
found at: www.randomhouse.co.uk

The Random House Group Limited Reg. No. 954009

A CIP catalogue record for this book
is available from the British Library

ISBN (from Jan 2007) 9781846051616

ISBN 1 8460 5161 4

The Random House Group Limited makes every effort to ensure that the
papers used in its books are made from trees that have been legally sourced
from well-managed and credibly certified forests. Our paper procurement
policy can be found at: www.randomhouse.co.uk/paper.htm

Picture credit: *Diff'rent Strokes* © Sipa/Rex Feature
Typeset by SX Composing DTP, Rayleigh, Essex
Printed and bound in Great Britain by
Mackays of Chatham plc, Chatham, Kent

For Charlie Michael and Michael John

Contents

Chapter One

Oscar's Lipstick

Ding Dong! Was that the doorbell? You can never be too sure. I didn't get up to answer it. I waited for it to ring again and confirm my suspicions. I waited and I listened. I listened by leaning my head forward and tilting it slightly to one side. Everyone knows that when you lean forward and tilt your head to one side the volume of life goes up.

Ding Dong! Now that made me jump, even though I was expecting it, like when I'm staring at my toaster waiting impatiently for my toast to pop up . . . when it does I jump, every time, never fails.

I've always disliked doorbells, but this has become worse since I got into showbiz. Most people who have experienced success have this fear of getting caught, found out, the-dream-is-over-type fear. My own version of the fear is that the Showbiz Police have come to take it all back. I imagine them stood at the door in green tights and holding a scroll like those blokes out of *Shrek 2*. There's two of them, one plays an introductory bugle, the other clears his animated throat:

'I'm sorry, Mr Kay, but I have orders to tell you that you've had a good run, sunshine, but the time has come for you to go back to your cardboard-crushing job at Netto supermarket.' He puts his hand out. 'House and car keys please.'

But I wasn't enjoying any kind of success when the doorbell rang in 1990. There was a completely different reason for my fear. It was my driving instructor ringing the doorbell and the time had come for my first ever driving lesson.

Raymond was his name. He was big burly fella, constantly tanned, like a cross between Bully from *Bullseye* and a fat Des O'Connor. If you can picture that, then I think you need help.

It wasn't the first time I'd met Raymond. He'd been my mum's driving instructor a few years before. I'd often seen my mum sat nervously in Raymond's Montego by the side of the laundrette, which was directly opposite our house. Incidentally, ours was a Victorian terrace house, a bit like Coronation Street but with a posh four-foot garden at the front. For some reason every gable-end house was a shop. We had a fruit shop at one end of the row, a chippie at the other (Elizabeth's beautiful fish, before she moved to Lytham) and directly opposite a TV-repair shop and the laundrette. I'd spent my life in that laundrette before we got a washing machine. My mum used to go in three times a week with three big bags and me in a pram. Apparently I used to sit in my pram singing 'Una Paloma Blanca' to the women. Years later me and R Julie used to play tennis up against the gable end of the laundrette during Wimbledon fortnight with the other local kids. That's where Raymond parked up smoking his pipe. Usually he'd be snapping at my mum because she was over-revving and couldn't find her biting point. But the advice must have paid off, because after three attempts my mum finally passed her test. We never bought a car though, we simply couldn't afford one. Nowadays my mum won't even consider it, she says there's too much traffic on the roads.

So going out in a car was a treat when I was growing up. I can still remember the excitement waiting for my Uncle Tony to swing around the side of the laundrette in his navy Sierra (well, if truth be told he wasn't my real Uncle Tony but my dad had borrowed his orbital sander once, so he was as good as). He was a tall, wiry man with a pencil moustache, a bit anaemic-looking. As long as I'd known him, he'd always looked as if he was at death's door, but he's seventy-two now and still banging on. He'll outlive us all. He'd take R Julie and me out for the day, usually to the seaside, or if it was raining he'd take us ice skating in Blackburn. I was just happy to be travelling in a car.

I was never a big fan of ice skating. I could never get the hang of it. That and the fact it's so bloody slippy out on the ice. I also think ice-skating rinks are a haven for paedophiles, skating around all day, hanging on to kids' heads, pretending to fall over. 'They should hang them on the Lottery', as my grandad used to say. When the bodies drop, the feet set the balls rolling.

I took a girlfriend ice skating once on our second date and I fell and broke my arm in two places. Luckily the whole disaster worked out for the best as the girl took pity on my incompetence and eventually she married me (I hasten to add there was a five-year gap between the broken arm and the wedding day).

Ding Dong! Hold on, I've got to answer this fecking door. I opened it nervously clutching my provisional.

'Hello, Peter, are you ready, son?' said Raymond.

'I suppose,' I said.

'Is your mum in?' he said, peering over my shoulder.

'Yeah, she's in the backyard bathing the hamster.'

'Mind if I say hello?' And before I could say 'no' he was halfway down the hall whistling the theme from *The Deer Hunter*.

Bloody hell, I wanted to get going, it was costing me £12 an hour for this and we were already down to £11.50.

I could see my mum through the kitchen window. She was in the backyard wearing pink Marigolds, struggling to hold the hamster in one hand and prise the top off the Vosene with the other.

R Julie had bought it from the pet shop beside the convent. We'd all been expecting a playful little thing, but as soon as my dad tried to stroke it, it took a chunk out of his wrist.

'Oooo, the vicious little swine,' my dad said as he ran to the medicine cupboard dripping blood everywhere.

After further investigation (R Julie borrowed a book on hamsters from the library) we discovered it was a Russian hamster and that they weren't the friendliest of creatures. I used to hear it moodily thrashing around in its cage, mumbling things in Russian. Often we'd wake to find bits of straw and tiny bottles of vodka strewn all over the kitchen floor. I'm joking of course, we never had any straw. Anyway, as with all the other pets we ever owned, eventually it fell victim to the Kay family curse and dropped dead. When exactly, though, we never knew, because it slept all day and nobody dared go near the vicious little sod so it could have been dead for weeks. In fact, if it hadn't been for me poking it relentlessly with a biro in the middle of the *Brookside* omnibus it might have lain there stiff as a board for months.

'Hello, Deirdre,' said Raymond. 'Have you not got yourself a car yet?'

'Hello, Ray. Have you got time for a cup of tea?'

No he hasn't got time, I thought as I shook my head violently

4

and pointed towards the souvenir Pope John Paul II clock on the wall in the kitchen.

'I better not, Deirdre I've got to take this lad up the bypass,' he said, winking at me. I gave him a nervous double take and had a quick check for a wedding ring.

'Is it a he or a she?' said Raymond inquisitively as he groped towards the hamster cage.

'We've no idea, nobody's ever got close enough to check because he –' and before my mum could say the word 'bites' Raymond was leaping around the backyard with the hamster's teeth embedded into his index finger.

I was now ten minutes into my first driving lesson and I hadn't seen hide nor hair of a steering wheel.

When I finally sat in the passenger seat of Raymond's Montego I couldn't help but stare at his blood-soaked bandage as it dangled over his gearbox.

'This is the handbrake, son,' he said with a quiver of discomfort in his voice and he pointed to the handbrake. I nodded in amazement but I knew damn well what a handbrake was, I'd seen enough episodes of *The Dukes of Hazzard*, plus I'd also released a handbrake myself – it was on a milk float at the top of Mercia Street in 1979.

We saw it parked at the top of the hill. The milkman was half-way down the street chatting to a woman and showing off his yogurts.

'Go on, I dare you,' said Jason Mullet. I said I didn't even know what a handbrake was, let alone know how to release one. 'It's the black stick in the middle,' said Troy Moran. 'Just pull it down and leg it, I double-dare you.' 'Now hold on,' I said, 'I might only be six years old but nobody is going to double-dare me and get away with it.' I checked to see if the milkman was still preoccupied then climbed into the milk float and delicately released the handbrake. And ever so slowly the float began to move. I quickly jumped out of the front seat and ran back to my so-called friends. All three of us stood with our mouths open and watched as the milk float advanced down the street, picking up speed and heading towards the milkman.

His attention caught by the rattle of a thousand gold tops, the milkman spun round in slow motion to find a year's wages charging towards him. He let out a high-pitched yelp, you know, the kind a dog makes when you fire an air rifle at its genitals (or maybe you don't).

Dropping his yogurts, the milkman leapt on board the milk float as it shot past him and, reaching for the steering wheel, managed to turn the float around 360 degrees. I looked on quite impressed with his manoeuvre until I noticed he was now coming up the hill towards us with thunder in his eyes. 'Stay there, you little bastards,' he shouted.

As if we would. We legged it – well, myself and Troy Moran did, but as Jason suffered from spina bifida we had no choice but to leave him. He tried his best but even he couldn't outrun a milk float travelling at two miles an hour. So he did what any respectable child of six would do in that situation and shopped the lot of us.

Later we were paid a visit from our local bobby, PC Hassan. He gave me a bit of a talking-to then offered me a Lion bar when I started to cry. But my dad gave me a clip round the ear when he got home from work. Happy days.

Thank God this was in the days before the ASBO had been invented, otherwise my life could have gone in a completely different direction and instead of writing this I could have been learning how to yacht with a bunch of glue-sniffers on taxpayers' money. Doesn't sound so bad when I put it like that.

So I got off lightly with the milk-float incident and hadn't touched a handbrake since.

'Don't be frightened of it, son, it's only a handbrake,' said Raymond. 'Just push the button in at the top with your thumb and lower it slowly.'

Then, slipping the gearstick into first, Raymond finally drove us away.

'Another one bites the dust,' said my mum as she dropped the dead hamster down the toilet. We'd been through that many pets by this point I'm surprised we weren't under investigation by the RSPCA. We'd had the lot: budgies, goldfish, two rabbits – Mork and Mindy (we'd been shot of them since Live Aid and we were still finding Maltesers behind the skirting boards), a tortoise called Flash. I could go on . . .

. . . in fact I will. The last family pet that we ever had was a dog called Oscar. He was a cross between a springer spaniel and a little bastard. Well, that's what my dad used to shout whenever he came downstairs and slipped at the bottom in Oscar's shit. He wasn't a bad dog, but he liked to eat CDs and get his lipstick out when visitors called round. It'd be very embarrassing for everybody concerned as he walked back and forth in front of the TV, smiling and his lipstick out glistening in the glare of the screen. It was quite a talent, in fact I was actually considering writing to *That's Life* but then he died.

That was a sad day. I was in the bath on a Sunday afternoon listening to Right Said Fred (don't ask) and the next thing I heard was R Julie shouting upstairs:

'Peter, come down here quick and bring the Dettol.'

I leapt out of the bath, ran downstairs to see Oscar taking his last dying breath in the backyard.

R Julie said he'd gotten out through a hole in the back gate, and managed to make it as far as Hibernia Street before he got into a fight with some other dogs. Well, I think it was other dogs because he had bite marks on his lipstick.

It was heartbreaking. Helpless and in pain, Oscar took one last look at us and then, to the sound of 'Deeply Dippy' echoing from the upstairs bathroom, he shit himself and died.

Bloody hell, I'm filling up. Writing this has brought it all back . . . just let me get a tissue . . . . where are they? . . . . That's better. I had to ring my Uncle Tony and ask him if he'd mind giving me a lift up to the pet crematorium on the other side of town (well, I say crematorium, it was more of an allotment with an oven). Uncle Tony wasn't best pleased as he was in the middle of watching the Grand Final of *Masterchef*.

We lowered Oscar into an empty Walkers crisp box – it was all I could find at short notice – put him in the boot and drove off.

We pulled off the main road and on to the set of *The Blair Witch Project*. We'd've been lost if it hadn't been for A4 Day-Glo cards with arrows drawn on them nailed to every third tree. Eventually, we came across a caravan sat in the middle of the woods with no wheels. We were greeted at the door by a white woman with dreadlocks carrying a shovel.

'What?' she said aggressively.

I nodded down to the box we were holding.

'Oh right, you better come in,' she said and retreated inside.

We followed her through some beads into her front room/

mortuary. There was a foul stench in the air. She motioned for us to come in further. Reluctantly we walked forward. The woman pointed to a 'No Smoking' sign on the wall by the door which was odd as neither of us was smoking. Then she pointed to a couple of other signs on the adjacent wall. 'Cash Only' and 'Two for a Tenner' were written in the same felt tip on the same Day-Glo card that we'd seen in the woods, only she'd made a bit of an effort with these and cut them into star shapes. I started to get the creeps. Well, I had every reason to, I was stood in a static caravan holding a dead dog in a crisp box.

Meanwhile, back on my driving lesson Raymond was still behind the wheel and cruising down a busy main road.

We slowed down at the pelican crossing and an Asian lady pulled up alongside of us in a Mercedes. Raymond shook his head.

'That shouldn't be allowed . . . look at her, she can't even see over the steering wheel.' Then he turned to me, looked me straight in the eye and said: 'If you ever see me driving round sat on cushions, shoot me.'

I had no idea what he was talking about – all I wanted to do was drive. Wasn't that the whole point of having a driving lesson, that you drove? In my head I was screaming, 'Gimme the wheel, fat boy,' but in reality I just smiled politely and nodded.

We drove to an industrial park on the outskirts of town and finally he turned to me and said:

'Right, now it's your turn.' Thank God for that, there was only twenty minutes left.

I found sitting behind a steering wheel a very liberating experience. It was the first one I'd sat behind since the dodgems at

Southport Pleasure Park. But this was much better, especially because I didn't have some gyppo hanging off the back of my seat asking me for a quid.

I'd spent my whole life dreaming of this moment. Ever since I'd played with toy cars as a child. Pushing them round on the floor in the back room at home, in and out of table legs, over my dad's slippers, making that engine noise, you know the one, the higher the gear, the higher the humming noise. I'd drive it as far as the tips of my fingers would stretch and then with a screech of brakes I'd spin it around and drive it back towards me. Matchbox, Corgi, I had the lot, sports cars, buses, even a London taxi. I'd line them up along the fireplace. Then they'd take part in the biggest race in the world until my mum shouted me for tea.

If I wasn't playing with cars then I'd be lying on the floor in front of the TV drawing them, designing them. I drew supercars, cars that could fly, cars that performed spectacular stunts I'd seen in James Bond films or anything with Burt Reynolds. I drew cars in every colour my bumper pack of felt tips would allow.

With this love of cars you can imagine my joy on Christmas Day in 1980 when Father Christmas brought me a 'Race 'n' Chase'. 'Yee-ha,' I screamed in the naff American accent that I'd seen in the advert a thousand times on TV (well, it feels like a thousand times when you're seven). It was a fantastic end to a tough few weeks. My dad had lost his job and some fella called John Lennon had been shot and everybody seemed to be crying all the time.

I couldn't wait to get it out of the box and play with it but all that had to wait till after we got back from Christmas Day Mass. I was so made up that Santa had brought it for me. With the usual threats from my parents of 'no presents' unless I behaved, things had been a bit touch and go for a while.

The emotional blackmail of Christmas has become an epidemic with parents these days.

They've successfully managed to twist a harmless folk tale into an opportunity for a bit of peace and quiet. I caught a couple of close friends of mine (who will remain anonymous for my own safety) telling their four-year-old son that if he saw the red light flash on the alarm sensor in the corner of the room it meant that Father Christmas was watching him and checking he was being a good boy. Then I watched the four-year-old tiptoe around the room with his eyes fixed on the sensor. And every time it lit up, he'd wave at it and smile. It's extraordinary what people will do for a bit of peace. It's almost as bad as the mother who told all her children that whenever they heard the ice-cream van chiming, it actually meant it'd run out of ice cream. Now that is cruel.

Eventually I discovered, like all children do, that Father Christmas didn't exist, only I had the grave misfortune of finding out on Christmas Eve.

I was lying in bed with one eye open, straining to hear the sound of sleigh bells, when instead I heard my parents shouting in the front street. I immediately jumped out of bed and climbed up on to my bedding box so that I could get a better look out of the window.

I could see my dad and he'd dropped what appeared to be a bin bag full of toys on the ground. I could make out an Etch-a-Sketch out of its box in the snow and a Tonka Toy Dump Truck.

'Bloody hell, Deirdre,' he shouted to my mum who was busy chasing a Girl's World doll's head as it rolled down the road and into the gutter.

Devastated, I climbed back under my duvet. How could they have lied to me all these years? How could so many people have kept it a secret from me? And why had they got me an Etch-a-Sketch when they knew damn well I wanted an Atari games console with free Pac-Man and Frogger?

I must admit I'd had been having my own suspicions about Father Christmas's existence.

The theory that one man could deliver presents to all the world's houses in one night? The magic-key theory? And one lone gunman firing from the top of the book depository when there was a second shot from the grassy knoll. Hold on, I've got all my theories mixed up.

Darren Martyn had said something at school about Father Christmas being 'a load of bollocks'. Then again, you could never believe anything he said. He came to school in a special taxi and was always touching his privates. He sells insurance now and drives a Mazda.

I'd also had my doubts when I was singing 'Jingle Bells' at the children's Christmas party down at the club. We had to sing it nine times as loud as we could before Father Christmas eventually appeared from behind the fire door. I knew something wasn't right as he was in a wheelchair and was wearing grey slip-on shoes. I'll never forget it.

But the shameful scene I witnessed in the front street that Christmas Eve confirmed my suspicions for ever. Crushed and inconsolable, I cried myself to sleep that night. It was just too much for a boy of nineteen to take in.

'Now put your left foot down on the clutch and lift your right foot up off the accelerator until you feel your biting point,' said Raymond. Biting point? Hadn't we just had one of them back at home with the hamster. But Raymond still kept chanting it over and over again. 'Biting point, biting point.' I didn't understand what he was saying. It was like being back in Electronics at school with Mr Booth, only now I wasn't trying to make a disco rope light, I was trying to drive a car.

'Lift your right foot up and put your left foot down, up, down, up, down,' he said impatiently. I was desperate to sing the 'Hokey-Cokey' back to him but I knew he wouldn't have been amused. I just did what he said and miraculously I started to feel the car come alive. My heart began to race as I felt the engine revving up and I thought, 'That's me, I'm doing that,' and with a huge smile across my face I raised my right foot off the accelerator, stalled the engine and we both lunged forward.

'Never mind,' said Raymond, 'let's take five,' then he got out his pipe and started to light it.

Take five? It's taken me three-quarters of an hour to get this far, you can't stop now. But we did. He chatted to me about a number of things, the previous night's episode of *Twin Peaks*, the effect that Velcro has had on our everyday lives and the death of Sammy Davis Jr to which he remarked, 'We was robbed.'

I was completely gobsmacked, infuriated and gobsmacked again!

Finally he let me have one more go at starting the car. I stalled it again. Then we swapped places and drove home in silence. Well, apart from Raymond whistling the theme from *Twin Peaks*.

He pulled up beside the laundrette.

'So same time next week then?' he said as I got out of the car.

I nodded back at him politely but inside I was seething. Twelve bloody pounds and for what? A quarter of an hour behind the wheel and two lungs full of pipe smoke.

Maybe I expected too much on my first lesson? I had thought he might have let me go for a spin on the motorway or maybe even drive through some cardboard boxes down a backstreet, like Starsky and Hutch. But no.

I had a few more lessons with Raymond, but things didn't really improve and I soon began to realise why it'd taken my mum three attempts to pass. We did get round to covering some basic manoeuvres – how to do a three-point turn and what pipe shag to buy from the duty-free shop in Ostend. But after nine lessons with Raymond I'd had enough. I'd also had enough of him smoking that bloody awful pipe. My clothes would stink when I got home and my driving was starting to become dangerous as I couldn't see out of the windscreen half of the time for tobacco smoke. My grandad was right when he said that anybody who smokes a pipe has got two arseholes.

The final straw came when he promised to show me some photos of his holiday to Bulgaria. I cancelled my next lesson, permanently. What a waste of time and money, and the question still remained: would I ever learn to drive?

Chapter Two

Trevor McDonald's Nose

I used to have a paper round every night after school. I'd be out delivering the *Bolton Evening News*, in all weathers. It was a proper paper round too, for paying customers. I wasn't pretending to deliver the free papers by dumping them in the canal and pocketing the money like some folk did. I'll not name names but you know who you are. No, I was one of the many devoted paper boys and girls of this country, staggering around the streets of suburbia developing a curvature of the spine and other irreversible damage to our already fragile lumbar regions.

God only knows what shape we'll all be in, or indeed what shape we'll *be*, in years to come. All of us walk this earth with the knowledge that our backs could go at any moment and like a human game of Ker-Plunk it'll only be a matter of time before one wrong move will send us all crashing to the floor.

And no doubt my back will go at the worst possible moment, probably in years from now when I'm in the middle of a special charity *It's a Knockout* tournament, live on ITV6. I'll be up to my eyes in mud, dressed as Mr Blobby scrambling alongside John Leslie OBE and I'll suddenly hear a crack.

Or it could happen when I'm simply changing the bin bag in the kitchen. With the remains of yesterday's Sunday dinner smeared all over my fingers, I wobble up the path in that fine rain (that soaks you through) towards the wheelie bin and suddenly feel a twinge. I fall to my knees in agony and that's when a million evening papers will take their revenge (and don't forget there was also a property guide on Wednesdays). I've come to the conclusion over the years that thanks to the *Bolton Evening News* my body is now a walking time bomb.

But the weight of my sack never bothered me when I was fifteen; it was just a paper round to me and the one thing keeping me going was the £3.50 wage I got at the end of each week. That was a lot of money to me at the time – after all I had nothing else to judge it by – but it would pale into insignificance when I left school and got my first proper, grown-up job in a factory down the road.

My mate's dad had pulled a few strings, in fact if truth be told he did his own puppet shows (I'm joking of course). He managed to get me an interview with one of the supervisors, well, I say interview, an unshaven bloke with a stutter drove up to me in a forklift truck, nodded his head and shouted,

'He'll d-d-d-d-d-do, you can s-s-s-start M-M-M-Monday.'

Imagine my shock when I discovered I'd get a wage of £3.50 an hour, not a week, but £3.50 an hour. I was as happy as Larry as I danced home in the rain (who's Larry?). My mind filled with thoughts of how I was going to spend my first big wage. What was I going to do with all that money? Why, learn to drive of course and buy the original soundtrack to the motion picture *Buster* on cassette.

I'd passed my new workplace almost every day of my life. It was on the main bus route into town past the Esso garage, the only one on the road with a deluxe car wash, opened by Henry Cooper. Further down was the Co-op, later taken over by Spar (so near so Spar) where my mum used to treat me to a Tunnock's Teacake if I was good and an empty cardboard box to play with when I got home. Then there was the Kazee's Silk Centre, Quintin's Electrical which was massive (my nana said they wouldn't be happy till they owned the whole block) and the ever-glorious pop factory. My heart would always soar if I saw one of the many lorries rattling out of the gates loaded up with a million rainbow-coloured bottles on its back. Enough chemically coloured pop to last you a lifetime. At the bottom of the road stood a huge white factory. I must have seen the factory workers filing in and out of the iron gates hundreds of times over the years, but never once had I imagined that I'd be joining them.

Called F.H. Lee's, the company mainly manufactured tissue products. It was owned by the ex-Manchester City and England player, Francis Lee. When most footballers hang up their boots they progress naturally into the lucrative world of football commentary, but Franny had decided that his financial security lay in making bog rolls.

Apparently Mr Lee visited his factory on the odd occasion, but our paths never crossed. One thing I do know is that he knew how to look after his workers. At Christmas everybody got the choice of three gifts: a big bottle of whisky, a big turkey or a big tin of Quality Street.* I of course opted for a stroll down Quality Street and was presented with my gift the last Friday before Christmas.

*Everything seems big when you're sixteen.

With my willpower intact I'd managed to keep the tin of Quality Street sealed ready to give to my mum. But when I went to clock out at the end of my shift while trying to hold the tin under my arm, I lost balance and watched on helplessly as it smashed to the floor in slow motion, sending the chocolates shooting off in all directions.

Funnily enough, I wasn't short of assistance when it came to picking them up. I just wish they'd been as eager to hand them back to me, instead of sticking fistfuls of them into either their pockets or their mouths, whichever came first.

Heartbroken, I trudged home in the snow with the dented tin under my arm and I still remember the look of confusion my mum gave me on Christmas morning when she opened a tin of Quality Street to find sixteen chocolates (all hard ones), three buttons and a paper clip. Bastards.

We had no luck with chocolates that Christmas. My Uncle Finton drove up from London in his metallic-green Jaguar on a flying visit. As he left (after eating us out of house and home) he pulled a tin of Quality Street out the boot as a parting gift.

I've no idea if Uncle Finton was aware that his chocolates were a year past their sell-by date but it didn't take us long to find out, when we ended up bringing in the New Year with severe stomach cramps and the shits. So memorable was our discomfort that such ailments are now referred to in our house as 'going for a jog down Quality Street'.

Mr Lee's generosity didn't just stop at Christmas, oh God, no. Every fortnight he gave his workers 'a pack'. This consisted of a large polythene bag filled up with every product that the factory produced. You were given six toilet rolls (in a choice of assorted colours), a patterned kitchen roll, some industrial cling film and two rolls of the finest aluminium foil this side of Wigan. Well, my mum was over the moon when I first brought it home, she'd never seen as much foil and cling film in her life. In fact, it's seventeen years since I worked at Franny Lee's and I'm sure she's still got some of that industrial cling film on top of the cupboard somewhere.

I was told that Mr Lee and his associates made the noble gesture in an effort to put an end to the huge amount of thieving that was going on at the factory. Apparently staff were increasingly prone to jamming kitchen foil down their knickers and smuggling it home. It's like my Uncle Ronnie used to say:

'If it's not nailed down, I'll nick it.' Perhaps not the best motto to live your life by, especially if you work for Securicor like he did.

The job I'd got was on the evening shift so I only worked from five to nine, which was a bit like the Dolly Parton song but reversed. My mum used to make me a packed lunch every night and I was ready for it, I can tell you. Two tuna-mayonnaise-spread sandwiches, wrapped in foil (there was going to be no shortage of that from now on) and a couple of mint Yo Yos.

'Be careful at work and don't forget to give me three rings,' she shouted to me on my first night as I ran for the bus.

I remember feeling very nervous as I approached the gates. It was that noise. It got louder as I got nearer. I'd heard the noise of machinery many times when I was growing up. My dad was a labourer at various factories around town and sometimes I'd walk home from work with him – well, he'd walk, I'd ride my Grifter. While I was waiting for him to clock off I'd stand outside the factory listening to that noise of machinery. It was loud enough standing outside the factory – how much louder must it have sounded inside? After all these years the time had come for me to finally find out.

I followed a few other workers into the canteen. I think it was a canteen, as there was a drinks vending machine in the corner of the room. I looked at the picture on the front of it. A bone-china cup and saucer were perched on a white lace doily. Fresh tea was being poured into the cup, and out of focus in the distance, beyond the terrace, there was a field. I could just make out the blurred shapes of women in saris picking tea in the baking sunlight. That's why I was somewhat disappointed when I pushed the button labelled 'Tea' and after forty seconds and numerous bangs I was rewarded with a polystyrene cup which hesitantly began to fill up with a liquid that looked like Bisto gravy granules mixed with saliva. A whistle blew somewhere and everybody got up to leave. I had a quick sip as I headed for the door and, as I'd suspected, it tasted sod all like the Queen's English tea that I'd come to love and respect over the years.

Like a little lost sheep and without making eye contact I got to the back of the queue. I followed the others as they clocked on. Eventually it was my turn but I started to panic when I couldn't find a clocking-in card with my name on.

'Don't worry, I've still not got one and I've been here a month,' said a voice over my shoulder. I turned round to be greeted by a blond-haired lad wearing a faded Curiosity Killed the Cat tour T-shirt (I think it was the 'Misfit' tour of '86). His name was Mick Santiago and we were to become work buddies over the next few months. In fact, we even stayed in touch after Mick got sacked for getting someone else to clock in for him. He was enjoying a weekend at the Reading Festival and would have got away with it if he hadn't been caught on camera dancing to Transvision Vamp in a crowd shot. Apparently one of the supervisors almost choked on his beer when he saw it on the big screen down the pub. Mick got his P45 first thing Monday morning, but I think he was more upset about being caught on camera singing 'Baby I Don't Care' than he was about losing his job.

He went on the dole and I didn't see him for a while. Then he turned up at my front door one night out of the blue and so I invited him in for a cup of tea.

He was wittering on about how he'd been on a weekend retreat with Jobseekers and had caught the clap off a black Swedish midget. He said he then spent six hours queuing at the STD clinic just to have 'some bird jam an umbrella up my bell-end'. Then he ate all my mum's ginger nuts and left.

I slammed the front door, ran upstairs and spent the rest of the night scrubbing the bog with every type of cleaner I could get my mum's yellow Marigolds on. I even gave it a splash with some holy water from Lourdes that I found under the sink. (Well, you can never be too careful, can you?)

The last time I heard of Mick he'd fallen for a girl down at the Church of the Nazarene and was playing bass in a Christian steel band. They were on a 'The Lord Loves a Sinner' tour performing at a variety of prisons the length and breadth of Great Britain.

But that's a different story. Right now he was taking me to meet the foreman. I turned the corner to find what I can only describe as a truly overwhelming sight. There were literally hundreds of women frantically bashing away on production lines – I could barely make them out for the tissue paper that hung in the air, like a sunlit fog. The other thing I couldn't fail to notice was the heat – it wrapped round me like a blanket. The noise was incredible now, a combination of machinery pumping out tissue product, screeching forklifts, the raucous laughter of the women and Bobby Brown singing 'My Prerogative'. To this day I still get butterflies when I hear that song.

'So who gave you the job? Was it Morris?' said Mick as he led me towards the foil room

'I don't know his name. He drove a forklift and had a stutter.'

'Yeah, that's Morris Minor, he's a d-d-d-dickhead,' he laughed. I smiled nervously; for all I knew Mick could have suffered from a stutter too. They all could.

Morris Minor (I was about to find out) was a nickname, after a hit novelty song that was around at the time called 'Stutter Rap'. The trouble was he had no idea people called him that.

'Hello, Morris. We met last week,' I said, hesitantly offering him a handshake.

'What the fuck do you mean Morris? . . . My name's Ian.'

It was then the penny dropped and I could feel Mick laughing behind me.

'I'm sorry,' I said.

'Yeah, well . . . just watch yourself, OK? Right, I want you to do a bit of shit shifting for me tonight.'

I didn't like the sound of that.

'I'm sticking you on the bins. Have you ever used a jack lift before?' he said as he nodded towards another lad pulling a pallet with one.

'Yeah, no problem,' I said confidently. Then I swear I had a look round to see who'd said it. I couldn't believe it was me, I'd never used one of those things in my life. I'd seen them down the supermarket often enough, being pulled round by blokes built like brick shithouses, but I'd never even touched one. What possessed me to say it I'll never know but within twenty minutes of being left alone with this thing I'd created a hole the size of a small crater in a plasterboard wall.

I glanced around. Nobody had noticed so, feeling strangely confident, I decided to try and drag a two-ton steel bin, piled high with rubbish, out to the crushing machine. I was quite proud of myself. I slid the forks underneath the bin. I jacked it up no bother at all, I even managed to drag it outside to the car park and then I lowered it . . . straight on to my foot. The following ten minutes were a complete blur and the next thing I remember I was sat in a pickup truck being driven by Morris Minor himself on my way to A&E.

'J-J-J-J-J-J-Just what d-d-d-do you think you w-w-w-w-w-were doing, you d-d-d-d-dopey prick?' he snarled at me at the lights. 'I thought y-y-y-you said you c-c-c-could use one?'

I just shrugged and mumbled, 'Dunno.' All I could do was stare at my big toe, which was starting to resemble something out of a *Tom & Jerry* cartoon. I could actually see it throbbing and it was beginning to turn a violent shade of maroon. I hadn't been in the job an hour and already I was going to get sacked. Good going, Peter.

Morris screeched into a disabled bay outside the A&E unit.

'Right, g-g-get out,' he growled. I hopped out of the truck with my sock in my mouth. Before I could shut the door, he had reversed and was starting to drive off with the passenger door still swinging.

'Hey,' I shouted to him, 'where are you going?'

'Back t-t-t-to work,' he b-b-b-barked (he's got me at it now).

'How am I gonna get home?' I said with tears in my eyes.

'Sweet J-J-J-Jesus,' he shouted and, reaching into his pocket, threw a ten-pence piece at me. 'Here, ring for a f-f-f-f-f-fucking t-t-t-t-t-t-t-taxi,' he said, and sped off.

As I picked up the ten-pence piece and put it in my pocket I glanced down at my big toe. It looked like Trevor McDonald's nose.

The accident-and-emergency unit was packed. Well, it was July, so it was full of kids with broken limbs. I was given a ticket and told to wait until my number came up. You know, like you do in Argos, where you have to wait and listen to that annoying recorded female voice repeating, 'Customer number five, to your collection point please.' (You obviously won't be getting the benefit of the impression I just did, but take my word for it, it's a very annoying voice.)

Hold on, my phone's ringing now . . . it was my nana. I bought her a boxed DVD set of *24*, Season One, off t'Internet, because she's a big fan of *CSI: Miami* and I thought she'd lap it up. I mean, it does keep you on the edge of your seat, I'm sure you'll agree. Anyway, she was calling to tell me that it doesn't make any sense and she's having trouble following the story. Now there's six discs in the box set and four episodes on each disc, hence twenty-four. My nana had put disc one in, watched an episode, then taken it out, then put disc two in and watched an episode, taken that out and . . . I could go on but I think you get the gist. 'I put the second one in and Kiefer Sutherland's wife's been kidnapped . . . it doesn't make any sense, Peter,' she said. I've just had to try to explain that there's four episodes on each disc. 'It's twenty-four, just follow the clock.'

Anyway, where was I? Oh yes, I was in A&E and had just got to the front of the queue for the payphone.

'Hello, Mum,' I said as normally as I could muster.

'Well, how's it going, are you on your break?' said my mum.

'Er . . . well, kind of, I'm at the hospital.'

'You're *where*? The hospital? Jesus, Mary and Joseph, what's happened?'

'I dropped a bin on my foot,' I said matter-of-factly.

'What kind of bin?'

'A two-ton steel one.'

'Oh my God.'

By this time my dad had overheard my mum's side of the conversation and was starting to shout questions over her shoulder.

'What's happened? Where is he?'

'It's R Peter. He's dropped a bin on his foot and he's down the hospital.'

I could see that my credit was running out on the phone (they just eat money).

'Tell him I'm coming down now,' shouted my dad.

'No, no, Mum, tell my dad to stay there, I'll be all right, my pips are going to go.'

'Oh my God, his pips, his pips are going now, he's losing his pips,' said my mum in a lather

'His what?' asked my dad.

'MUM, PLEASE TELL MY DAD I DON'T WANT HIM TO COME DOWN!' I shouted after her, but it was too late, she'd gone. 'Shit!'

I hung the phone up and turned round to find half the A&E staring at me. Lord knows what they made of that conversation.

The last thing I needed right now was my dad coming down. He was always the same. Whenever I had any kind of an accident he would somehow find it funny to wind me up. When I was a child and I'd fall over and cut myself, I'd come staggering in from the backyard sobbing, snot dripping down my top lip, and sure enough my dad would look at the blood on my knee or elbow and shout to my mum:

'Deirdre, go and get the saw out of the shed, I'll have to cut it off,' and then I'd start wailing like a banshee.

I fell for it every time, hook, line and sinker, and now this sadist was sat on a bus on his way to A&E.

It was the first time I'd been at the hospital since I was struck down with a water infection the previous summer. I went to watch Genesis in Leeds and to cut a long story short, I caught thrush off an Orangina bottle. A few days later I started to notice a burning sensation when I passed water (and I don't mean when I cycled past the reservoir). The burning was getting worse. I thought I was going to set fire to the bathroom curtains at one point. After much denial I finally went to see the doctor. He was a big, bearded fellow with a booming voice and reminded me of Brian Blessed. In fact, if this book is ever made into a film Brian Blessed would be the perfect actor to play the doctor.

I told him about my burning sensation and for some reason he weighed me. 'Fifteen stone, my God, boy,' he boomed, 'you must have balls made out of ivory.' Then he handed me some dolly mixtures out of a jar on his desk and sent me to see a urologist.

On reflection this isn't a very big role for Brian Blessed. He's only got one line and although it's a good one, with plenty of booming, it's really not worth an actor of Brian's pedigree getting out of bed for. I'll give it to Paul Shane from *Hi-De-Hi*.

I had to take a sample of urine with me when I went to see the urologist at the hospital. I couldn't get anybody else's so had no choice but to take my own. I'd never given a sample before and the letter I'd been sent didn't specify how much they required. My mum wasn't available for advice so I filled up half a bottle of

Lucozade and put it in my rucksack and headed for the hospital. I got to the packed waiting room in the outpatients department, reached inside my bag for the bottle and found that most of its contents had leaked. It must have been all the jigging about I'd done running for the bus. I had half a mind to write a strong letter of complaint to Lucozade regarding the state of their screw-top lids. The reception nurse wasn't overimpressed either as I passed her the piss-stained bottle with see-through label.

After a wait of ninety minutes (thanks to Thatcher) I finally got to see the urologist. She (and by 'she' I do mean a lady) asked me about my condition.

'A couple of questions for you, Mr Kay. When you pass water is it a trickle or is it a good healthy jet?'

I had to confess that I'd never really noticed. It was an uncomfortable thing for a lad of fifteen to discuss, especially with a female doctor. I was just incredibly shy. Then I slipped out of my dungarees (I'm kidding) and climbed up on to the table.

'Lie on your side, Mr Kay, and pull your knees up into your chest.'

Pull my knees up into my chest? I thought, Christ, you'll be lucky, I haven't seen my ribs since we lost Shergar.

'High as you can, Mr Kay,' she pleaded, 'and try to breathe deeply.'

Breathing deeply was the easy bit. I don't remember her asking me to roll my eyes back into my head and bite the back of my knuckles but that's what I did when she inserted two of her fingers into my anus.

'Good God in Heaven!' I said, trying to disguise it with a cough and almost severing her fingers.

'Is that tender, Mr Kay?' she asked.

'Tender? It's brilliant, Doctor . . . Er . . . is there any chance you could do it with a bit of a rhythm?'

I'll not disclose what happened next. Suffice to say I wasn't invited back to her outpatients clinic.

Fast-forward one summer and I'm back here once again. Same hospital, different table. With my toe still throbbing I lay in the curtained cubicle, studying the nurse in front of me as she held a large needle over a naked flame.

'Where are you going to put that?' I asked nervously, as the end started to smoulder.

'Through your toenail,' she replied.

I gulped loudly

'It's either that or you lose the nail,' she said.

That's when I started to think, do I really need a toenail, I mean, do they actually serve any purpose in life? But before I could arrive at any kind of conclusion my train of thought was derailed by the sound of my dad charging through A&E.

'Where is he? Down here?' There then followed a shriek – 'Sorry, love, wrong curtain' – then our curtain tore back and there he stood. He turned his attention to my toe, took a sharp intake of breath, smiled proudly and said:

'I think I better go and get a saw. It'll have to come off.'

The next day I was back at work, limping dramatically. I think Morris must have taken pity on me because I was taken off shit-shifting duty and put to work on a line with the women.

I was sixteen, I was naive and I had never heard filth like it in all my life. These women were mothers, grandmothers, but their endless barrage of filth and sexual innuendos would have made Bernard Manning blush. It was certainly an education for me and they were far worse than any blokes I've ever worked with.

But despite their passion for smut and their obsession with grabbing my arse every time I tried to reload the foil machine, I learned to love them all dearly and have nothing but fond memories of my time spent with them.

Later, when I settled into working with them at Franny Lee's, I used to bring my radio-cassette player with me. It was quite a heavy piece of kit from the days when the general consensus seemed to be 'the bigger, the better'. Size mattered and seeing a half-naked male stagger down a beach with a stereo the size of wheelie bin on his shoulder wasn't an uncommon sight at all in the late 1980s.

My stereo wasn't as big as that, but it still needed eighteen double-D batteries. I honestly don't know how I managed to carry it to work with me every night. I brought it with me because I'd seen some documentary about the Second World War with all the women working in the munitions factories and singing along to *Workers' Playtime* on the wireless in a very British way. I suppose I wanted to re-create that camaraderie. And then when I turned round to find the room engaged in a singalong to Andrew Gold's 'Never Let Her Slip Away', it made dragging my stereo to work worth it.

Occasionally, I got a lift home from Donna Moss, who worked on kitchen roll and drove a Metro. I was grateful for the lift, especially having the stereo in tow. We became good friends over the summer. One night when she confessed to being let down by a babysitter I was more than willing to offer my services. Well, after all it was the least I could do. She'd saved me a fortune in bus fares.

I'd met her children already. They were lovely girls. Granted I didn't have much experience in looking after children but by the time Donna left the house they were already settled in bed. My job was done.

I nosied through her record collection and apart from the latest album from Debbie Gibson and the single 'Japanese Boy' by Aneka that I found jammed down behind the drinks cabinet, everything seemed in order. It was then I remembered what Donna had said to me just before she dashed out to her waiting taxi: 'Just help yourself to whatever you like.' Two minutes later I was opening a family-sized tin of corned beef and settling down to watch *Quantum Leap* on BBC2. Heaven.

Call me eccentric but I just fancied a corned-beef sandwich. Only problem was I'd never opened a tin of corned beef before in my life, let alone a family-sized one. I knew that there was some sort of key involved and that you had to drag it around the side of the can in order to open it. But with my attention distracted by the television, I looked down to find I'd wandered off-course. The key had now spiralled out into mid-air, so in a desperate effort to get it back on-course I decided to grab the tin key and drag it round the tin. I watched in astonishment as the razor wire sliced my through my hand and blood ejaculated up into my face. 'Ow, that hurt,' I thought as I stared at the wound.

A sudden realisation enveloped me and without thinking I let out a scream. I was rapidly becoming dizzy as the blood drained from my stupid brain. I reached for some kitchen roll (she should've had plenty) but all I got was an empty cardboard tube. Sod's Law. Just like your shoelaces always snap when you're in a rush to go out.

As I drunkenly swayed around the lounge to the theme from *Quantum Leap*, I heard a child's cry on the baby monitor. 'Shit!' My scream must've woken the children. I climbed the stairs in an effort to settle them. With hindsight, staggering into a child's bedroom in the middle of the night covered in blood was probably not the wisest move I've ever made.

With the children now screaming for mercy I ran downstairs to the kitchen to try to find some Farley's Rusks. Lord only knows why I thought two girls aged five and seven would want Farley's Rusks. A warm blanket and therapy would have probably been a preferred option.

Frantically I swung into the kitchen, thumping through the cupboards, my blood smearing the white Formica, like a scene from *Scream*.

I heard a door slam. A front door.

'Hiya. Only me, I forgot my purse.'

It was Donna. She was home! Before I had a chance to explain she was halfway up the staircase. I closed my eyes and heard her scream.

Well, I don't blame her, would have screamed if I saw my children sat up in bed sobbing with their faces smeared in blood.

Leaping the complete length of her staircase she kicked open the lounge door like a Ninja to find me cowering next to her serving hatch.

Before I knew it, she had punched me and pushed me out of the front door. I passed out.

Donna was always frosty with me after that night. She stopped offering me lifts home and never again asked me to babysit for her.

A friendship lost. All for a bloody corned-beef sandwich (NO PUN INTENDED).

Chapter Three

The Moon Landings of '84

I carried on working at Franny Lee's for another six months but I had to leave after the management decided they wanted to change to 'Continental shifts' and I refused to wear a sombrero. I'm joking of course. Truth is I couldn't do the new shift hours because I'd just started at college and the hours of my course clashed. I'd enrolled on a BTEC in Performing Arts. It was the first of its kind to be set up in Bolton and you can get any images you may have of *The Kids From Fame* out of your head straight away. Don't forget this was Greater Manchester in the early 1990s. It was more drug-taker than star-maker and the only time I ever saw someone on a car roof it was during the poll tax riots.

I found enrolling on a performing arts course quite a difficult decision to make, because while most of my friends would be studying for their A levels, I'd be walking against a strong wind in a black leotard pretending to be a mime. It really didn't feel like a sensible road to take, but then again sometimes the right road never does. (Oh, that was a bit deep.)

I'd always enjoyed making people laugh. All through school I'd been the class clown, a role that I revelled in. I even have a school report that reads: 'Peter seems unable to resist trying to amuse the children around him.' The teacher wrote that in 1978 when I was five years old. Even at that age I had a feeling for where my vocation in life was going to take me. Even then I kind of knew my talent for comedy was more of a vocation, a calling. That may sound really wanky, but I knew the time had now come for me to seize the day. That was the scary part.

Show business felt a million miles away from Bolton. I'd no connections in showbiz. In fact I'd never even met anybody in showbiz, not unless you count Fred Dibnah and he'd only waved at me from his steamroller as he drove past us at the Bolton Show. None of my family had ever been entertainers. My grandad liked to play 'The Ballad of Davy Crockett' on the comb and tissue paper every now and again but we never had Hughie Green knocking on the front door.

But I liked to perform as a child. I enjoyed the attention – well, providing the attention was getting laughs. When I was three or four I'd put on shows for the family. My sister and I would hang a duvet over a clothes line that we had in the back room and pretend it was a stage curtain. I'd then give her a nod, she'd kick the plug on the record player, and simultaneously lowered the pulley on the clothes line, causing the duvet to rise majestically and reveal me in some costume or other (usually a pair of my dad's wellies and a plastic cowboy hat).

My poor family then had to sit and watch as I lip-synced badly to a song from my *Muppet Show* LP, marched up and down with a mop over my shoulder to the theme from *Upstairs, Downstairs* or performed impressions of Frank Spencer and Louis Armstrong. Every credit to them, they always clapped and cheered and the memory of their false smiles will stay with me for ever.

I never got much of a chance to entertain at school – well, not legitimately anyway. We hardly ever did any shows or plays and I blame the nuns for this. Nuns featured very heavily in both my primary and secondary educations and I speak from bitter personal experience when I tell you that nuns and showbiz don't mix (apart from *The Sound of Music* of course but that goes without saying). In fact I never understood why we didn't perform *The Sound of Music* as a school production. We already had half the costumes and I'm not referring to the Nazis either. No, a show like *The Sound of Music* would have been far too daring for the Sisters of the Divine Virginity, so instead we had to play it safe by doing the Nativity every bloody year.

I didn't just have nuns teaching me, I had humans too, real people, and they'd do their best each year to try and freshen up the age-old story of the Nativity. They'd experiment with different ways of staging. One year the Three Wise Men arrived on BMX bikes and a couple of years before that, after the success of *The Wiz* at the cinema, a few radical members of staff decided to black up the cast, including Mary and Joseph. I'll never forget the stunned reception we received from the clergy on the opening night. It was controversial for 1979, even making headlines on the front of the local free paper. The nuns weren't happy bunnies and had to catch a bus to the Bishop's house to apologise in person. You've got to remember this was ten years before Madonna did her notorious 'Like a Prayer' video.

I on the other hand would have happily blacked up just to get out of the choir and on to the stage. I was sick of singing the same songs every year. Granted I got to sing the odd solo here and there on 'Silent Night' or 'Little Donkey', but there was nothing I could get my teeth stuck into. Then luckily Stuart Regan got suspended for solvent abuse and I was given his role as the Innkeeper. I had one line to learn and no time to waste.

In full costume and make-up I sat nervously in Class 3 waiting for my first big moment. Eventually I felt the cold hand of a nun touch me in the darkness. She led me towards the dimly lit stage. My chance had finally arrived. I knew what I was meant to do but for some reason I didn't want to do it. With a packed hall out front I decided that instead of telling Mary and Joseph that there was 'no room at the Inn' I would offer them an en suite with full English. The nuns were not amused but the audience loved it. What a wonderful feeling it was to stand onstage and listen to that sound, the sound of laughter. I felt happy, I felt safe.

After primary school I made a huge move of a hundred yards up the road to my big school, called Mount St Joseph (and apparently the nuns sometimes did). I got off to a reassuring theatrical start by bagging a pivotal role in that year's production, *The Times They Are A-Changin'*. Inspired by the Bob Dylan song, it was specially devised by the staff and pupils in order to celebrate fifty years of the nuns' occupation of the convent (which is currently being converted into a Muslim girls' school at time of going to print).

It was really more of a revue than a show. There were songs from the Second World War for the pensioners, Brendan Crook stuck on a false beard and mimed to Bob Dylan and I had the privilege of walking on the moon. Well, I say the moon, it was a couple of white duvets, but I couldn't have cared less. It was a magical experience for a boy aged eleven. With strobe lights flickering, I had to walk across the stage in slow motion to the theme from *2001: A Space Odyssey* and plant a big flag in the middle of some cotton wool. It was brave of the nuns to use strobe lights. They were a revolutionary piece of equipment in 1984 and still carry a medical warning today. I had to admire the nuns for showing such balls and everything would have gone according to plan if Alison Heggarty hadn't had an epileptic fit on the last night. Scene-stealing bitch. Everybody missed my flag because they were too busy trying to watch the nuns hold her tongue down with a shatterproof ruler.

Miss Scott, who was then head of drama, made a drama out of the whole 'strobe light' fiasco and left. There wouldn't be a school production for another four years, unless you count *Toad of Toad Hall* and I don't because it was shit! And I'm not just saying that because I didn't get a part.

Then came the winter of my discontent, a truly desolate time for performing. We got to read the occasional play in English but even then nobody would dare attempt a character voice or even do an accent. But I wouldn't class that as drama and any kind of performing was never really encouraged by the nuns; the general consensus within the school seemed to be that if you liked acting you were either a puff or a snob. I was neither.

But then, miraculously, after much deliberation, the nuns decided they wanted to go over the rainbow. After calling a press conference in the convent, they announced that the end-of-year production would be *The Wizard of Oz*, the only snag being I was now in fifth year and any rehearsals would clash with my all-important final exams. But I couldn't miss a chance to be in *The Wizard of Oz*.

I heard that they were holding auditions after school so I decided I'd call in after my paper round. Coincidentally my paper round circled the houses surrounding the school. In fact, I used to deliver a paper to the convent, something that I dreaded after a few of the older, more senile nuns tried to coax me inside to watch *Jesus of Nazareth* with them.

The nuns were obsessed with *Jesus of Nazareth*. We used to have to sit through nine hours of it every Easter, the annual 'Jesus of Nazarethathon' as we liked to call it. Now don't get me wrong, I think *Jesus of Nazareth* is a monumental piece of work. The definitive version of the Jesus story featuring a galaxy of stars from stage and screen and you'll never find a finer Jesus than Robert Powell from *Holby City*. But after watching nine hours without a break I personally felt as though I'd been on that cross with him.

We used to take our revenge in RE when Sister Matic read from the Bible. We'd take turns interrupting her.

'Then the soldiers took Jesus to see Pontius Pilate –'

'You mean Rod Steiger, Sister?' someone would ask.

'Yes, that's right, my child,' she'd say, slightly thrown but flattered that we were so interested. She'd continue 'Meanwhile, Judas was –' Another interruption.

'You mean Ian McShane, Sister? From *Lovejoy?*'

'Yes,' she'd snap, now cottoning on to what we were doing. She composed herself and continued: 'As Jesus hung from the cross he looked down to see a centurion looking up at him –'

'You mean Ernest Borgnine, Sister, from *Airwolf*?' She'd lose it now and throw a board duster in the general direction of the voice. No sense of humour, nuns, 'nun' whatsoever.

Anyway, where was I? Ah yes, I was about to gatecrash the school auditions for the *The Wizard of Oz*. I'd come up with a plan. As I got to the end of my paper round the auditions would be coming to a close. The whole plan hung on one of the teachers spotting me at the back of the hall and then persuading me into having an audition. In particular the lovely Miss Scott. She was back and raring to go after a couple of years in rehab.

I arrived at the back of the assembly hall in time to catch the last of the auditions. *The X-Factor* was no match for this as Mark Dempsey stomped round the stage singing 'If I Only Had a Brain' with a hare-lip.

My plan worked like a charm. Miss Scott saw me lurking at the back of the hall and invited me over for a chat. Ten minutes later I was reading the part of the Cowardly Lion and did I do it justice? Of course I did. I hadn't been sat up watching *The Wizard of Oz* on video all night for nothing. Not only did I get offered the part but I also got a round of applause. As the clapping subsided, Mr Lawson (the deputy head) shouted to me from the back of the hall.

'Bravo, very funny . . . but how funny will it be in twelve months when you can't get a job because you've failed your exams?' I could have swung for the miserable bastard. I wanted to reply with a witty comment, I wanted to tell him that in twelve months' time I'd be working at Franny Lee's factory packing cling film for £3.50 an hour but I couldn't think of a witty comment or predict the future, so I just shouted,

'Oh, I'll be all right,' and gave him a half-hearted thumbs up.

I hated Mr Lawson. He wasn't a nice man. In fact, I thought he was a bit of a bully. He'd strut round school like an arrogant Jimmy Tarbuck. The nuns thought the sun shone out of his fat arse, but all I wanted to do was kick it. We'd sit around at dinner thinking of different ways to destroy him.

He used to hate pupils wearing their coats in school as it wasn't part of the school uniform. They had to be in your bag and out of sight otherwise he'd confiscate them and give you a week's detention. Total knobhead.

So one night, after school, myself and a few of the other lads called into a jumble sale on the way home and bought a load of ladies' coats three sizes too small. It was worth it just to see the look of confusion on the pensioners' faces as we handed them our money and left.

Bright and early next morning the seven of us turned the corner in our brand new old coats. It was like the opening scene from *Reservoir Dogs* as we strolled past the convent in slow motion. I was particularly fond of my pink PVC lady's mac with its matching tie belt and press studs.

And sure enough, as we approached the gates, Mr Lawson swooped into position with a smug grin all over his fat face. He held out his hand and without even arguing we took off our coats and handed them over. Lawson was loving it.

'Don't think you'll be seeing these again until the end of term,' he said gloatingly. 'I can only be pushed so far, boys.' I'd like to have pushed him, into a threshing machine.

We then went round the corner, took our real coats out of our bags and put them on. Lawson was so jubilant in his victory that he failed to notice our fashion sense was a trifle odd. I mean, how often do you see seven fifteen-year-old boys walking to school wearing an assortment of ladies' coats three sizes too small for them?

But we were in for the long con and three months later on the last day of term we tasted victory ourselves when we saw a furious Lawson staggering round the convent gardens carrying a mountain of ladies' coats.

'Well, they must belong to somebody,' he repeatedly said to

passing pupils whilst attempting to hand them a pink PVC mac. They just walked off mystified. Apparently he ended up giving the coats back to the local jumble sale.

I found the rehearsals to *The Wizard of Oz* easy enough – every Sunday afternoon and a couple of evenings a week, after school. The hard part was revising for my exams. I've never been good at any kind of revision or dissertation. I start off with every good intention but within five minutes I find myself distracted, watering plants or putting my CDs in alphabetical order . . . sorry, I just noticed my Lighthouse Family CD was in with the Beatles.

I'm not good at exams either. In fact, I even tried to cheat on an exam once in third year. I'd just seen a film at the pictures called *Spies Like Us* with Dan Aykroyd and Chevy Chase. It was OK, a few funny bits, but there was this one scene where they tried to cheat during an exam and that's what gave me the idea.

I was in the middle of revising for my dreaded Chemistry exam. I decided to put my plan to the test. On the day of the exam, I got a scrap of paper and delicately wrote down some answers in the smallest handwriting I could muster. I scrunched the paper up into a tiny ball and then pondered where I could hide it. It had to be somewhere I could whip it out with ease if I was stuck for an answer in the exam. My trouser pocket was too obvious, so was my shirt sleeve. For some reason, and I still can't figure out why to this day, I decided to stick the ball of paper in my ear.

Delicately, I balanced the paper on the edge of my ear, then I sneezed violently and it shot down into my ear and got stuck. I immediately started to panic which is the worst thing you can do in an exam. I grabbed a sharpened pencil and attempted to fish it out but I only managed to push it further into my head. By this time the other pupils were becoming distracted by the commotion.

I looked over to Sister Zar Doin-it in a desperate effort to catch her attention. Eventually she glanced up from her copy of *True Detective* to see me now out of my chair, slapping the side of my head like a maniac. With tears in my eyes and the answers in my ear she sent me to see the nurse.

Our resident school nurse was a she-male, a fella in drag, who only made an appearance a couple of times a year, to check six hundred kids' heads for nits and to dish out the annual TB injection. By now hyperventilating for fear of going deaf, I knocked on her/his door. Stinking of nicotine, 'it' opened the door.

'What's up?' it snapped. Sobbing, I concocted a pathetic story about how I'd been a slave to earache the last few weeks and had only placed paper in my ear because I'd run out of tissues. I don't think it believed a word I was saying for one second. It mumbled something in Latin, looked into my ear with its reusable lighter and advised me to go to hospital. Bloody hell, not the hospital. They had to get my mum out of work. What a complete balls-up.

At the hospital, my mum and a nurse had to pin me to the floor while a doctor ferreted around in my ear with the biggest pair or tweezers I'd ever seen in my life. I felt like one of the Borrowers. Finally, after what seemed like an hour, the doctor started to drag the paper out of my ear. The noise was deafening. Then suddenly there was a pop, like a cork coming out of a bottle as he removed it from my head. I just prayed to God he didn't open it up and try to read it.

Things didn't work out too bad in the end because I missed my Chemistry exam by going to the hospital. And I managed to get my left ear syringed into the bargain. I've been able to hear perfectly out of my left ear since.

The Wizard of Oz was approaching fast and the nuns weren't happy when I told them I was going on holiday to Ireland for a fortnight with my mum. This meant I'd end up missing some important rehearsals. But what could I do? We'd had it booked for months. I promised them I'd be back in time for the dress rehearsal.

I'd been going over to Ireland most of my life. Normally we'd fly over but because of the cost we could only go every couple of years. Flying used to be expensive. It's hard to imagine that today with all these budget airlines popping up everywhere. Nowadays you can fly halfway round the world for sod all. I hear people saying,

'How can they afford to fly so cheaply?' and I say,

'Try reaching for your life jacket under your seat when you're flying into the sea and you'll soon find out.' What do you want when you're paying sod all for your flight? Safety?

This particular Easter the airline prices had got so expensive that we decided to go on the boat from Liverpool instead. Never again. It takes an hour to fly to Belfast on a plane from Manchester. It took eleven hours on the boat. I didn't realise that they travelled so slowly until I ventured up on deck after we'd been sailing for four hours and found I could still see the Liver Building.

It was an overnight crossing and we had toyed with the idea of getting a cabin and our heads down for the night, but my mum's sister Roisin had made the same trip a few weeks previously and said that the non-smoking lounge had long leather seats that were comfortable enough to sleep on.

I don't know what my Auntie Roisin's idea of comfort was, but we didn't get a wink of sleep all night. The sea was very choppy and we spent most of our crossing sliding up and down the leather upholstery in a storm. We looked like a couple of extras from *The*

Poseidon Adventure. It was awful, so awful in fact that last night, when my mum asked me where I was up to with my book and I replied, 'The boat trip to Belfast,' she immediately closed her eyes, shook her head and mouthed the word 'awful'.

As well as enduring the discomfort of the leather seats, the howling wind and the freezing temperature, we also had to listen to the shittiest compilation tape in the world . . . ever. It was on a continual loop for the entire journey. In the middle of the night I resorted to trying to smash the speaker above my head with my shoe and I still get nauseous when I hear 'Moonlight Shadow' played on the pan pipes (mind you, wouldn't anybody?)

Thankfully I had a lovely time in Ireland, but then again I always do. The way of life is much slower over there and it usually takes me a couple days to unwind, but once I've adjusted to it, peace and relaxation are the order of the day. I can honestly say that I'm rarely happier anywhere else in the world.

It does amaze me, though, how laid-back everybody is. You've just got to go with the flow or the lack of it as the case maybe. We used to stop at my granny's and some days we wouldn't even get round to leaving the house. We'd have every intention of going out but family would call and after copious amounts of tea and cake we'd always end up falling asleep in front of my granny's big open fire. Next thing you know you'd wake up to the theme from *Prisoner: Cell Block H* and the day would be over.

When I did manage to leave the house and get out into the fresh air I'd usually find myself walking down the hill into the local town, Coalisland in County Tyrone. I don't wish to sound patronising but it always seemed to me as if time had stood still – the bus, shops, even the public transport, on the rare occasions it appeared. In fact, apart from the barracks with its sixty-foot-high corrugated-iron fence that looked as though a spaceship had landed in the middle of the town, nothing had changed since 1947. One day I paid a visit to the library and hired out a cassette with my granny's library card. It was an audio cassette of the comedy series Porridge starring Ronnie Barker. I'd seen *Porridge* a few times growing up – it was usually on on Thursday nights after *Top of the Pops*. My parents would laugh at it a lot but I didn't understand it. As I got older I became more familiar with the movie version of *Porridge* that they made in the late seventies.

It held special memories for me as it was one of the few times we all went to the cinema together as a family. My dad took us to the Odeon one night after school. *Porridge* was on a double bill with *Rising Damp – The Movie*. I remember my dad falling down in between the seat he was laughing that much.

Maybe that's why I like it so much. I think it's inevitable we inherit some of our parents' tastes. That day I hired *Porridge*, took it back to my granny's house and listened to it, I laughed as hard as my dad had at the Odeon all those years before. What impressed me the most was the sharp and witty dialogue, delivered with such impeccable timing. From that moment on I became a lifelong fan of *Porridge* and it opened my eyes to the comic genius of Ronnie Barker. It also ignited a spark deep down inside me. Perhaps one day I might be able to be a comic actor like him.

Our holiday drew to a close and it dawned on us that we'd have to endure that bloody awful boat trip back to Liverpool again. Throwing caution to the wind we decided to book a sleeping cabin for the return journey. We also plied ourselves with a cocktail of anti-sickness tablets and sleeping pills before we left my granny's.

Drugged up to the eyeballs, we said our emotional goodbyes and headed for the boat. Little tip for you, always check the date and time on your ticket before you leave. I sarcastically mentioned this to my mum as we stood on the docks watching 'our' boat sail off into the distance. That's the last thing I remember before I passed out.

The rest is just a hazy memory. I do have a vague recollection of my Uncle Rory giving me a fireman's lift up my granny's path but the rest is a blur. After sleeping for seventeen hours we woke around teatime the next day, said our now not so emotional goodbyes once again and made a second attempt to catch the boat. This time we made it.

But because of the previous day's cock-up I got back a day late for the dress rehearsal. I was in the nuns' bad books and Miss Shambo the school choreographer was furious. She'd spent the weekend teaching the rest of the cast some important dance moves and I'd missed them.

I've no idea how familiar you are with *The Wizard of Oz* but while on their way to the Emerald City, Dorothy and co. are attacked in a forest by some creatures known as the 'Jitterbugs'. They're insects of some kind, or in our case third-year girls in tank tops and ra-ra skirts with their faces painted green. The Jitterbugs supposedly possess your body and make you dance until you drop, or in my case, just drop. Because Miss Shambo said it was too late for me to learn the dance routine and that I'd just have to sit on the stage like a good little Lion while everybody else cavorted around me to 'Wake Me Up Before You Go-Go' by Wham!

'Don't you think it'll look stupid with everybody else dancing except me?' I said to Miss Shambo.

'Yes, I do, but everybody else has rehearsed the steps.' As far as I was concerned I might as well sit on the stage holding a sign up saying 'Sorry, folks, but I was on holiday when they rehearsed this'. In fact, I actually started to make one in Art but ran out of glitter.

Opening night, I nervously sat backstage having some last-minute fur stapled to my helmet and listening through the air vent to the audience filing into the assembly hall. It was my first big performance since the moon landings of '84.

Before I knew it I could hear the orchestral strains of 'Ding Dong, the Witch is Dead' and then, once again, I felt the familiar cold hand of a nun as she touched my tail and she led me towards the darkened stage.

'We'll have to stop meeting like this, Sister,' I whispered into her veil, but she gave me no response.

I leapt out from behind a cardboard bush and roared 'Put 'em up' in my best American accent. It got a few laughs. So far so good. Then came the Jitterbugs. Wham! started playing right on cue and I immediately dropped to the floor as Miss Shambo had ordered, but as I sat watching the cast jitterbugging around me, I thought, hold on, this isn't right, and I could feel the adrenalin rushing through me. There was only one thing to do, so I leapt to my furry feet and like a Lion possessed I began to dance. I hadn't a clue if what I was doing was good or bad, but what I did know was that it was getting big laughs from the audience.

With the laughter ringing in my ears, I jumped off the stage and danced out into the audience. I had no idea why, or where I was going, I just knew that I was on to something good. I headed towards my family. 'Hello, Mum,' I shouted and gave her a wave. By this time the place was rocking and the audience were in hysterics. They knew this wasn't in the script.

I danced passed the Mayor and the governors, all the while avoiding eye contact with Miss Shambo who was sat in the corner furiously scribbling notes. I made my way back on to the stage and noticed a couple of trees representing the forest (well, they were actually second-year girls with American tan tights over their heads covered in bits of green tissue paper). I had an idea forming. I knew it was quite naughty but if I pulled it off it would bring the house down. I danced to the back of the stage, straight up to a tree and cocked my leg up. The room exploded. I held my leg in the air for a few seconds pretending to urinate.

'Aw, you're dead, Miss Shambo's going to kill you!' said a girl's voice from inside the tree, but I couldn't have cared less. The sound of laughter was deafening now and with that kind of a reaction what I was doing couldn't be all that bad. But Sister Sledge gave me a right bollocking during the interval. She collared me backstage and said,

'Is that what you're going to be when you grow up, a comedian?'

I wanted to say, 'Yes Sister, it is,' but it was hard for me to talk with her hands round my windpipe.

Ten years later in Marks & Spencer I bumped into that same girl. She said hello, I said hello back.

'You don't remember me, do you?' she said. I had to confess I didn't. 'You pissed on me in *The Wizard of Oz*,' she replied, a little bit too loudly for my liking in the middle of Blue Harbour. 'My mum and dad always said you'd end up a comedian,' she added and walked off.

Wham! reached their climax and I returned to my original position at the front of the stage and sat back down. The whole room shook with applause. It felt good.

Being in the show seemed like academic suicide at the time. In fact, that's exactly what it turned out to be. I got one GCSE in Art and Dorothy went back to Kansas.

But I've never regretted it for a second. Performing in the show opened my eyes again to the true potential I had for making people laugh. Not only was I glad that I followed my instincts and played the part but I also got to keep the Lion costume (and wear it sixteen years later on the road to Amarillo).

Chapter Four

A Highland Toffee and a
Packet of Three

I once overheard an actor being interviewed on TV-am. The telly
was in the next room but I heard the interviewer (I think it was
Richard Keys) ask what advice he had for any budding actors who
may have been watching and fancied having a go at it.

'I'm afraid you can't just have a go at acting,' the actor snapped
back at Richard. 'If you want to be an actor then you've got to eat,
sleep and breathe acting, that's if you want to be any kind of
success.'

I remember that scaring the shit out of me. I didn't want to eat,
sleep and breathe acting, I just fancied having a go at it. You can
imagine my relief when I ran in from the kitchen to discover that
the actor being interviewed was Burt Kwouk. But nevertheless it
did make me think, maybe I was fooling myself on this performing
arts course?

College could be fun sometimes, I have to admit, but I was
finding it hard to settle in and I wasn't really enjoying myself. The

other students were friendly enough but they seemed pretentious and angry. It was the first time a performing arts course had been set up in Bolton, and of course like all things new, there were a few initial problems. In this case the staff members. It felt as though nobody had actually sat down and thought about what running a performing arts course would entail. As time passed by we slowly began to get more and more suspicious about the tutors' qualifications. Did they know anything about performance? One tutor in particular took us for theatre workshop every Tuesday afternoon. I'll call him Mr Delaney (as that was his name). Unfortunately for him he was a severely cross-eyed man, who we discovered also taught horticulture to disabled people on the other side of town. He'd then drive over to us for the afternoon session with soil under his fingernails and spit on his shoes.

Straight away we didn't see eye to eye. In fact, it was more eye to ear where he was concerned. He'd already thrown me out of one of his lectures because I said I thought that Shakespeare was only famous because of his last name. God forbid you'd have an opinion.

Mr Delaney resented me for being funny. I remember he completely blew his top in a lecture once. Grabbing me and leaning right into my face, he shouted,

'I crack the funnies in here, Mr Kay, and don't you forget it.'

The truth was Mr Delaney wasn't funny. His jokes were just a series of smutty innuendos and double entendres. He also had a fascination for all things farcical. He thought it was hysterical and he would drop everything (including his trousers) at the slightest hint of performing a farce.

Personally I can take or leave farce. All that running around half naked and tripping over next door's dog never did it for me.

I was never a huge fan of *Fawlty Towers*. I enjoyed the sarcastic, witty banter between Basil and Sybil but I was never too keen on the farcical element. When the guest dies in 'The Kipper and the Corpse' I really just want Basil to call a meeting of all the guests and announce that tragically due to circumstances beyond his control a guest has sadly passed away in the night. I do realise this ruins the whole point and would cut the episode down to ten minutes but I'd prefer that to twenty minutes of Basil and Manuel running from room to room with a dead body in a hamper. It drives me mad.

So you can imagine how frustrated I was to discover Mr Delaney had entered us for the annual Bolton Drama Festival* and told the organisers that we'd be performing a farce.

The play was called *The Wages Of Sin* and coincidentally it was written by an Andrew Sachs. Now whether this was the same Andrew Sachs who played Manuel in *Fawlty Towers*, I'm still none the wiser.

I was cast as Lord Peregrine Fortune-Mint, a wealthy eighteenth-century landowner with a shotgun and a penchant for the type of scantily clad maids who like to bend over. Not unlike Mr Delaney who also seemed to have a lingering enjoyment of the maid-bending-over scenes. In fact, it was all we ever seemed to rehearse.

'Now watch what I do,' he'd say in his thick Wigan accent. Then he'd approach the maid gropingly from behind with a naughty look on his face. Licking his lips and outstretching his hands, he leaned forward. Just then his wife walked in and caught him.

I'm referring to the character's wife, of course, not Mr Delaney's.

---

* Well, it said 'annual' on the banner hanging between British Home Stores and the Cenotaph, but it turned out to be the first and only drama festival that Bolton ever had.

She was shacked up with a marriage guidance counsellor in Clitheroe or so I heard.

Delaney spent so much time perfecting the maid scenes that he seemed not to notice the dwindling attendance figures, as one by one students resigned from the course. This meant that Delaney had to step in at the last minute and play the narrator, a part that he openly relished. Before you could say 'Ooo-er, Missus,' we were off to the Bolton Octagon for our first and final performance. The show was a farce, on more than one level. My heart sank when I saw the quality of some of the other performances that night. They were all thoughtful, funny pieces written and performed by children, some of them half my age. And then there was us. Students from Bolton's prestigious performing arts course, topping the bill with an out-of-date farce and a cross-eyed gardener.

But, as Freddie once sang, 'The Show Must Go On'.

The script required my character to have a moustache and, as funds were short on the old make-up front, I decided to take a trip to a local fancy-dress shop. I was after a real corker of a moustache and luckily they had one very much like the one I'd imagined in stock. Sadly though, it was light brown instead of black.

'We haven't had any black ones in for a while,' the girl behind the counter confessed. 'I get them from a friend of mine in Hull. She's a taxidermist and –'

I quickly raised my hand to shush her as she'd already provided me with too much information. I counted my change and made for the door.

'Can I interest you in some fake dogshit?' she shouted. 'Two for one this week only?' But I was gone.

Backstage, I eyed up some black-coloured greasepaint on a shelf in the dressing room. I fingered some out of the pot and smeared it on to my light brown moustache. It did the trick and with my newly blackened facial hair I winked at myself in the mirror and headed for the stage.

The lights dimmed, the audience fell quiet and through a small slash in the curtains I could see Delaney taking centre stage. There were a few initial chuckles from the audience but they quickly subsided when they realised that they were in fact Delaney's real eyes and not for comic effect.

Personally I was glad to hear any kind of laughter from the audience as I knew how barren the comic desert was that lay before them. Delaney, in his role of narrator, proceeded to introduce characters:

'Please would you welcome Lord Peregrine Fortune-Mint.' That was my cue.

I bounded out from behind the curtains to take my opening bow. So far so good. Next it was the turn of my wife, Lady Penelope Fortune-Mint, and sure enough Sonia Cassidy entered as gracefully as a baby elephant and took a bow.

The script then said we embraced and kissed. We'd choreographed it over a hundred times in the boiler room at college. I took her hand, spun her towards me, leaned her back and gave her an enormous kiss on the lips. Then I tilted her up and span her back out to face the audience. That's when they started to laugh and laugh and laugh. I was astonished by the reaction, it was only a kiss. Maybe I'd misjudged the play after all and the night wasn't going to be as painful I'd envisaged. But then I turned to the equally confused Sonia to find that she now had a moustache. Shit! The black greasepaint had rubbed off on her top lip during the kiss and now I realised why the audience was hysterical.

But Sonia was still confused. Subtly I nodded towards her top lip but she was helpless without any kind of reflection. We got through our lines as best we could despite the distracting howls of laughter. I could see Delaney angrily glaring at me from the side of the stage. Well, I think it was me but I couldn't quite tell, as he had one eye on Sonia and the other on my shoes. Either way I knew I was in for a bollocking.

After the show I couldn't tell who was more upset, Sonia or Delaney. I apologised to them both, and tried to reassure them that at least it had got big laughs but neither one of them was having it. My only regret was kissing her so soon. If I'd have known it was going to bring the house down I'd have saved it for the finale.

Something else happened to me that night as I waited nervously in the wings. It was the first time I'd ever done any kind of performing outside of school and occasionally I found myself glancing around, looking for a nun to take hold of my hand and lead me to the stage, but I suddenly realised that those days were over and that's when it hit me. I missed school.

It became clear to me why I'd failed to settle into the performing arts course. Deep down I expected to be returning to school. It was as if I was on a long holiday and soon it would be September. After twelve years of education this sudden change was a slow shock and a massive adjustment. What I was feeling was grief. It wouldn't have been so bad if I hadn't enjoyed school so much, but I did, and now all I wanted to do was go back.

But I couldn't even return for a visit because the nuns demolished the school the day after I left. Well, not them personally, but as far as I was concerned they might as well have driven those JCBs themselves. It was sacrilege.

School had been a very happy time for me. Sure, there were ups and downs, but on the whole I seemed to spend most of my time either laughing or making other people laugh. I also made some brilliant friends who I still cherish to this day. Well, two of them.

I walked up to the school one night during the demolition, climbed over the construction fence and jumped down into what would have been the Art department. Art was the only subject I passed in the end and that was only because I slipped the moderator twenty quid. I'm joking. Actually I was quite good at it and I'd come a long way from drawing cars on the front-room floor with my felt tips. (My mum still blames me for ruining that carpet.)

I continued walking through what remained of the school. It was eerily quiet and very surreal, especially when I found an empty bulldozer sitting in the middle of the dining hall. The nuns would have had a fit if they'd seen it. They'd mopped that floor every day for the last five years.

Contrary to popular myths I was also quite partial to a school dinner. I understand where Jamie Oliver OBE is coming from but personally I could never get enough of chips, beans and Turkey Twizzlers.

And you couldn't argue with the prices. When I was at school you could get a starter, main meal, pudding and carton of Vimto all for less than 50p. You've got to go to prison to get value for money like that these days.

I was also a sucker for seconds, even though it wasn't allowed. I'd tell the nun on checkout that she'd given me the wrong change. She'd give me another 50p and I'd get straight back in the queue and buy another dinner. Magic. You can never have too much Manchester tart. Paddy McGuinness will back me up on that one. Only he won't be talking about the pudding.

If the dining hall was full and you just fancied a quick snack you could always opt for a tuck-shop lunch. Within easy reach of all amenities, you could pick up a carton of orange, a bag of cheesy corn puffs and a Texan, again for less than 50p. I sound like the presenter of a travel programme now. Our school tuck shop used to be run by Sister Swingout. She was an elderly nun but sharp as a tack when it came to business. Aided and abetted by two girl prefects, she had a strict no-nonsense policy and I would often find myself at the cold end of her ice pops.

Nevertheless, we'd get great enjoyment from winding her up. Confusing her by asking for sweets that didn't exist.

'Have you had any Purple-Headed Warriors, Sister?'

or

'Have you got any of those Strawberry Strap-ons, Sister?'

She'd just shake her head in confusion.

And if we weren't inventing confectionery, then we'd just ask her for things she didn't sell like 'A Wham bar and twenty Benson & Hedges please, Sister', or 'A Highland toffee and a Packet of Three'. She'd just swear at us in Latin and chase us away with her mop.

I tried packed lunches for a few months but they weren't for me. I never found two spam sandwiches and a Munch Bunch yogurt very filling. There's only so much you can cram into an *A-Team* lunch box and I'd still always end up having a proper hot dinner as well. I was a growing boy at the end of the day.

But all that was gone for ever and there wouldn't be any more school dinners. I sat aloft the bulldozer, looking around at the empty room. What a waste. Surely they could have used this building for something else, evening classes or maybe they could have turned it into an enormous Whacky Warehouse for kids.

It wouldn't have needed adjusting that much, just fill the library up with coloured balls, stick a bumpy slide on the side of the convent and they would have made a fortune. I think the nuns would have probably objected, not that there were that many of them left to object any more, as the Sisters of the Divine Virginity were falling short on their recruitment drive. Well, what did they expect? There were no bright colours, no sex and no dental plan. I mean, what's the incentive? We used to send them a valentine card every year from Jesus, just to keep their spirits up.

This decline had been taking place for the last ten years, since someone had decided to change Mount St Joseph from an all girls' school into a mixed comprehensive. The nuns had had things cushy until 1980 but then the lads arrived and it all went tits up for the nuns. Talk about a shock, they'd never seen such behaviour in all their holy lives. And by the time I arrived in '84 things had gone from bad to worse. The nuns were dropping like flies and the defiant ones were on double novenas. It reminded me of that film *Dangerous Minds*, but without the rapping or Michelle Pfeiffer.

There were a few rotten apples in my year and when I say rotten I mean proper mentalists, who thrived on rule-breaking and bucking the system. They would go to any lengths to tip the nuns over the edge of insanity. From setting desks on fire to urinating on books (or vice versa). Every day was a different box of delights at Mount St Joseph.

They even shot a pigeon once with an air rifle, then left it on the steps of the convent in a Nike shoebox, and all because the nuns wouldn't play 'Relax' by Frankie Goes To Hollywood at the school disco (well, it had been banned by Radio 1 at the time).

I shudder when I remember the awful things that we did. I sometimes think there must have been devilment in the air during the summer of '73. As some of these kids were evil. It's hardly surprising, though, when you consider that most of them were probably conceived to *Dark Side of the Moon*. And what chance did I stand? Gary Glitter was number one with 'The Leader of the Gang' the week I was born.

(That's freaky, I just looked down at the word count at the bottom of my computer screen and it was on 666. Jesus!)

But I have to be honest with you and tell you that despite all of their badness these mentalists were very, very funny. I was no angel myself and even though I wasn't in their league, I was still great friends with all of them. I've tried keeping in touch with some of them over the years by going on Friends Reunited, but I don't think they're allowed access to t'Internet in prison.

It has to be said: some of the disruptive behaviour and stunts were quite original at the time.

Like when we deliberately arrived early for an RE lesson just so we could draw a mural on the blackboard. Using coloured chalk, we painstakingly drew the image of an Arizona desert road heading off into the distance up the centre of the blackboard. We drew a cactus, a few people and finally we drew a huge articulated lorry heading straight towards us. Then we flipped the blackboard over, took our seats and waited patiently for Sister Matic to arrive.

We were giggling with anticipation when eventually Sister turned in her seat and flipped the blackboard over revealing our mural. Then we'd take great delight in shouting,

'Sister, get out of the way quick, there's a truck coming.'

She always failed to see the humour in our pranks, even when we traced a full sized image of Pope John Paul II out of our RE book on to the blackboard. I thought she would have been made up sitting beside the Pope.

But disruptive behaviour almost always resulted in our being detained after the lesson for a talking-to and frig me, do nuns like to talk? I think *all* teachers do. They love the sound of their own voices, so much so that sometimes we could end up being detained for ages. So we came up with a sure-fire plan that would get us out of there fast. We used to fart on them. Seriously. We all used to push as hard as we could and eventually we'd create enough of an odour that they'd have no choice but to release us. It might seem a bit drastic on reflection but it worked a treat every time. Except for when Danny Thorncliffe followed through in Metalwork but I don't really want to talk about that (well, not yet anyway).

Another stunt we pulled was in Chemistry with Sister O'Mercy. Again we turned up early for class and hid ourselves behind the big wooden benches in the science lab. The lesson began and Sister O'Mercy slowly got more and more concerned as to why her class was half empty. Ten minutes went by, she'd glanced at her Rolex and mumbled something in Latin and still we were hiding behind the benches, each of us in position, poised with our textbooks and pens in our hands ready.

Then eventually she turned to the blackboard for a few seconds and that's when we all popped up into our seats simultaneously. She turned back and freaked out. Where? How did they get in here so fast? And we just casually copied from the board as if we'd been there all the time.

Sister O'Mercy never turned up for Chemistry the following week. Apparently she packed her bag and jumped over the convent wall in the middle of the night. The last I heard she was scaling Ben Nevis dressed as Bugs Bunny for muscular dystrophy.

But, as I say, it wasn't just nuns that we had teaching us, we had humans too. One of my favourites was the French teacher, Miss Plum. We all turned our desks around in her lesson once and then told her that she was at the wrong end of the classroom. It was a stand-off and as usual she burst into tears and went to get Mr Lawson. Of course, by the time they both returned we were back facing the right way. Bloody hell, we did some horrible things.

But the worst one I can think of is the time somebody (and I'm not saying who) dressed the school crucifix up for the end-of-year assembly. Whoever it was must have been planning it for a while. It was a highly skilled operation that took guts and incredible dexterity. How they managed it I'm still none the wiser but I'll never forget the looks of hysteria on the nuns' faces when the curtains rolled back revealing Jesus nailed to the cross wearing a woolly Bolton Wanderers hat and a purple body warmer. The prefects were wheeling the nuns out with oxygen masks. What I still can't figure out is how they got the body warmer over Jesus's outstretched arms without ripping it? I'm not suggesting that it was a miracle for one second.

But unbeknownst, to us, our carefree, fun-loving days were numbered, as over on the opposite side of town a rival Catholic secondary school called St Bernadette's was sinking slowly into the ground and in their infinite wisdom the local education authority had decided to merge that school with ours.

The reason for doing this was not because they'd found subsidence in the girls' toilets, it was because there was a more elaborate plan about to be unveiled that would hopefully put an end to this persistent disruptive behaviour once and for all, the plan mysteriously called Mode II.

We were all summoned into the assembly hall at the end of third year for an important discussion. There were a couple of blokes in suits from the education authority already in there and our headmistress, Sister Sledge, stood at her podium and told us that because we were a 'special' year (I took special to mean full of nutters) we were going to be presented with the unique opportunity of choosing one of two academic options.

Choice number one was simple: 'Just do your coursework and study hard for your all-important final exams.' OR (and this is when I half expected the stage to light up and turn into the set of a game show): 'You can choose Mode II, a revolutionary new option where there'll be no coursework and no exam. Instead you'll be given the opportunity to gain experience in the some of the important things in life like Painting & Decorating, Car Maintenance and Gardening, to name but a few.'

But it didn't end there. In the pamphlet they provided it said that 'you will be continually assessed by staff throughout the duration of Mode II and if your grades are sufficient you'll be awarded with a qualification equivalent to a GCSE'. 'So, why not do what's right for YOU and choose Mode II?' I think they fell down a bit on the tag line but other than that it sounded perfect for me and I couldn't wait to sign up.

But my parents had a different opinion.

'Gardening instead of exams? That can't be right,' my dad said as he studied the pamphlet during *The Disabled Krypton Factor.*

Mum agreed with him. 'They just want to get rid of all the troublemakers,' and she was right. I knew that but I still fancied doing it.

'Not a chance,' my dad said. 'Fixing cars and decorating – what a load of crap. They're luring a bunch of idiots over to a school that's sinking and then letting them all sink . . . Now bugger off, will you, I'm trying to watch this bloke land the space shuttle with his feet!'

So I didn't do Mode II and my mum and dad were right. All the nutters signed up and like lambs to the slaughter they joined a sinking St Bernadette's. School wasn't the same any more. We still had a laugh but all the controversy had been sucked out of our lives.

I'd still see my old friends each night as they dismounted their Mode II bus proudly wearing overalls stained with oil and silk emulsion. They seemed so grown up all of a sudden while we were doing boring coursework. Our jealousy didn't last long and I have to admit I was relieved a few months later when Danny Thorncliffe flipped his lid and took four nuns hostage with some turps and a Bunsen burner.

Mentally, the cheese had slid off Danny's cracker a long time ago. I remember saying that when I saw him trying to headbutt wasps in the convent gardens. But taking hostages was the final straw. When he blew up the science lab he made it on to the local TV news.

Danny was suspended but had the last laugh when he sued the education authority for damages and won. He reckoned the cuts he received to his face as a result of the blast ruined any chance he might have had of becoming a male model.

The last time we were all together was when the school was entered for a local design project. Every Thursday for a few weeks, Mode II students were invited back to our school (much to the nuns' disgust) and Mr India, the head of the Craft and Design department, put us into groups.

I was crap at Craft and Design. I'd only taken it as an option because I'd been a dab hand with Lego and because Mr India promised I could build my own hovercraft and travel to school in it. I never got any further than dismantling my nana's U-Bank for parts. I ended up getting a U in my final exam and I think I only got that because I spelt my name right at the top of the paper

Our task for this project was to design and build 'something' that could travel thirty feet – that was the brief. It could be any shape or size. It could be powered by any means. It just had to travel thirty feet across the assembly-hall floor, four weeks from that day, in front of our parents, some governors and possibly the Bishop, depending on whether or not he was back from the World Cup.

I was put into a group with some of my old friends from Mode II and it was great being in a lesson with them again. In fact, we were only together for five minutes before we set the fire alarm off. Danny Thorncliffe had just got out of the burns unit and we were teasing him by throwing lit matches at his bandages. Happy days.

The first thing we had to do was pick a name for our group. Mr India said that ideally it should have something to do with speed and dexterity. Everybody else chose names like 'Supersonic' and 'The Hurricanes'. After a deliberation of ten seconds we came up with 'The Very Fast'.

I have to confess we did nothing but piss about for three weeks. Every time we saw Mr India coming we'd each grab a pair of masonry goggles and stand round the lathe looking busy. But when I realised we only had three days until the competition and my mum had booked the day off work I began to panic. We had designed nothing.

Mr India gave everybody an appraisal and we hung our heads in shame when we saw what the other groups had come up with. 'The Speed Demons' had risen mightily to the challenge with their remote-controlled, jet-powered land cruiser. By incorporating the guts of a Dyson and over three hundred ball bearings that they'd 'found' in a skip behind MFI, they'd managed put the cast of *Robot*

Wars to shame. Quite an achievement when you consider that *Robot Wars* would not be invented for another fifteen years.

I was personally very jealous when I saw what 'Red Rum and Co.' had come up with. It was just a bloody wooden ball, the clever sods. They'd sculpted it out of pine in the woodwork room and were planning to roll it down the hall. Everybody hates a smart-arse.

Eventually Mr India got round to our group and when he saw what we'd done (or rather what we hadn't done) he totally lost the plot. I felt bad because he was a gentle soul. He let the kids call him Pablo and played the guitar whenever we had a power cut but now we'd let him down.

'I can't believe you've done nothing. You've had four weeks.'

We just shrugged pathetically. He kept repeating himself over and over. We even tried farting on him in an effort to make him stop but the poor bugger had inhaled so many toxic chemicals over the years that his sinuses were dead. Danny Thorncliffe on the other hand, pushed a little too hard and followed through. What a stink. So there we were, stood in front of Mr India, with tears in our eyes. Luckily he mistook them for tears of regret and granted us a twenty-four-hour reprise.

That night after watching *Wacky Races* I had a dream. If we took a piece of wood about a foot long, drilled two holes in it and then threaded a couple of axles through the holes, then placed four wheels at the end of them, then (and here's the genius bit) we attached a powerful spring to the back, maybe, just maybe, if the laws of physics allowed, we could push the coiled spring up against a wall, hold it tightly and when we let it go, it would hopefully shoot forward . . . thirty feet? In theory anyway.

Well, it was just a dream but goddammit, that's all we had.

The Very Fast · Mark 1

The contraption took about an hour to make, which was handy as it was now the presentation day. We needed a decent spring, though, for the back. Simon Birch (or Fingers as we called him) managed to come up with the goods. He never revealed where he got it from but I noticed the town hall clock had stopped working a few days later. Maybe it was just a coincidence that his dad worked as a security guard there.

Quickly we screwed the spring to the back of the wood and cleared a path in the metalwork room. Time for the acid test. I pressed the vehicle against the wall, coiling the spring as tight as I could. I held my breath, counted to three and let rip. It shot forward all right, about four feet. We stared at it in silence until Danny Thorncliffe pulled out a cigarette, lit it calmly and said, 'We're fucked lads.'

'No we're not,' I said, but I could feel the group glaring at me.

'It's supposed to travel thirty feet,' said Fingers.

But before I could answer him, I was distracted by the sight of the Lord Mayor's car pulling into the staff car park.

The assembly hall was packed with proud parents and dignitaries as they strolled round the room with plastic cups filled with fair trade coffee. Each group had been designated a table allowing them to display their designs and plans with pride. I noticed some of the groups had coloured charts and elaborate files filled with notes on technical data. We were huddled around a single piece of A4 with a sketch of the contraption in blue biro. I was so embarrassed, I wouldn't even let my mum come over for a chat.

We drew the short straw and were last to go, which only added to the pressure. Each of us made several uneasy trips to the toilet. Fingers was in such a state of despair that he climbed out of the bog window and never came back.

Red Rum and Co. rolled their wooden ball across the floor to rapturous applause. I thought that they should have been disqualified just for being smug.

Finally, after what seemed like an eternity, it was our turn. Mr India made his announcement:

'Last but by no means least, would you please show your appreciation for "The Very Fast".'

There was some sarcastic laughter at the mention of our name, but I was confident that would cease once they'd witnessed our endeavours.

The room watched on in silence as we pushed each other forward as group leader. I swear if Mr India hadn't deliberately cleared his throat a fight would have broken out between us.

Reluctantly I was pushed to the front and all I could hear was the sound of my Adidas Kick trainers squeaking as I walked to the centre of the hall. I took up my position, grabbed the pitiful contraption with my hands, and then with all of my might I threw it across the hall floor towards the finish line.

Now, you're not going to believe this but we came second. I swear to God. We were totally shell-shocked when the judges announced their decision. I still can't believe it twenty years later. I just flung the contraption across the floor and we came second. I don't think the wheels even touched the ground and the spring flew off halfway down the hall and caught a nun on the shin.

Red Rum and Co. beat us with their smarmy wooden ball but we couldn't have cared less, The Very Fast had come second. And as if things couldn't get any better we were given a Double Decker each and a five-pound voucher for WH Smith's. Brilliant!

Chapter Five

Catholic Intercourse

Some of my favourite memories of school are the occasional trips that we went on. Every year on the last Friday in May eight coaches would leave the convent packed with hyperactive children and head for Alton Towers. (In case you're unaware, Alton Towers is a successful theme park in the heart of the Staffordshire countryside that will hopefully now furnish myself and my family with a few free passes for giving them a mention.)

The nuns sent us away on that particular day because traditionally it was the same day that the fifth-years left school and they liked to celebrate by throwing eggs and flour over each other in the front street. That's why the nuns thought it best to keep the rest of the school out of the way. Damage limitation I think they call it now.

I was always very excited and found it hard to sleep the night before the annual trip to Alton Towers. My head would be crammed with plans, such as which ride we should go on first and the curious expectation of what the new ride would be like. Because a new ride was unveiled every year, which usually meant some obligatory horror-story gossip regarding a friend of a friend's cousin's nephew's brother who'd had his head cut off while riding this new ride, but whatever the rumour it wasn't going to deter us from queuing for three hours and going on it eight times in a row.

That was the only thing that bugged me about theme parks, the bloody queuing. On a bad day you'd spend most of your day queuing and would end up going on only a few of the rides. These days you can pay more and get one of those special 'fast track' passes that allow you to go straight to the front of the queue. It'd be great if the management at Alton threw in a few of those free day passes as well.

We'd be put into groups and designated a teacher as an escort. I used to enjoy the teachers' attire on school trips because they would always turn up in their play clothes. We'd be in hysterics at some of the fashions they'd arrive in. The bluest blue jeans in the world, I'm talking sky blue now with gigantic turn-ups, so big, kids could have hidden in them and been smuggled into the park for free.

Another memorable school trip was to the Isle of Rhum in third year. I wasn't actually supposed to be going on that particular trip but I got a phone call from Mr Fitzpatrick, my History teacher, telling me that Paul Jarvis had just been suspended for headbutting a nun, so a vacant place had come up.

I was keen to go but the problem was I'd never been on a hiking type of trip before and I didn't have any of the right equipment. Well, I had a woolly hat and some fingerless gloves, but that was about it. Mr Fitzpatrick said he could lend me some hiking boots out of the school store but what I really needed was a good, strong, waterproof coat ideal for walking up mountains in the November rain. I rang round a few friends but most of them wouldn't be seen dead in a waterproof coat. It was late Friday evening, all the shops were shut and we were going early Saturday morning.

Luckily my dad overheard my plight as I chatted on the phone in the hall. He said he'd have a word with my Uncle Tony. They were going out for their usual Friday-night game of snooker and if anybody could lay their hands on anything at short notice my Uncle Tony was the man.

Time was getting tight, I wasn't holding out much hope and then I got a call from my dad. He was phoning from the payphone down at the Labour Club.

'Peter, it's your dad.' (He always said that in case I didn't recognise his voice.) 'I've got you a coat. It'll be there for you in the morning.' Then the phone went dead.

I got up early, it was about half three, went downstairs and got the shock of my life. True to his word my dad had got me a good waterproof coat – it was hanging off the kitchen door in all its glory. The only problem was it was a luminous Day-Glo orange and had 'Motorway Maintenance' written on the back in big yellow letters.

I charged upstairs, two steps at a time and burst into my mum and dad's room.

'BLOODY HELL!' my dad shouted. 'Turn the light off.'

But the light wasn't on, it was the glow of the coat lighting up the bedroom.

'I can't wear this,' I said.

'Why not? It's a bloody good coat, that,' said my dad. 'What else do you want on a Friday night? Millets was shut! Now bugger off, I'm trying to sleep here.'

He was right. I had no choice. I had to like it or lump it.

Everybody had a good laugh at my coat. I wasn't surprised. I stood out a mile wherever I went. When we pulled over for a brew at Carlisle Services a foreman in charge of a motorway road gang tried to give me a written warning for playing Pole Position in the mini arcade.

By the time we reached Scotland and the Highlands, where most of the land is National Trust, it had gone beyond a joke. There was I strolling around a conservation area wearing a luminous orange coat with Motorway Maintenance written on the back of it. It certainly got a few of the locals' tongues wagging, especially when I pretended to gesture the layout of a new four-lane bypass.

On the way to Rhum we stopped off to get some food rations and unbeknownst to Mr Fitzpatrick we hid three boxes of ribbed Durex in the bottom of his shopping trolley. I'll never forget the look of embarrassment on his face when he got to the checkout and the cashier tried to swipe them. He was mortified, particularly as he had three schoolgirls bagging up for him. We made the rest of the journey in complete silence.

I also went to France with the school. Now that was a hellish journey – it took us two days and four nights (you do the maths). I was just grateful that the coach had a video player on board to help pass the time. It was wall-to-wall films the whole journey. We watched the lot: two *Karate Kids*, *Teen Wolf*, *Back to the Future*, *Grease* (four times – which is probably the reason why I dislike the film so much today). Well, I think you'd have felt the same as me if you'd have had Catherine Profitt and Fiona Sedgeley singing 'Summer Lovin'' in your ear at half five in the morning. I even tried to bribe the driver into leaving them at Watford Gap to no avail.

I'm surprised he didn't take the money in hindsight, as he was a dodgy bugger. We hadn't even finished boarding the coach in

Bolton and he was already on the mike reading out the obligatory list of coach rules.

'Don't even think of using the toilet on board unless it's an emergency and even then, if you do, no solids. I don't want any of you messing about with the emergency exit at the back of the coach. I had one young boy fall out en route to Legoland and he's now fed through a straw, so think on,' he said.

Don't breathe, Don't smile – you'd think we were going on holiday or something. It was one rule after another, but the rule he kept banging on about at every opportunity was, 'Don't bring any cans of pop on board the coach as they can easily roll under my foot pedals and cause a major road accident.' Then the cheeky snake pulled over for a toilet stop right in the middle of some barren French desert, in the arse-end of nowhere, opened the boot and began to sell us 'warm' cans of Rola Cola for a pound each.

Later in the journey we managed to talk the teachers into watching *Beverly Hills Cop*, but we only got three minutes into it before it was hastily ejected by Miss Hoffle-stien (our Jewish French teacher) after she heard 'Get the fuck out of here' three times. She replaced it with a punishing double bill of *The Jazz Singer* and *Yentl*. I was just grateful *Schindler's List* hadn't been made otherwise we would probably have had to sit through that too.

There was another uproar when we watched *The Terminator*. It came to the classic sex scene between Sarah Connor and 'the goodie' bloke from the future – I forget his name now but he was in *Aliens*. They started to shag and you could have cut the atmosphere with a special atmosphere cutter. The teachers all started to cough nervously and look round at each other and then

Mr Almond (the French Geography teacher) climbed down behind the driver in an effort to turn off the video. The video player was situated on a shelf directly behind the driver's seat. Mr Almond had to pull back a pair of curtains and stretch over the driver's shoulder in order to work the controls.

The screen went blank and there was a huge boo from everybody on board. But the boos were replaced by cheers when the picture flickered back on and they were still mid-shag. Then the picture paused and all we could see was 'the goodie' fella left holding Sarah Connor's breasts in mid-air. There were more cheers and then the whole coach exploded in hysterical delight when they started to shag backwards in slow motion. The noise of wolf whistles was deafening. Then the driver came on the microphone.

'Hey, keep it down, I'm trying to drive here,' he shouted.

Mr Almond got back into his seat, saw what was on the screen, turned red with embarrassment and climbed back down to the video recorder shaking his head.

The screen went blank again for a few seconds and then the picture came back on but now they were shagging forward in slow motion. The bus erupted once again with wolf whistles and cheers. We overheard the driver on his mike telling Mr Almond to 'leave it alone and sit the fuck down before we crash'. Poor Mr Almond reappeared looking more defeated than ever, having subjected us to the longest sex scene in motion-picture history.

Mr Almond was dogged with bad luck on that school trip. Unbeknownst to him he was robbed outside the Eiffel Tower when a thief unclipped his bumbag and ran off with three hundred quid's worth of traveller's cheques, then he got his genitals stung by a jellyfish on a day trip to the beach and had to be rushed to Le A&E because his balls were swelling up to the size of grapefruit.

I don't know if it is just the Catholic religion but I was brought up to believe that sex is a sin. It was always an awkward subject to discuss in front of adults, even worse in front of nuns. I'll never forget the excruciating experience when the time came for sex education at school. I knew there was going to be trouble when I noticed all the science textbooks had been glued shut on the chapter entitled 'Reproduction'. Then the nuns made us take notes home in order to get our parents' permission before we could learn the facts of life.

Personally I thought having nuns teach sex education was a bad idea to begin with. I mean, let's be honest they're hardly experts in the field, are they? I wish I could say the same about priests but hey . . . let's not go there.

The nun that we had taking us for our painful journey into the facts of life was Sister Act II. She opted for the slide-show technique, but I've got to tell you, 'What Mr Bee and Mrs Flower got up to in the garden' was one of the most embarrassing things I've ever had to sit through. Not only was it dated, juvenile and patronising, but it was confusing too.

Afterwards she turned off the projector and flicked on the lights. 'So is that all clear to you now?'

Clear as mud. There was a stunned silence. I mean, how you could get a lady pregnant by hovering round a daffodil was beyond me. She'd lost us and she knew it.

'It's Mother Nature,' she said, desperately attempting to elaborate. All God's animals 'do it' . . . some of you must have witnessed dogs doing it in the street.'

'You mean shit, Sister?' said Clive Whitworth, sticking his hand up.

'No,' said Danny Thorncliffe, 'She's talking about shaggin' aren't you?'

But by now Sister Act II seemed unsteady on her brogues and had moved over to the science lab window for a little fresh air.

Things weren't much better for me at home when it came to the facts of life. My mum had sent away to the *Daily Mirror* for a leaflet by Claire Rayner. Occasionally when we were all watching television as a family a sex scene would rear its head and my mum would say,

'That reminds me, I must let you read that leaflet I got off Claire Rayner . . .' (as if she was a personal friend of hers.)

I could have died of embarrassment. I just smiled politely and uncomfortably reached for something to read, the back of a box of tissues, anything just to distract me from the sex scene on the TV. Equally embarrassed, my dad would be quickly flicking over to something less provocative on the other channel, usually two rhinos shagging on BBC1.

I ended up reading the Claire Rayner leaflet myself one weekend when my mum was away at my Auntie Barbara's in Milton Keynes. I found it hiding at the bottom of my mum's knicker drawer one Saturday night after *Tales of the Unexpected*. I lay on the bed reading it, but I was still none the wiser. It was full of foreign words I'd never even seen before like 'labia' and 'clitoris'. I couldn't even pronounce them let alone find them on a woman. Hopefully I wouldn't need to for some time, I was only eleven and I didn't fancy burning in hell just yet.

But just when I'd given up any chance of discovering the truth about the Facts of Life good old Channel 4 decided to start screening adult films late on Friday nights. It was known as the 'Red Triangle' film season because they had a red triangle in the corner of the screen throughout the film to let viewers know the material was X-rated.

Millions of confused adolescents like myself gave a resounding sigh of relief as the season became a haven for us. With black-and-white portables flickering in bedrooms up and down the country, suddenly, between the subtitles, it all made sense. I wrote a letter of gratitude to Gus McDonald at *Right to Reply* but he never read it out.

Meanwhile, back at school, the nuns decided to follow up on sex education by taking us into the hall and making us sit through a slide show on abortion. I still recoil now when I think of the graphic images they forced upon us that day. Mr Bee and Mrs Flower were replaced by coloured slides on a twelve-foot screen of aborted foetuses (and just before dinner too). They even passed round a plastic replica of an aborted foetus so we could see the size for ourselves.

At the time we all just accepted it as the norm (and I don't mean that fat bloke off *Cheers*), but looking back the nuns were completely out of order for subjecting us to that. Not only were we eleven years old but the thing that infuriates me the most when I think about it now is they never gave us both sides of the story. It was just one biased opinion after another. Clearly the nuns were against abortion but instead of shocking us into having the same opinion as them they should have given us all the facts. They knew that those images would have an impact on us at a tender age, and believe me, they did.

The nuns never mentioned the argument for pro-abortion once and they quickly bundled Natalie Cunningham out of the hall when she informed them that her sister had had an abortion. I half expected to see Natalie's head impaled on the school gates at home time – come to think of it I never did see her again . . . shit!

It made me realise how dangerous Catholicism could be. When I was at school I was always told that if I was bad God would punish me and in the same breath I was told that God would forgive me for my sins whatever they were. It was a bit like being slapped one minute and getting a big cuddle the next. Catholicism sure knew how to mess with a child's head.

The confusion began to get me down but still I never once questioned my faith. Now I don't want to get all *Da Vinci Code* on you (and I'm sure the publishers, Random House, would prefer if I didn't either, they've have had enough drama with Dan Brown in the dock without Peter Kay ending up in court again! I say again as I did jury service in '96. And I lost a fortune on bus fares that the court wouldn't refund, the swines.) But over the years I've come to the conclusion that Catholicism is rife with hypocrisy and confusion. It's preyed on people like myself while people like myself were busy praying. (Do you like what I did with the word praying there? Hey I don't waste my evenings.)

For example, I was always taught to go to church every Sunday and we did until my mum discovered a loophole in the Bible. It basically says keep the Sabbath day holy; it doesn't actually say anything about having to go to church. So we just used to watch *Praise Be!* with Thora Hird and have a sing-song.

I also believe that a man called Jesus did walk the earth at one time but I don't think he was the superhero that the Bible makes him out to be. Could he really turn water into wine? Did he raise people from the dead? Well if David Blaine can't survive under-water in a tank for seven days without needing medical attention, then I very much doubt it. I think Jesus was just an ordinary person like me and you (well, I'm comparing you with myself in the hope you're not a mentalist). I belive that Jesus spoke about peace, he spoke about turning love into hate, tears into laughter, war into peace and – hold on a minute, this is Johnny Mathis. Jesus's teachings spread and quickly he built up a passionate following. People hung on to his every word, some would even walk for miles just to catch a glimpse of him. I can only imagine it must've been like that for Henry Winkler when he played the Fonz in *Happy Days*. Ultimately Jesus's success bred contempt, people of power weren't fond of this hip and trendy preacher and before you could say 'Happy Days' Jesus was beaten, whipped, nailed to a cross and crucified. They didn't understand him, so they murdered him, in their ignorance and fear.

But Jesus had the last laugh. Apparently two days later on Easter Sunday he came back from the dead. Well, he'd have been daft not to with all those chocolate eggs knocking around. I mean, look at me, I bought three Yorkie eggs from the Texaco garage just because they'd been reduced to a quid. Pig that I am.

Later, after the crucifixion, Judas, who shopped Jesus for thirty pieces of silver (about £16.50) could no longer live with the guilt of his betrayal, committed suicide by hanging himself from a tree. A scene that ITV decided to cut out of *Jesus Christ Superstar* in their infinite wisdom, when they showed it last Easter Sunday afternoon. So not only did it look as though Judas didn't have a conscience but it also looked as if he got away with it.

The reason I'm telling you all this is that basically I believe in the same principles as Jesus or, as they've now become known in the last few paragraphs, 'The Johnny Mathis Principles'. And these fundamental teachings are at the core of most religions.

Basically we should try to follow the fundamental rules that were laid out for us in the Ten Commandments (obviously use your own judgement when coveting your neighbour's ox). Treat others like you would like to be treated (that obviously excludes people like Gary Glitter). And try to stand up for old people on public transport every once in a while (no matter how badly they may smell of piss and biscuits). If we all did this then I'm confident that the world will be a better place for all of us.

One thing I've never been keen on is the Catholic Church continually turning to its parishioners for funding. I think people should support their parish when it comes to the odd broken window or maybe the annual trip to Lourdes but why doesn't the Vatican dip its hand in its deep pocket when it comes to the missions and training new priests? Why do the parishioners have to fork out all the time?

The Catholic leaders seem to sit on all of this wealth in the Vatican, and why? What good does it do? Why are all of these priceless possessions gathering dust when the riches they would provide could be put to better use elsewhere? The Catholic leaders tell us that they're there to honour God, but it just doesn't make sense to me when Jesus supposedly led a meagre life of virtual poverty.

The one thing that illustrates my point better than most is the final scene at the end of *Indiana Jones and the Last Crusade*. (I can't remember much of the film as I was on a double date with Paddy at the time and he was trying to get to second base with Geraldine Sloane. He thought he had his hand on her bust for most of the film but when the lights came up at the end it turned out to be her handbag. 'I thought she'd had her nipple pierced,' he confessed to me later on the bus home.) After chasing after the Holy Grail for most of the badly CGI'd film, Indiana Jones's quest finally reaches its climax in a cave of some sort. The Holy Grail takes the form of Christ's chalice but instead of one, they are presented with a choice of two. The stupid greedy Nazi goes for the most expensive-looking chalice but it's the wrong choice and falls to his death (with a badly dubbed scream). But thankfully R Indy knows his stuff, he's studied the subject. He knows that Jesus didn't have a pot to piss in and so he chooses the knackered-looking chalice and lo and behold it's the Holy Grail.

I quizzed Sister Matic about this in RE when we got back to school after half-term, but the only answer that she could provide was 'Insolence', which she screamed at me before throwing a board duster at my head. I was lucky – twenty years earlier she probably would have just pulled out a gun and shot me for asking such a question.

That reminds me of a very funny story I once heard the late, great Dave Allen tell. He said that when he was a child his parents sent him away to a Catholic boarding school deep in the Irish countryside. They drove him up to the gates, he got out with his suitcase and, frightened, he walked up to a huge pair of wooden doors. He banged on the knocker as hard as he could and eventually a fierce-looking nun answered the door.

'Yes?' she bellowed.

'Er . . . my name is David Allen, Sister, and I've come to stay,' he replied nervously.

'And are you going to behave yourself, boy?' asked the nun.

And then Dave Allen said that he looked over the nun's shoulder and saw a man nailed to a cross hanging from a wall, and said,

'You bet your sweet arse I'm going to behave myself, Sister'

I was a great admirer of Dave Allen. He liked to send up the

Catholic Church and his material was considered very controversial at the time. I certainly sympathised with his humour, being educated by the nuns and having served as an altar boy for a total of seven years, man and boy. I would like to say that I did it for the love of Our Lord Jesus Christ but it was actually because Jason Wallace told me that he'd got a tenner from a widow for serving a funeral.

After a while, though, I discovered he must have been lying because I did a whole raft of funerals and never got paid once. I even used to pretend to cry. I could have got a BAFTA for the heartbreaking performances I gave up at that crematorium.

Being an altar boy also meant that I was on call twenty-four/ seven. I'm surprised the priest didn't issue all the altar boys with beepers like they have on *ER*. Because whenever a funeral came in and the nuns got a call, I was dragged out of school and sent up to the church to serve. To hell with my education, Jesus is calling. One minute I'd be in PE, walking across an upturned gym bench and the next thing you know I'd be kneeling beside a coffin pretending to cry.

I also had to serve Mass every Sunday. My mum was so proud, though, seeing me up there in all my altar-boy regalia. Being on the altar gave me the chance to be in front of the congregation every week and was my first experience of being in front of a large crowd. And believe me, I played in front of some packed houses – we could have about seven hundred people in some Sundays.

But if truth be told it wasn't a very glamorous profession; in fact, it was hard work. We had to help the priest serve the Mass, wash his hands, pour his wine, shake his bells – we rarely had time to kneel down. If it'd said 'Slave Wanted' in the job description I'd have given it a miss.

One job I hated doing was the Eucharistic plate. This was a solid silver plate that you had to shove under each member of the congregation's chins when they came up for Holy Communion. It was a disgusting job – I had to deal with bad breath, rotten teeth and I saw more tongues than a cut-price prostitute.

And tongues of every shape, size and colour too. In fact it would be a good Sunday if you caught sight of a pink one. Especially when everybody had been out on the ale the night before. Most tongues would be purple or puce and you could smell the drink even before they got to the altar rails. Some of the congregation would still be drunk. I remember the priest saying 'The body of Christ' to a bloke who was clearly still legless, to which he replied, 'Cheers.'

We used to get what we called 'the shakers' too. These were mostly old people. God forgive me but how their tongues could shake. It'd be like a scene from *The Exorcist* some Sundays. I'd have to chase their tongues round with my plate in case they dropped the Eucharist on to the carpet. I remember one old dear shut her eyes and said 'Amen' and her teeth slid out of her gob. I had to crawl under the bench to get them back for the dirty bitch.

But there were some perks to the job too. I could bag the best palms for my mum on Palm Sunday. The best ashes on Ash Wednesday. I also managed to get my mum some holy water from Pope John Paul II's private vestry in Rome. My mum loved her holy water, she used to pour it into a font the shape of the Virgin Mary on the wall near the front door. We used to bless ourselves every morning before we went to school. Only, one time she got the holy-water bottle mixed up with some white spirit that sat next to it under the sink and we had to go to school stinking of turps.

I like to think that by serving on the altar I've more than done my bit towards securing my place in heaven. And what a vision of heaven it is too. Millions of people queuing in single file up an endless white marble staircase, there's plenty of mist and tireless angels fly to and fro on administration duties. If you've ever seen the film *A Matter of Life and Death* with David Niven then you'll know what I'm on about. And if you've never seen that film then you've certainly missed a treat. Take a tip from me and keep a lookout for it. They usually show it in the afternoon before Channel 4 racing.

Hopefully, I shouldn't have to queue up for too long before I get to the pearly gates (like I say, being an altar boy is a bit like having one of those fast-track passes that Alton Towers do, remember wink, wink). And my idea of heaven if that I get to settle back in front of a large television and watch the best bits of my life all over again. All of my friends and family can sit with me too and hopefully we'll be able to settle any outstanding arguments about who said what and when. I can also stop the tape once in a while and go for a swim in a pool full of Vimto. I always wanted to do that especially on a summer's day, so I could swim and drink at the same time. I might as well request it when I get to heaven because I wrote to *Jim'll Fix It* in 1982 and heard sod all back.

I know it might seem hypocritical of me to talk about a heaven after all the criticism that I've thrown at Catholicism, but at the end of the day I can believe what I like, it's my life. I like to believe in a God of some kind, in some sort of higher being or force. Personally I find it very comforting plus it also gives me somebody to talk to on long train journeys when there's no phone signal.

And if I do get to my heaven and find that it doesn't exist then it'll be much too late to do anything about it and hopefully I will have lived a deluded but happy life. I also won't be able to complain to anyone because there won't be anyone there . . . except maybe Jonathan Ross because, let's face it, he's fecking everywhere these days. In fact, he's around a lot more than Jesus Christ.

Chapter Six

The Holy White Triangle

I was never a fan of PE at school and I don't recall asking to be physically educated. It just seemed to happen and before I knew it my mum was sewing my initials on to the front of a gym bag and I was being forced to leap over a horsebox and perform a forward roll. That's what they classed as games. My idea of games were Connect 4 or Ker-Plunk. If it had been up to me physical education wouldn't even have been on the curriculum. It would just have been something that you did after school if you hadn't got a life.

I would rather have spent the time learning something more important like first aid or sign language, two subjects that should be on every school timetable in the world surely? PE was just an opportunity for the fit kids to show up the fat kids. Not that I'm saying I was a fat kid. I've always been naturally big-boned, or cuddly as Mum preferred to call it as she fed me my eighth Wall's Viennetta. There's always been a stigma attached to being overweight, especially when it comes to physical education. I was the last to get picked for any kind of sports and then even that usually resulted in a heated argument between the two team captains.

'We're not having him, we had him last week.'

It was a vicious circle and I was at the centre of it.

'Oh, don't mind me, you just argue among yourselves,' I mumbled as I filed my nails.

They could bicker as long as they wanted as far as I was concerned. I think the reason I developed a lack of enthusiasm towards PE was because people who liked PE had a lack of enthusiasm towards me. But I didn't mind, because the longer they bickered the less time we'd have for games. And anyway, it didn't matter because whoever got me I'd still always end up being put in a goal of some kind.

It turned me off football for life. I don't completely hate the game, I like watching the World Cup, particularly when they show the highlights to music with some Cameroon player doing a funny dance when he scores or footage of the England team blubbing when they get kicked out (as if it's come as a shock to them).

I think the public was given a wrong impression of me when I did the John Smith's 'Ave it' advert a few years ago. It was the one where all these highly skilled footballers performed various ball skills in a circle – balancing it on the back of their necks, flipping it into the air – before finally one of them passed it to me and I just toe-bunged it over a garden fence. The director wanted it done it in one continuous take, so we all had to get it right. It only took two takes to film. On the second take I was so impressed that I'd managed to boot the ball, I shouted out, 'Ave it!' They decided to keep it in and that's how the Ave It! catchphrase started. It became the buzzword during the World Cup of 2002, shouted at me wherever I went. Slowly this began to fuel the myth that I was a football fanatic. I got invited on to a load of football talk shows and also to a lot of games. I declined them all until I got a chance to take my nephew to Manchester United. He's a massive Manchester United fan. It was his eighth birthday and I knew he'd be over the moon. I told him I was just taking him to the Manchester United shop to get him some merchandise for his birthday. We went to the shop and bought a few things, but then instead of going back out of the main entrance, I led him out of a fire door and up a staircase. We went through another set of fire doors and came out in the directors' box.

My nephew's eyes lit up as he gazed up at the footballers in the room. I hadn't got a clue who most of them were but I did recognise Bobby Charlton, Denis Law and the late George Best. And I could feel the hairs go up on the back of my neck. We must have looked like a right couple of freaks stood in the corner with our mouths gaping open.

We had a couple of cracking seats in the directors' box – the view was amazing and so was the atmosphere. So long as no one tried chatting to me about the offside rule I knew I'd be OK. Then I felt my nephew's elbow poking me in the ribs.

'What's up?' I asked.

He just gestured past me with his eyes. I turned round to find a familiar-looking man sat by the side of me and we exchanged smiles. I turned back to my nephew and whispered to him,

'Who is it?'

'It's Roy Keane,' he whispered back out of the corner of his mouth.

I turned back to smile again and this time he held out his hand and offered me some spearmint.

'Go on . . . Ave it!' he said and laughed.

Manchester United played badly that day. My nephew was fed up with the result. What I found awkward was that every time Leicester scored Roy Keane would get increasingly irate. He'd sigh and tut, look at me and shake his head. The more they lost the louder he got. I'd just shake my head in agreement with him and mumble comments like 'What are they playing at?' and 'Come on, lads, what are you doing? You're throwing it away,' but I hadn't got a clue what was happening. I was more interested in one of those airships that was hovering above the ground rotating a variety of birthday messages.

Ironically, my nephew plays football in the same playground where I used to avoid it twenty years earlier.

I preferred to spend my playtime over in the corner of the schoolyard behind the boiler discussing the latest video releases with Darren Leech and Ryan Shannon. We were video mad – video recorders were all the rage at the time, the new big thing. Everybody was getting them. We used to compare notes about what films we'd seen, what was coming out and who could get what on pirate. It always tickled me that expression – pirate. 'A mate of mine can get it on pirate.' *ET* was the pirate video that everybody wanted to watch at the time. My dad managed to get hold of a copy. The quality was absolutely appalling but the whole family and a few of the neighbours gathered to watch it in our front room. You couldn't make head nor tail of it, let alone cry. I think my dad cried, though not because ET went home at the end but because the pirate copy had cost him a fiver from a bloke down the club. It wouldn't have cost that much more to go to the cinema and watch it properly in all of its glory.

Darren Leech was heavily into video nasties. If it was banned you could bet he'd seen it. *The Burning, The Evil Dead, The Driller*

Killer – quite an achievement for a boy of ten. He'd regale us with the stories of the latest slasher film he'd seen, acting out the scenes for us in violent detail, and he'd always drag his stooge over, poor old Barry Clegg, and force him to play the part of the victim.

I'd like to tell you that these dangerous games had no long-term damage on either of the boys but I'm afraid I can't. The last time I saw Barry Clegg he was collecting trolleys in the rain at Safeway's and Darren Leech is currently on remand for attacking his stepfather with a two-speed hammer drill. I rest my case, Your Honour.

Our video recorder was a Panasonic, model number NV 2010. (That'll probably mean nothing to you but it meant everything to me.) I loved that video. In fact, when my parents told me they'd paid their deposit for it at Rumbelows, my eyes lit up and for the first and only time in my life I performed a backflip (I was quite supple for a big lad).

I could hardly contain my excitement on the day standing at the window waiting for the delivery truck to arrive. The video was so big it took two of them to carry it into the lounge (or the best room as my mum liked to call it).* It was a true silver dream machine. What a beautiful beast. It had a twenty-one-day programmable timer and came with a remote control on a wire. I was speechless, all I could do was stare at it, as it sat nestled in its new home, a specially constructed pine video unit from MFI that my Dad had put together the weekend before. It also sported a top drawer with enough room for over thirty VHS tapes.

*I don't know if any of you ever had a best room. We lived in a two-up two-down terraced house. The place was cramped enough without my mum putting one room aside for best. We were only ever allowed in the lounge for special occasions, like birthdays and Christmas. It was ridiculous.

That night we recorded *Top of the Pops* and *Tucker's Luck* (a piss-poor spin-off from *Grange Hill*) and we watched them back to back three times in a row, just because we could. I remember my dad losing his mind as one point because I pressed the pause button.

'Don't do that, you'll break it,' he roared at me from his armchair.

He would go mental if I pressed the pause, fast-forward or rewind buttons. It's as if the manufacturers had included them in an effort to encourage parents into bollocking their children a bit more often.

I was hooked, and slid helplessly into the world of home video. While other lads were buying the latest sports gear and doing keepy-uppy in their backyards, I was buying blank videotapes and scouring the TV guides, with a black felt tip in my hand, searching for things to record.

The lads at school were very materialistic when it came to sports equipment. They were always trying to outdo each other with the latest trainers or sports bags. It had to be a name – Adidas, Reebok or Nike. My sports bag just said 'sport' on the side of it. Nothing else. People would sometimes ask me what kind of sport I liked. I'd just point to the bag and say I like sport, all sport, sport in general.

We weren't the richest family by far but it's not that we were poor. It's just that I wasn't arsed when it came to all that label competitiveness. I was probably the only person I knew who enjoyed wearing a school uniform. To me they were like overalls and I couldn't see the point of getting your normal clothes dirty when you had a uniform to wear. If you paid 10p on the last day of term you were allowed to wear your own clothes. Most schools do it (and I think they do it in the armed forces). I'd turn up in my uniform and they'd say,

'Why are you in your uniform? You could've worn your own clothes for 10p.'

I'd say,

'These *are* my own clothes,' and they'd walk away confused, but I knew I was right.

I only succumbed to materialistic temptation once. I had to go to the optician's. I wasn't keen on going as the last thing I needed in my uncool life was a spazzy pair of National Health glasses, but my mum insisted. She'd caught me squinting my eyes watching *3-2-1* (well, who wouldn't, it was shit). While we were walking back from the opticians, we passed a local sports shop and I fell in love with a pair of Nike trainers in the window.

They were white and when I say white I mean blinding white. The golden rule in '87 was the whiter the trainer, the cooler you were. My mum bought them for me as an early birthday present. I put them on and went back to school in the afternoon. Usually if I had a morning appointment I would have tried to blag the whole day off school. But now I had my new white Nike trainers to show off, I strolled down the road and through the gates like John Travolta in *Saturday Night Fever*.

There were a few stares and mumbles as I walked by but I didn't care. It was a beautiful summer's day. There wasn't a cloud in the blue sky above me and I was cool for just once in my life. I got to class and before I could sit down Big Mouth Gareth Riley decided to take the piss.

'Hello, Kay, I like your new Nick trainers.'

A few stifled laughs followed.

'If you open your eyes smart-arse you'll actually see they're Nike,' I replied smugly.

'No they're not, they're Nick's.'

He said it so indignantly that I had no choice but to casually glance down and read them. Shit! He was right. They were Nick trainers, a piss-poor copy of Nike for piss-poor people who couldn't read. Perhaps the trip to the optician's wasn't a bad idea after all. Ah well, at least I got to be cool for about ten minutes.

But 1987 turned out to be the summer of being uncool for me and the trainers incident wasn't the only embarrassing thing to happen. As you've probably gathered I wasn't a fan of physical education. In fact, I would say and do anything in order to try to get out of my weekly games lesson. Fake illnesses, throw myself down flights of stairs. I even paid Steven Marshall a pound once to write me a note supposedly from my parents excusing me from PE. He was famous for his adult handwriting. I was so convinced my plan would work that I even got the note laminated for future use. But old Mr Donaldson, my PE teacher, was no fool – he already had a stack of similar letters in the same distinctive handwriting.

Undeterred and desperate, I tried the oldest trick in the book and told him that I'd forgotten my PE kit. He just calmly walked over to the corner of the changing room and said,

'That's all right, Mr Kay, just get something out of the bin in the corner.'

PLEASE GOD, NO, NOT THE BIN! The bin was a huge red barrel that had sat in the corner of the changing rooms since before the school had been built. A skull and crossbones had been scrawled on the side of it. What lurked inside the bin fuelled the nightmares of every boy in the school who had ever contemplated skiving off PE. It was full of dirty, discarded and stinking PE kits.

Now whether these PE kits had been discarded on purpose or by accident wasn't clear, but one thing we did know was that the rancid smell that emanated from that bin was enough to put you off lying for life. I can still taste it in the back of my throat today. It was a mixture of stale sweat, urine and heartache.

Teachers understood the power of that bin. They knew no child would ever succumb to the suggestion of getting something out of it. In fact, they'd sooner cut their own hands off or, as I did, hastily reconsider.

'Whoops, sorry, sir . . . oh look, I've just found my PE kit here at the bottom of my bag, well, what do you know, it was there all along,' I said sheepishly, pulling a creased pair of shorts from under my *A-Team* lunch box. I'd sooner play football in a creased pair of shorts than a pair stinking of somebody else's shit.

We never had a football pitch at school so every Thursday we used to walk over to the local park.* The only problem was this was *my* local park and that would cause me an enormous amount of embarrassment over the years. Occasionally friends of the family crossing through the park would see me, and suddenly I'd hear, 'Yoo-hoo, Peter,' and because the pitch was a public right of way the game would have to stop while a lady pushing a pram or pulling a tartan shopping trolley would come over for a chat about the

---

*Mr Donaldson our PE teacher would take it upon himself to stop the traffic on the busy main road as we all crossed. We'd find it highly amusing because more often than not he'd get a beep from an impatient motorist which was usually followed by some abuse like 'Move, you wanker'. Fair play to Mr Donaldson, he always stood his ground. Well, he did until the wing mirror off a passing lorry clipped the back of his head and sent him arse over tit into the gutter. The nuns rushed him to hospital with concussion and thankfully PE was cancelled for a fortnight.

weather or Britain's involvement in the bombing of Libya. It didn't make me a very popular person with my teammates.

Then, as if that wasn't bad enough, one day a German shepherd came into my life. It was an ordinary afternoon just like any other. We were playing football in the park, I was in goal as usual, when from out of nowhere a German shepherd appeared and mounted me from behind. I didn't even know his name. I'm joking of course.

Please don't expect me to try to explain to you why this German shepherd chose to mount me because I don't have any answers. All I do know is that it started to happen every week and it always seemed to happen when the other team was just about to score. The dog would appear out of thin air and start to shag my leg.

I was becoming a nervous wreck. I couldn't sleep and whenever I did the dog would appear. I'd wake up in a frenzy in the middle of the night, kicking the duvet, trying to shake this damn dog from my leg. I didn't know the dog, I'd never seen the dog before, but it was starting to take over my life. I took to riding around the park on my bike after school in an effort to find out who owned the dog. I'd take a carrier bag full of leftovers from my tea with me as a peace offering. And I'd have them swinging from my handlebars as I searched for the dog, but I could never find it and it still only showed up during football for a quick game of hump my leg.

Thursday would come around too quickly and we'd all trudge over to the park. I'd be on edge, trying to hide myself in the middle of a group, my eyes darting from left to right, searching for the horny mutt.

Eventually I'd have to take up my usual position in goal. I'd have a quick chat to Darren Leech about his latest video nasty and before you could say 'I Spit On Your Grave', the other team would be screaming towards me in a frenzied attempt to score. At that very moment the dog would appear from out of the blue and climb on. Unbelievable! I'd be trying to shake it off and save a goal at the same time but resistance was futile. They'd score and the dog would bugger off.

Bewildered, I staggered to my feet and shouted to the others,

'Did you see it? Did you see it? It did it again.'

But while the other team was busy charging back up the pitch celebrating, my team were just hurling abuse at me. But what did they expect me to do with a German shepherd clinging rhythmically to my thirteen-year-old leg?

We ended up playing in a different park in the end after my mum wrote an embarrassing letter of complaint to Sister Sledge. I never saw that dog again but even today when I drive past a German shepherd I find my leg involuntarily starts to shake.

I always wanted our school to have a swimming pool. Other schools in Bolton had them, so why not ours? Apparently the year before I arrived the school had been given some money from the education authority and the pupils had the chance to vote between having a swimming pool or a recreation centre. The morons chose a recreation centre. I only saw the inside of it about six times in all my time at Mount St Joseph. In the end the nuns ended up using it as a storeroom for their religious stuff, like candles, hymn books and a ping-pong table. What a waste. I wish they'd have chosen a swimming pool, because swimming was a sport that I could do.

I was taught to swim on Tuesday evenings at High Street Baths in Bolton, an old Victorian building that has since been demolished. I had a lot of affection for the place but have to admit it was a shithole. It was dangerously decrepit and out of date even by the standards of the 1980s.

After the success of the 'Ave It! football advert I was asked to film a second one for John Smith's bitter campaign. This one was to be set at the European Championships and I was to play the part of the diver. A few days before filming I got a call from the producer just before I went down to London. He chatted to me about what I'd be expected to do during the filming at the swimming pool at Crystal Palace. Then casually halfway through the conversation he said,

'. . . and of course when you jump off the top of the diving board the director will be expecting you to bomb into the water.'

'He'll be asking me to do what? Bomb?' I said.

'Yes, you know, bomb, like you used to do off the diving board at the local baths when you were a kid.'

'My local baths used to dream of having a diving board mate,' I said. 'We never even had a slide, all we had was a handful of half-eaten, white polystyrene floats that you could hang on to in the water,' I said. 'I've never bombed in my life, not unless you count that taxi drivers' Christmas party I did over in Blackburn last July.'

Perhaps I'm such a keen swimmer because I used to go to swimming lessons twice a week at High Street Baths. My mum and dad used to take me on Tuesday nights to the 'Barracuda' Swimming Club, and I went there with the school one afternoon a week.

We had professional instructors at the Barracuda Club – well, as professional as you could get for 30p a session. I managed to collect most of my badges, 125-metre breaststroke, 125-metre crawl and an all-important life-saving certificate. Well, all-important was what they told me, but I've still yet to save a black rubber brick from drowning while coincidentally walking past the side of a canal wearing a pair of pyjamas. Nevertheless, I wore my badges with immense pride after my mum had sewn them on to my navy-blue trunks with red piping down the side. The trunks also sported a secret inside pocket (for what reason I'll never know).

The afternoon swimming trip with the school was a much more relaxed affair. We used to have a laugh in the changing rooms, the usual childish pranks. Turning the showers to cold while people were in them and hiding each other's clothes. I remember I once found a pair of underpants on the floor and we took great amusement in throwing them at each other and then it turned into an improvised game of football. By now they were sodden. Clint Kennedy decided to take things a step too far and slap any unsuspecting persons entering the changing room round the back of the head with the soggy underpants. It was funny until he almost blinded a bloke coming in with his son.

This bloke lost his mind (and almost an eye). Clint got a major bollocking off the nuns and would be banned from going swimming for the rest of the term. They would also force him to write a letter of apology to the bloke and his son.

At the time, though, we all found it very amusing, until on closer inspection I realised that the offending underpants were actually mine. They must have fallen out of my bag on to the floor. Cold and damp, I had no choice but to put them in a carrier bag and walk home commando.

The main difference between the Barracuda Swimming Club and school swimming was that, as I said, at the Barracuda we had professional instructors teaching us, but when we went with the school it was left to the nuns. Far be it for me to generalise, but nuns are to teaching swimming what pensioners are to power-lifting – in other words, useless.

I'm just glad I had the Barracuda Club, otherwise I would probably still be in armbands doing the doggy-paddle.

Sister Scissors* hadn't got a clue about swimming. She'd try to coach us as best she could, motioning breaststroke movements to us by the side of the pool. We used to find it very uncomfortable because every time we'd complete a circuit we'd come back and face Sister squatting by the side of the pool offering encouragement to us and the closer we swam towards her the more we could see her big white knickers. We had no choice but to look up her vestments.

We'd swim off deliberately slowly, desperately trying to delay our journey back. But we'd inevitably have to swim back towards her.

'Hurry up,' she'd shout. 'Open your eyes, Peter Kay! You're swimming into the wall.'

I really didn't want to glimpse her holy white triangle again. It took the fun out of swimming.

Sadly Bolton doesn't have a public swimming pool in the town centre at the moment, somewhere for families or kids to go to. We did have the Water Place for a while but that was demolished a couple of years back, I don't know why, it hadn't really been open that long.

I was thirteen when it first opened, I went with some girlfriends of mine from school. I wasn't supposed to be the only lad but my mate dropped out. I'd never been swimming on my own with a group of girls.

I raced into the changing rooms and ripped my clothes off. I didn't want to be last in the pool to a bunch of girls. I already had my trunks on underneath so that I could get into the pool in

---

*I've just hit rock bottom on the whole nun-naming thing.

extra-fast time. I stuffed my clothes into a locker, shut the door and then noticed that there was no number on the locker. In fact, there weren't any numbers on some of the lockers in my block. In a rush to get the building completed in time, the builders had forgotten to put numbers on all of the lockers.

Because I was in a rush I decided to just count where my locker was, fourth across, second row up, great, and then I dashed over to the YTS locker-room attendant in the corner of the changing room and thrust my key at him. I actually did a double take when I glanced up at him because he looked remarkably like Fatima Whitbread. I think he was used to getting this reaction because he stared back at me with venom.

Then grudgingly he looked over his shoulder to the 'I Ran the World 'clock on the wall.

'You've got an hour,' he said, and passed me a red rubber band to wear on my wrist. As I ran off he shouted. 'Don't run,' after me.

Then I was faced with a dilemma that I have every time I go swimming: how do I get across that freezing cold pool of four-inch shallow water without getting my feet wet? (Why do they always make you walk through that before you get to the pool?) Maybe I could clamber round the edges? At least I would avoid those plasters I could see floating on the top of it. Maybe I could leap it? No, too far. The ironic thing is that this pool of cloudy fluid has been deliberately put there for you to cleanse your feet before you enter the pool. I don't hate much in life but I hate that water. I'm making myself feel sick now so I'll move on.

I managed to beat the girls into the pool and after an hour of splashing and playing tag I heard a booming voice over a tannoy system: 'Red bands out please, red bands out.' That was us, time to leave.

I got out of the pool and reluctantly tiptoed through the obligatory pool of shallow water again. It was much worse the second time. Shivering, I went over to the attendant and got my locker key from him. I half expected him to be practising the javelin but he was just slumped in his chair reading a film magazine with Sigourney Weaver on the cover in *Aliens*.

I went back to the lockers and counted, four across, two up, put the key in, turned it but nothing happened. I tried it again but still it wouldn't budge. I tried several more times, starting to panic. I may have been victorious beating the girls into the pool but at this rate they'd already be on their second cup of chicken soup from the vending machine.

I went back over to the locker attendant and told him that I couldn't open my locker. I saw the look on his face, he really didn't want to help.

'Are you sure it's your locker?' he said patronisingly.

'Yes,' I said.

'Because some of them haven't got any numbers on them yet.'

'I know.'

'Well, why did you use one of them?'

Why didn't you put a sticker on them saying they were out of order, you lazy Fatima Whitbread lookalike? I never said this, I just thought it loudly in my head.

He sighed, slammed his magazine down and walked over to my locker. He tried it himself, twisting and turning the key every which way but loose.

'See,' I said.

'Are you sure it's yours?' he said.

'Yes, I know four across and two up, I know which one it is.'

This was getting beyond a joke. By now the girls will have grown up, got married, had kids and be back at the same vending machine drinking chicken soup with their own children. (Slight exaggeration there for comic effect but I'll allow it.)

Just as I could feel pneumonia creeping into my lungs I thankfully heard a voice over the PA again, this time asking for all 'yellow bands' to leave the pool. I saw a flash of concern in the attendant's eyes.

'Wait here,' he said and ran off.

He returned with an enormous pair of industrial bolt cutters and without so much as flinching, he snapped the lock off the front of the locker and went off to greet the yellow bands from the pool with his usual apathy.

The locker door swung open on its crooked hinges and revealed to me a white string vest, a pair of tan-coloured open-toed sandals, a trilby hat . . . I could go on but I think you get the picture.

'This isn't my locker,' I mumbled to myself in shock.

I re-counted the lockers, put my key in the one below and, hey presto, it opened. Quickly I grabbed my clothes, legged it over to a cubicle and locked the door. What a palaver!

The last thing I saw as I sneaked out of the changing rooms was the shocked expression of an elderly naked man as he stood facing his vandalised locker.

'What the bloody hell happened here?' I heard echoing behind me as I fled out the door.

I've never understood blokes like that old man, strolling around naked with everything swinging in front of all and sundry. I know it's a male changing room but there's no need to parade it about. I think they must get some kind of a kick out of it. I mean, call me old-fashioned but on the odd occasion that I'm ever in a changing room and I have to get naked, I do it discreetly with a towel round me or in a corner with nobody looking. I don't get my cock out and stop for a chat; I keep my head down, literally.

The other thing that pisses me off are blokes who bring their kids into the changing rooms with them. I understand that they probably don't have a choice but there are very few things worse in this world than turning round in the shower to find a strange child watching you soaping up your nether region. Again, it's bang out of order and I find it extremely uncomfortable.

But even worse than that is when blokes strike up a conversation with me when I'm naked. Now I agree that conversation is a dying art form but never, I repeat never, in the memory of mankind will you ever catch me striking up a conversation with a naked man.

'So what you up to then, Peter?'

'Well, right now I'm drying my balls.' Get the picture?

Don't get me wrong, I'm not homophobic, I'm not scared of my house and for your information I watched *Brokeback Mountain* twice on the flight to Corfu last year. (Well, I had no choice, *Herbie: Fully Loaded* was broken.) But even I like to draw the line occasionally.

Some chancer did it to me again the other week. He strolled over to me in the changing rooms and his opening gambit was:

'So, Peter, how's it hanging?'

Words failed me, people.

Time for a brew I think and then onwards and upwards to the next chapter!

Chapter Seven

Music Was My First Love . . .

(that's if you don't count Carol Farrell who broke two of my ribs trying to 'Do the Hucklebuck' at a school disco)

Her lifeless body lay on the roof of the limousine, crushed. Everybody knew the old McKenna building was over forty storeys high and she must have fallen from the top in order to cause that kind of damage. Every window in the limousine had been shattered and I could hear the shards of glass crunch under the cop's shoes as he wearily tried to hold back the few onlookers that had gathered, too little, too late.

I lit myself a cigarette in the glow of the police lights but it didn't do anything to calm my nerves. That was the last thing I needed to see on a day like this. I shouldn't have seen this. I wouldn't have seen this if I'd stayed with Melissa. I looked at my watch. She'd be sipping her orange juice right about now, watching the sun rise up over the San Fernando Valley. What was I doing here? Hold on, who is this? Who am I? This isn't my life . . .

Sorry about that, I don't know what happened there . . .

In third year we got the opportunity to learn an instrument. I decided to have a go at the saxophone as it had always struck me as being very cool. Black sunglasses, jazz and all that, but that myth was soon shattered as I staggered down the road with a saxophone case banging on my legs as I walked. It was huge, in fact it was almost as big as me.

A Welsh music teacher tutored me for an hour every Monday. I can't remember his name but I remember he was a miserable sod. I think he'd left his sense of humour in a jazz club somewhere, as well as his looks. It seemed as though he was wearing his head upside down. Very strange.

He also had no patience.

'Your fingering is all wrong, Mr Kay,' he'd shout at me like Mr Shorofsky (from *Fame*). 'You must practise your fingering all the time.'

I wanted to show him a couple of fingers. I was only learning 'Three Blind Mice' for God's sake, it was hardly 'Baker Street'.

I succeeded in keeping up the lessons for three weeks, and was actually quite proud of myself, and then it all went wrong when I tried to clean my instrument. I only did it because I thought it'd make the Welshman happy. I remember it was a Sunday night because I could hear the theme from *The South Bank Show* coming from the telly in the back room (we flicked it off after the theme – that was the best bit).

I filled the kitchen sink with hot soapy water, squirted in some Fairy Liquid, got a fresh scouring pad out, put on my mum's Marigolds and plopped my tenor sax into the sink. Splash! I was just about to start scrubbing when my mum came into the kitchen and shrieked,

'What are you doing?'

'I'm cleaning my saxophone,' I said.

'Well, you don't use Fairy Liquid.' she said. 'If you want to clean it, use this,' and in saying that she leaned into the cupboard and pulled out a bottle of Jif cleaner.

Phew, that was close, I thought to myself as I squirted it up and down the saxophone.

'That'll get a proper good shine on it,' she said and then went to bed.

Cut to a close-up of the Welsh music teacher, inspecting my saxophone in horror.

'You washed it in the sink?' he said.

I nodded proudly. I even went as far as to stroke it for him in an effort to demonstrate the shine.

He held the saxophone aloft, studying it like Jack Klugman used to do with a dead body at the beginning of *Quincy, ME.*

'Let me get this straight, you washed it in a sink with soap and water?' he said.

'No,' I said, 'not soap, Jif.'

'JIF?' he bellowed again. This time he made me jump.

Yeah, Jif, bloody hell, what's his problem? I was only trying to make him happy. He snatched the saxophone out of my hands.

'You can't clean a tenor saxophone with JIF, you stupid boy,' he shouted.

I thought 'stupid boy' was a bit uncalled for, but now didn't seem like the right time to mention that to him, especially with him turning maroon and foaming at the mouth.

'I only wanted to clean it,' I said

'You've done more than clean it, you've broken it.' And with that he put the saxophone to his lips and blew. There wasn't a sound. Personally I'd have loved it if a few bubbles had floated out of the end of it.

'It can it be fixed, can't it?' I asked him.

'I hope for your sake, yes,' he said. 'Now get out of my sight!'

I quickly gathered my stuff together and left, never to darken his music room door again.

I bumped into him a few weeks later in the convent gardens. I asked him if he'd managed to repair the saxophone. He said it'd been sent away and he'd let me know. Well, twenty years have passed and I've still not heard from him and between me and you I honestly don't hold out much hope.

I have images of the Welshman wandering round music-repair shops with a saxophone case under his arm, like J.R. Hartley in those Yellow Pages adverts.

That was my first and only venture into the world of musical instruments. Tragic really when I think how much I love music.

I realise that music is part of all of our lives to some degree but I've really let it rule mine. I still can't embark on a car journey without hand-picking a certain selection of music tracks to suit the right mood, season, weather. I find that everything has a bearing on what I play. I might only be nipping to the Late Shop for a bottle of semi-skimmed milk, but it matters nevertheless.

Apparently, my mum used to play music all the time when she was pregnant with me and when I was a baby. We only had a few LPs* (as they were called then – in fact they still are by my nana). One of my earliest memories is of my mum playing the best of the

*My nephew recently found a box of LPs in the attic and said, 'Wow, look at the size of these CDs Grandma.' We all laughed because it'd hadn't occurred to us that he wouldn't have seen one. He'd never actually seen a record player before or ever heard of cassette tapes. And when I attempted to explain the concept of the 'eight track' to him he just left the room, laughing and shaking his head. Mind you, so did everybody else in the seventies.

Carpenters, Simon & Garfunkel and the Beach Boys to me, and for some reason the original soundtrack to *Paint Your Wagon*, all in rotation, all of the time. I have the vaguest recollections of her dancing around the room with me in her arms, and I'd listen to them as I lay on the floor, drawing on a piece of wallpaper with coloured crayons. The sun always seemed to be shining.

As I got older my mum and dad's record collection gradually became integrated with mine. In my teenage years I decided to revisit those worn-out LPs. Delicately sliding them out of their tatty paper sleeves for the first time in a long time. And as soon as I played them, a door swung open in my mind and all those priceless memories came flooding back.

Hearing them again evoked a powerful aching inside me for a time that was long since gone. What really freaked me out was when I discovered I knew all the music off by heart. I found myself humming along to the tunes, sometimes even singing the words. This music was part of me. And on reflection they weren't bad albums to have grown up with either.

I remain fascinated by the moods and the memories that music conjures up. I hear a certain song and suddenly I'm transported somewhere else. Just off the top of my head, for example, if I hear 'Don't Stop 'Til You Get Enough' by Michael Jackson, suddenly it's July 1979 and I'm back at Butlins holiday camp in Filey, it's raining and I'm drinking out of an 'I Shot JR' cup that I got for my birthday (they were all the rage).

If I hear 'Walk the Dinosaur' by Was (Not Was). I'm back in the school minibus on my way to Aberystwyth on a field trip. We're all listening to the Top 40 on the radio, Stuart Finnegan hits me in the face with a torch and cuts my nose, the hyperactive prick. Not a particularly good memory, that one, let's try another one.

When I hear 'Mistletoe and Wine' by Cliff Richard, I immediately think of Christmas . . . That was a joke.

If I hear 'White Lines' by Grandmaster Flash (which isn't very often these days), I'm immediately transported back to March 1984. It's snowing heavily and I'm about to ride the waltzers for the first time on one of those travelling fairgrounds. It knocked me sick. I puked on some gypsy bloke's hand and ended up missing *Shine On Harvey Moon* because I was sat on the couch with my head in a bucket.

I could go on but I think you get the picture. Every song has a story and that's the way it'll always be. Even this week on the radio they've been playing the new song called 'Trouble' by Ray LaMontagne and no doubt it'll always remind me of this time now, writing this chapter. It'll remind me of this afternoon, the spectacular weather I can see outside and here I am sat in the kitchen typing this to you. I've either got to be extremely dedicated or mad. I'll let you be the judge of that.

Of course I had toys when I was a child but I think the family record player was my favourite. It was a navy-coloured box with a flip-up lid, quite common at the time. It had a handle on the side, suggesting that it was portable (if you were a weightlifter) and it had four speeds, 16, 33, 45 and 78, the latter being my favourite because of the comedy value in being able to speed up certain records and make Simon & Garfunkel sound like Pinky & Perky.

More records started to appear in the house as the years passed. *The Best of Henry Mancini and his Orchestra*, for example, I loved that one because it had the *Pink Panther* theme on it. Then my dad came home with a Danny Kaye album, on which he performed selected works from Hans Christian Andersen and 'Tubby the Tuber'. My mum's favourite LP was the *TV Times Album* featuring the themes from *Magpie* and a *Bouquet of Barbed Wire* (filth). That album was played constantly. I hold it directly responsible for the long-standing obsession I have for TV themes.

The first LP that I ever bought was a BBC sound-effects album, *Disasters*. It seems a worrying choice on reflection. I was only eight. It was £2.30 from WH Smith's and I had saved up my pocket money for ages to buy it. Sound effects fascinated me. There were car crashes, collapsing mine shafts, inner-city riots (with or without petrol bombs), cattle stampedes, all the classics. Guaranteed to break the ice at any party. (I never went to many parties.)

I bought it because I'd now graduated to a Philips cassette player that my dad bought from the catalogue. It also had a built-in microphone feature that enabled me to play the *Disasters* album on the record player and also record myself on the cassette player, and make my own little plays and news bulletins. I was hooked. I'd spend the whole of the summer holidays writing and recording plays that always ended with a mine shaft collapsing or a riot (with petrol bombs). It was 1981 and riots were all the rage that summer.

We also had the bog-standard recordings of my sister and me singing a variety of nursery rhymes and hymns. 'I Can Sing a Rainbow' and 'Walk with Me, Oh My Lord'. I dug them out recently and transferred them on to CD for my mum as a Christmas present. It was actually quite emotional for us when we listened to them again after all of these years because my mum thought a lot of them had been lost. (It was also quite a cheap gift.)

I soon realised I could put the recording feature to better use and I started to record my family. Unbeknownst to them I recorded them almost all of the time. I know it may sound a bit strange and possibly even quite sinister, but I really had no ulterior motive other than to listen back to them. It sounds really stupid to confess that but even at such a young age I was absolutely fascinated by real-life conversations and I still am. What people say, how they talk over each other, how a conversation can spiral from one subject to another. I also loved the silence. The pauses that naturally occur in conversation can sometimes be funnier than the conversation itself. You couldn't write it but I could capture it and save it for ever on my TDK 90s.

Mind you, I say you couldn't write it but the creators of *The Royle Family* came damn close. It was one of the best comedy series I'd seen in a long time when it was first shown on television. I was fascinated by the way they managed to replicate real conversations. They were so similar to the ones that I had recorded of my family over the years. I laughed at the series first time round, but I've watched it again recently and have found it far funnier than I did ever before, like the comedy has distilled and got better.

I was particularly fond of the real-time aspect to the show, which allowed for pauses in conversation to happen and that 'fat' for me is the funniest thing in the series, its greatest strength. I had nothing but admiration for the series' creators and luckily I've had the privilege of getting to know them over the last few years. In particular Craig Cash. I told him of the recordings I used to make of my family and even managed to play him some. It was like listening to something that he'd written, the rhythm of the speech, the discussions that we were having, it was all so similar.

I always used to play my recordings back to my family later – 'Is that my voice?' they'd say 'Oh, do I really talk like that? I sound awful' – and they'd laugh. People like to eavesdrop on conversations. Why do you think reality television has become such a big success (and I'm talking about *Big Brother* now not *The X-Factor*)?

My family got used to me recording their conversations over the years. It became a part of our everyday lives, like living in a real life *The Truman Show*.

'He's taping us again, this lad, I know he is, where have you hid it?' they'd say.

I even stopped hiding it after a while and would just sit the cassette recorder on the table at mealtimes.

I've kept these recordings from Christmas, birthday parties, etc. The memories that they evoke are priceless and can sometimes be very emotional as well as funny, especially as some of the people on them are no longer around any more. I find that even the recordings that once seemed a bit boring are priceless now. Moments captured, that I can listen to and treasure.

One of my favourite recordings is of the time my dad was about to saw through a piece of wood and he asked me to sit on the end of it as a weight. You can hear him on the recording:

'Peter . . . Peter, come here and sit on this for me . . . and don't move whatever you do.'

I oblige and sit on the wood. You can then hear my dad start to saw. I remember it so vividly. He was halfway through sawing the wood and I got bored. I forgot all about his previous instructions about not moving, and with my attention wandering I decide to go for a little walk, perhaps hoping to finish off building my Lego windmill in the back room.

My dad carries on sawing and doesn't realise I've gone until the unweighted wood tips up and he saws straight into his leg.

'BLOODY HELL!' he says in the recording. 'What did I tell you? Don't move, I said. Jesus Christ! Deirdre, get the cloth quick.'

All hell breaks loose. He'd only grazed the skin, he didn't even have to go to A&E.

Later that night I played the recording back and we all cried laughing, even my dad 'saw' the funny side of it (if you'll forgive the pun).

Another recording I cherish is from Christmas 1988. It was one of the last times we were all together as a family and I recorded it at my grandparents' house on a Boxing Day afternoon. You can hear the end theme from *Jim'll Fix It* playing on the TV before we decide to play our traditional family game of charades, or as my mum says on the recording, 'Are we playing Give Us a Clue?'

After a while it's my nana's turn to have a go and though she plays it every year she still insists on talking all through the charade.

'It's a film . . . and a book . . . and it's two words.'

'You're not supposed to talk, Mum,' my dad says, but she's not listening. She's in full flight now and she begins to fling herself round the front room, making gestures with her arms. Then my grandad asks her,

'What it's called?'

I don't know what he was thinking, I mean, what did he expect her to do, tell him and then sit down? You're supposed to guess, that's the whole point of the game. My nana ignores him and carries on, but we're all still none the wiser.

After ten minutes of complete frustration you can hear my nana say,

'Hold on.'

She goes into the kitchen and you can then hear the slamming of cupboard doors.

'Here it is,' she shouts victoriously from the kitchen.

My dad is already in hysterics now in anticipation of what she'll return with. She re-enters the front room carrying a dessert bowl and as my dad slides off the armchair choking with laughter you can hear him shout out '*Oliver Twist*'.

Every Sunday morning after we came back from eleven o'clock Mass we'd watch *The Waltons* and have a big family breakfast. My dad never came to Mass, so he would've already made a start on breakfast by the time we got back from church. Well, I say made a start – he would've turned the grill on.

It's not that my dad didn't go to church, he just preferred to go to the evening Mass because he 'couldn't be doing with all that bloody singing after everything' and also because he could bunk off after Holy Communion and sneak into the Willows for a pint.

He did have a point about the singing. They do sing an awful lot at church and it does sometimes seem that if somebody so much as coughs it's an excuse for another song. Especially at Christmas and Easter where the general rule seems to be the longer and more musical the Mass the more holy it is. The length of Live Aid pales into insignificance next to some religious celebrations I've attended.

Anyway, one Sunday we sat round the table chatting and subtly I managed to switch the tape player on to 'record' again. My dad told a fascinating story about the time he got mugged coming home from work. I don't think he really intended it to be a funny story and that's probably what made it even more humorous. A stifled laugh is always funnier.

'It was a cold Friday night in winter, I'd just been paid and was walking home from the rope works,' he says. (Incidentally, my dad worked there for many years. The only perk he ever got was an abundance of free string and washing lines. We couldn't shut our airing cupboard we had that many. I had no idea why he kept bringing them home, as we never had a use for them. Maybe he just kept doing it because they were free?) 'Two lads jumped me from behind in the backstreet. One of them headbutted me to the ground, while the other one robbed me. Then they made off with my wages. I managed to get a look at them. It was the Critchley brothers off Tittenhurst Road. They were always up to no good. I crawled to my feet and I somehow managed to stagger home, I really don't know how because I was in unbearable agony.'

That bit always makes me laugh when I hear it. He makes it sound like he's describing a scene from *Shane* or *High Noon*.

'I came in the front door and when your mum clapped eyes on me she had a fit. "Oh my God," she said, "what happened to you?" I told her I'd been mugged on the way home from work but that I'd managed to get a good look at them. Then I went straight to the shed in the backyard and got myself a piece of wood with a nail in. "Where are you going with that?" your mum said. I said, "I'm going to sort out the two rascals who did this to me." Well, I never said rascals but you know what I mean. Then your mum started begging me not to go, not to take the law into my own hands, didn't you, Deirdre?'

'No, I did no such thing, you could have done what you wanted for me, I wasn't bothered,' my mum says, which is very funny because it really knocks the wind out of my dad's sails for a few seconds. He's trying to come across as the Charles Bronson of Bolton, a vigilante with a grudge and my mum flatly refuses to play along, she just continues clearing the breakfast table. 'I just told you to just go to the police, but you wouldn't listen,' she says

'Anyway, so I went out looking for them. I got to the bottom of Croston Street and just as I'm walking up Daubhill, I spies a panda car coming towards me, so quickly I threw my wood into a doorway, I think it was Graci's Wine Store . . . you know next to the paper shop?'

You can tell from the silence in the conversation that I clearly have no idea where he means, but still he persists on getting the geography right. 'It's on the same side as the dry-cleaner's, you cross the lights by the Co-op near that special school where they make brushes. You know? . . . Next to what used to be that Calor Gas place before it blew up, they sell halal meat now?'

You can hear me say 'Oh yeah' but you can tell I still haven't the faintest idea where he is talking about.

'Anyway, you probably won't remember where it was, this was before you were born.'

That'll explain why I hadn't got a clue.

'The police must have seen my wood and they pulled over,' he says.

'And you were still covered in blood,' my mum adds.

'Oh aye, I was. "What are you doing with that wood?" the copper said. I said, "I'm looking for the two blokes who did this to me." "Well," he says, "you'll only get yourself into trouble taking the law into your own hands. Do you know who did it?" I said. "Yes, I do." "Right, well, get in," he said, "and we'll go and have a look for them."

'Meanwhile, back at home your grandad had called round to borrow some plates off us and he asked your mum where I was. She said, "He's been mugged coming home from work, he reckons it was those Critchley lads from off the lane, so he got a big piece of wood out of the shed and he's gone looking for them.

I begged him not to go, pleaded with him, but he wouldn't listen to me." '

At this point on the recording you can hear my mum shouting from the kitchen: 'Will you stop lying, I never said no such thing,' to which my dad replies, 'Bloody hell, Deirdre, give it a rest, will you, I'm trying to tell the lad a story here.'

So my grandad went out into the night to try to stop my dad from beating up the Critchley brothers. The only problem was Grandad only had a rough idea which house they lived in. My dad meanwhile was cruising around in a police car when a message came over the radio. 'Calling all cars, calling all cars,' (well, that's what my dad says in an American accent), 'we're getting reports of a disturbance at a house on Tittenhurst Road, some bloke's forced entry and we need medical assistance.'

'I don't know why but as soon as I heard that over the radio I knew it was your grandad,' my dad says in the recording. The police car swung round and headed for the house on Tittenhurst Road. Not sure of the address, my grandad had kicked the wrong front door in to find an old lady on the floor clutching her chest. The Critchley brothers were actually next door. They heard the commotion through the wall and legged it out the back before the police showed up with my dad. What a palaver!

'It upset your grandad, that,' my dad says. 'And he started with his angina soon after.'

'Did they never catch the Critchley brothers?' I say.

'No, but they got their comeuppance. The eldest one got done for drink-driving – he knocked a nun down on Green Lane and got ten years for manslaughter. The other one was a bit slow. He got done for armed robbery. He held up a butcher's shop on Christmas Eve because his mam had forgotten to get a turkey.

Serves them bloody right. Never forget, what goes around comes around, son.'

Then you can hear my dad take a final gulp of his brew and the end theme of *The Waltons* from the telly in the corner.

Chapter Eight

The Vinyl Countdown

In 1978 my dad had joined a record club at work. He and a few of his mates had decided to get a kitty together so they could buy and record the latest albums. It was the only time I ever saw my dad really get into something that even resembled a hobby (except for the time he tried to grow moustache, but then gave up because everyone said that he looked like a nonce). It was through this record club that I first started to become aware of the many different types of music. When my dad went out playing snooker on a Friday night my mum would let me sneak on to his record player and listen to the latest albums he'd got from the record club.

I think my dad knew that I listened to them, but he didn't mind just so long as I didn't scratch any of them or destroy his pride and joy. His 'pride and joy' being his Bush Stereogram featuring chrome cassette player and VHF radio. It was a stunning piece of equipment. Upholstered and finished in a sumptuous dark mahogany wood effect, each speaker weighed the equivalent of an nine-year-old boy (and I would have known as I was nine years old at the time). I'd slowly remove each record out of its protective paper sleeve then, with the delicacy of a bomb-disposal expert, I'd gently place them on to the turntable.

I'd put my dad's ginormous headphones on and sink back into his armchair. The headphones didn't fit round my head they were that big.

But I didn't care. I was lost, transported to a different world. Every Friday night. I visited the Hotel California with the Eagles, I served time in Folsom Prison with Johnny Cash and I got lost in the Bermuda Triangle with Barry Manilow.

And there were many others. I can remember being completely terrified and captivated when I first heard Jeff Wayne's musical version of *The War of the Worlds*. And I couldn't stop looking at the incredible artwork that came inside the gatefold sleeve as I listened to it over and over again.

I'll never forget the Friday I first listened to Meat Loaf's epic *Bat Out of Hell* album. I played it so loud that the sound bled out of the side of my dad's headphones and was louder than *The Gentle Touch* on ITV. R Julie was furious and threw a glass of Vimto at my head. Luckily she was an extremely bad shot and it managed to completely miss both my head and my dad's pride and joy.

The record club opened my ears to a whole new world of musical giants. Elton John, Queen, Genesis, Steely Dan, the stunning soundtrack to *Superman The Movie* by John Williams, ELO, Supertramp, Blondie, Neil Diamond and the Clash (obviously the last two weren't together). Quite an eclectic mix of music for a boy of my age, but I devoured the lot.

I now had a hunger for music to feed. So I joined my local library who fortunately had just started hiring out music on record and cassette. I hired everything and anything you could think of, from early Sinatra to the late Frank Zappa.

Foolishly, the library also provided the public with 'reservation cards' which enabled you to order music of your choice. I must have been responsible for using up their entire yearly budget as every weekend you'd find me in the music shops of Bolton armed with a fistful of 'reservation cards' and a biro.

I'd spend hours scribbling down the names of the latest releases. Then I'd return to the library and hand in my reservation cards. I managed to build up a vast music collection (and the library didn't do too badly out of it either). I also spent so much time in the library over the years that people were beginning to think I was either unemployed, homeless or library staff, and in a few cases all three.

One album I used the reservation cards to order was the original soundtrack to Mel Brooks's *The Producers*. I had always had a particular fondness for that film ever since my mum had let me stay up late one night and watch it on TV. I was eleven then and I thought it was the funniest thing that I had ever seen. I fell in love with everything about it, the script, the characters, the music. To paraphrase a line from the film, 'It was everything I'd ever wanted in a movie.' When I eventually got the soundtrack from the library I played it constantly, drove my sister mental. It wasn't just 'Springtime for Hitler' in our house, it was Summer and Winter too.

For many years I harboured a secret ambition to turn *The Producers* into a stage musical. I even went so far as to write a rough stage adaptation for it in an old Geography exercise book. Then I read that David Geffen or someone had bought the rights and that was that. As you'll probably be aware, a stage adaptation was made a few years ago and thankfully it was written and devised by its original creator, Mel Brooks, with great love and affection.

I never saw the show on Broadway but I did get to see it when it eventually came to the West End in London with the brilliant Nathan Lane and Lee Evans. *The Producers* turned out to be one of the best shows I've ever seen. I thought it was very, very funny. If you haven't seen it then I highly recommend you go, because it's a great night out. The funny thing was, it actually surpassed the original film for me. Maybe I might get a chance to be in it one day . . . who knows?

Another ambition I secretly harboured when I was younger was to be a disc jockey. Well, what's the point of having all this music and not being able to celebrate it with people? Isn't that what music is supposed to be about? I found myself loitering with intent around the DJ at school discos. Martin St Clair was his name and his nickname was 'the saint' (I bet he was up all night thinking of that). He'd been wooing girls for years with his flashing lights and his fancy white telephone-cum-headphone system. They adored him, hanging around the stage all night requesting the latest hits and swooning over his naff Anglo-American accent that lay somewhere between Cincinnati and Burnley.

The ironic thing was I didn't want to be a DJ becuase I wanted to be adored. I didn't even want to speak. All I wanted to do was play the music and enjoy myself watching others enjoying themselves.

But first I had to penetrate 'The Saint' and he was a hard nut to crack. He was a fortress of false tan and Hi Karate but slowly we came to an arrangement. He'd let me play a couple of songs and in return I'd hump his speakers back to the convent at the end of the night, leaving him free to sip Top Deck shandy out of a flask lid and sign autographs for 'the gals' (as he called them), in the front street outside school. The main road would be chock-a-block with cars, filled with parents impatient to pick their sweaty, hyperactive children up and get back home in time for *Tenko*.

All good things come to those who wait (except for my Uncle Gavin who got knocked down by a cement mixer while on his way to receive a new kidney). It was a simple process of elimination and Martin 'The Saint' St Clair had no choice but to hang up his headphones at the end of the summer. He was almost seventeen, he'd completed his O levels and was now ready to step out into the big wide world or, in his case, hospital radio. My loitering paid off and in September of that year, I took his baton and stepped up to the mike as his natural successor. And then every Thursday between the hours of seven and nine you'd find me on stage playing records as happy as a pig in shit. I held those kids in the palm of my hand with classics like 'We Don't Have To' – Jermaine Stewart, 'I'm Your Man' – Wham! (on 12-inch) and the ever-faithful 'Dancing on the Ceiling' by Lionel Richie. Even Sister Sledge used to make an appearance (and I'm talking about the nun, not the band). She'd sit at the back of the hall smiling and knitting, yes, you read that correctly, 'knitting'. Occasionally she'd tap her brogues along to the beat and I swear once she actually asked me to play the Communards' 'Don't Leave Me This Way'.

It brought me enormous joy to stand up there every week playing those songs. I'd never known a thrill like it (you've got to remember I still hadn't kissed a girl properly at this point and you can't count Mandy Sharples as she bit my tongue and spat in my mouth).

I loved to see those shapes spinning on the dance floor, faces full of pleasure and satisfaction all because of what I had chosen to play. Give the correct selection of tracks in the right order and you could elevate the people to the moon (and back).

Not that it was just thrown together, oh God no, we used to spend hours putting those playlists together. When I say 'we' I mean myself and Paul (my best mate then . . . and now). We also used to spend hours hanging around the music stalls on Bolton Market, buying warped ex-jukebox singles for 50p a throw. Until Paul came up with the clever idea of recording the music off the radio then hooking a cassette player up to the turntables – we saved ourselves a fortune. Now all we had to do was record the Top 40 on a Sunday evening and nobody would be any the wiser just as long as we managed to fade the track before Tommy Vance spoke.

When I eventually left school I continued being a disc jockey part-time. I did the occasional family function but with one proviso: if they hired the equipment I'd bring the music. I never took any payment, apart from perhaps the odd bit of buffet and a glass of Coke. I had a good run for a few years and at one point I genuinely contemplated making a go of it professionally, as it seemed like the closest I'd ever get to showbiz. But what I was soon to discover was that it was a lot tougher doing a disco for a wedding reception than it was doing it for the school. Mainly because you never got pissheads coming up to you at school telling you your music was 'shite' (well, apart from the occasional nun who'd been at the altar wine).

But when I DJ'd at weddings I used to get it all the time. There'd always be some prize knobhead who'd stagger over to me full of buffet to have a look through my record collection.

'That's shit, that's shit, shit, shit, shit, shit, Lionel Richie, shit, Wham!, shit, shit . . . more shit.'

Then I guarantee you he'd ask me to play some obscure track for him, a dark and dreary B-side from twenty years before that reminded him of an ex-girlfriend who'd broken his heart.

I'd smile deafly and never put it on. Then he'd spend the rest of the night trying to make sure I played it for him. I'd keep nodding and giving him the thumbs up until he'd threaten to glass me so I'd have to play it. Then I'd have to watch in horror as the dance floor emptied in one fell swoop, people walking back to their tables throwing venomous looks towards me and shaking their heads in disgust. To top it all the dickhead who asked for the record wouldn't even have the courtesy to get up and dance. He'd just sit in his chair nodding, raise his pint up to me for the chorus and wink.

I also came to the conclusion that I was jinxed. Every time I seemed to hire the equipment something went wrong with it. Like the time I hired the world's most sensitive CD player. It just jumped all night long. If you moved, it jumped; if you fluttered your eyelids, it would jump. I spent five hours walking around the stage like a friggin' astronaut. The bride and groom thought I had piles.

Another night I was booked to DJ at a fiftieth for a fat woman called Jean, who claimed she was my aunt because she'd been to water aerobics twice with my mum. I arrived to find that the hire company had dropped off the equipment but had neglected to leave me any lights. After a few fruitless telephone calls and numerous answer-machine messages sprinkled with expletives, I had to resort to paying one of the bar staff a tenner of my own money just to sit by the door all night and keep flicking the light switch on and off in time to the music.

The final straw came when I tried another hire company and turned up at the evening wedding reception to find that I had no power lead. They'd left me everything else except a power lead. With pains in my chest I frantically tried to track down a lead from somewhere while the bride, the groom and two hundred of their lovely guests sat and listened to the local radio. Luckily one of the bar staff found that a lead on a standard three-pronged kettle plug would do the trick, but my joy was short-lived when it slowly began to dawn on me that household kettle leads are only a foot long.

With tears in my eyes I dragged my equipment over to a plug socket in the corner of the room, where I then spent the remaining few hours on my knees trying to get the party started. All people could see was the top of my head and latecomers thought I was a midget. I couldn't stand up straight for days after that night. Bruised and beaten, I decided to throw the disco towel in once and for all.

My head had also been turned by live concerts. The first one I ever went to was the Four Tops on their 'Indestructible' tour live at the Manchester Apollo. They'd had a resurgence in the charts with 'Loco in Acapulco' and had proceeded to wheel out the old hits once again. I really enjoyed them, but then again it was my first ever concert. I would have probably enjoyed the Wurzels live at that point in my life. My only criticism was that the support band did longer than the Tops themselves.

I saw Hall & Oates, Phil Collins, Prince (supported by the Pasadenas who got bottled by the crowd at Manchester City football ground as soon as they came onstage), Lyle Lovett and Was (Not Was) who supported Dire Straits and who were actually much better, David Byrne who was amazing both times I saw him and totally different, and U2 – I've seen them live many times over the years and what I find astonishing is that they always manage to outdo themselves every time.

But Billy Joel has always remained my favourite. I've seen him live so many times. In fact, he's about to tour the UK again in the next couple of weeks for the first time in twelve years and I'm going to try to go to every one of his shows, writing permitting of course.

It all started when my dad bought me an EP of 'Uptown Girl' on 12-inch in the November of 1983. It was a Saturday afternoon and I'd been out all day collecting bonfire wood all day. My dad came home from town on the bus at teatime and handed me the record. I was made up and played it over and over again. I'd seen the video on *Saturday Morning Starship* with Bonnie Langford and Tommy Boyd and thought it was brilliant.

I got his follow-up single, 'Tell Her About It' (again on 12-inch – they were all the rage), for a Christmas present. It was another big hit and even though I knew very little about him, he was becoming a favourite in my house. The following summer Billy Joel came to the UK to play some dates on his 'Innocent Man' tour. I was too young to go but I was able to watch and listen to him with my dad. It was one of the first times that a concert had been broadcast live simultaneously on TV and radio. I recorded it on one of my dad's TDK 90s off Radio 1 in glorious VHF. I still have the cassette and have even managed to get hold of a VHS copy of the show.

I was hooked. Maybe it's because my dad liked him too, but I thought it was the best thing I had ever seen and have remained a dedicated fan ever since.

As you've no doubt gathered over the last few pages, music is so integral to my life and my comedy that I can't begin to imagine any of my work without it. It's hard for me to envisage my stand-up without the wedding DJ playing his music at the end of the show or any episode of *Phoenix Nights* without Jerry singing one of his awful medleys with Les Alanos.

So you can probably imagine my excitement when I discovered that I was being sent to work in a record shop for my work placement when I was at school in fourth year.

When Mrs Divine asked each of us in our Careers lesson what we wanted to do in life, most of us hadn't got a clue. But when she got round to me and I thought about her question for a few seconds, I replied,

'I'd like to be a nursery nurse miss.'

Everybody laughed but it was one of the rare occasions in my life when I was being serious. I always thought of myself as being great with children. I liked to make them laugh and I genuinely thought I'd be good at.

'A nursery nurse?' she scorned back at me. 'But you're a lad.'

'And?' I said, but Mrs Divine was having none of it. She assumed I was just trying to act the clown as usual but she was wrong.

She sent me to Edwin P. Lees for a fortnight. It was a electrical shop in the town centre, a kind of Dixons without the glamour. I remember feeling gutted when she told me where I was going. I thought, you can't put me with kids so you're putting me with washing machines, marvellous. I don't think she could have got me further away from a child if she'd tried.

I didn't relish the idea of selling white goods to the public for a fortnight. I knew nothing about vacuum cleaners, chest freezers and tumble dryers. But luckily God was smiling down on me on my first day. The shop manager wasn't too keen on having a work placement crowding up his precious shop floor. He decided to keep me out of sight, so he shoved me upstairs into the record department.

It wasn't in the same league as HMV or Virgin but they still stocked the Top 40 and all of the latest releases. I was to work with Regina. She'd run the record department single-handedly since 1961. And now, because of 'these new-fangled CDs and laser discs', the future was starting to look bleak.

The main problem with the record department at Edwin P. Lees is that nobody knew that they had one. The shop was widely known for selling white goods and when I told people I was working in the record department there, the general reaction seemed to be, 'Oh, I thought that had shut down years ago'

As a result of this we had at the very most three customers a day, possibly twelve on a Saturday, which Regina considered to be a rush.

She was a lovely lady, a trifle stern and old-fashioned in her approach but then again so would I be if I'd been trapped upstairs in a morgue of a record department for over a quarter of a century. She also sported a grey beehive of a hairdo, which most people found visually distressing; it was like being served by the bride of Frankenstein.

Regina had very little time for contemporary sounds. OMD and KLF were just letters to her and when a customer once asked her about Aztec Camera she directed them to a local photography shop.

Granted, she may not have known how to jack her body or pump up the jam, but she did know how to create a fan-shaped poster display for the new album by Brother Beyond to cover up a rising-damp stain on the wall above the Folk & Country section.

To be fair, even though we had very few punters her mission to turn them into customers never wavered. She lived faultlessly by the motto 'If they'll browse, they'll buy'. She even felt-tipped her motto on to a piece of paper and stuck it under the counter (out of the customers' view of course). Derren Brown was no match for Regina when she tapped into a customer's mind. Casually she'd start by mentioning the state of the weather and ten minutes later some unsuspecting customer would be walking downstairs bewildered, clutching a carrier bag full of cassettes, albums and a laser disc of *The Eagle Has Landed*. Problem was, they never came back after they'd once been duped by Regina into buying a load of shite they didn't need.

I was the complete opposite of Regina, in that I hated ripping people off. I knew from the other music shops in town that Regina's stock was vastly overpriced, and on the odd occasion she left me alone I made it my moral duty to inform the customers of any discrepancies in value for money. For example: 'Why don't you try the Vinyl Countdown?' I'd say. 'I was in there the other day and I saw the very same album for half the price.'

I would have appreciated it if a shop assistant told me the truth when I went shopping. I just wasn't cut out for the dog-eat-dog world of retail. Maybe what I did was slightly dishonest, but with a fresh taste for deceitfulness I was about to take it to a higher level.

Now, I've never stolen anything in my life – well, not unless you count the odd sweet from the pick 'n' mix down the multiplex, but then again everybody does that . . . don't they? Well, if you don't you should, especially when you go to the counter and realise the prices they're charging – 14p for penny chews.

I'll stop digressing to tell you that I'm not proud of the actions I took during my time at Edwin P. Lees. All I can say in my defence is that I'm a human being at the end of the day and human beings make mistakes.

What I'm about to tell you, I've never told anybody else – well, not that many. But hey, isn't that why you buy an autobiography, for moments of truth like this? I just hope you don't think less of me as a person and I just pray that one day we'll be able to look back at the whole sorry episode and laugh at it together.

I was now into my second week of the work placement. Regina and I had established a working relationship and a modicum of trust had built between us. She'd nip into town on the odd occasion to do some errands and trust me to hold the fort. That's when the shit hit the fan.

Leaving a music nut like myself alone in a record department is like leading a smackhead into a pub full of dealers. I had all the music I could ever dream of at my disposal and absolutely no way of adding it to my own music collection . . . unless I could devise a cunning plan.

That was the moment, dear reader, that I fell to the dark side. I figured that if I could just 'borrow' (and 'borrow' is the key word here) a few selections of music, then I could take them home, copy them (with my high-speed dub facility) and return them to their rightful place on the shelf the next day. Surely there wasn't a court in all the land that could construe that as theft? I was merely borrowing the music after all, rather like the library service that I'd grown so fond of on the other side of town.

I hand-picked a few choice cuts of music, such as the original soundtrack to *Dirty Dancing* and Wet Wet Wet's *Memphis Sessions* (hardly worth taking the risk on reflection).

Then, and here's the cunning bit, I decided to smuggle the music out of the building by shoving it down the front of my pants. I stuck to cassettes for obvious reasons. Shoving a couple of LPs down there would have given me an indiscreet square bulge and probably given the game away slightly.

Regina never noticed a thing, not even me sweating like a pig and grunting my goodbye in fear as I left the shop. I was a nervous wreck and remember feeling dirty with guilt as I ran across town to the bus station. Perhaps it was because I had *Dirty Dancing* down the front of my pants, who knows?

Once home, I felt safe and I ran upstairs into my bedroom to copy the cassettes immediately just before the fraud squad kicked my front door down. I could feel the threatening gaze of a thousand Catholic eyes staring down at me from heaven. My dreams were filled with dead nuns wagging their fingers and chanting, 'We knew you'd end up like this.' I could hardly sleep.

I came in early the next morning and slipped the cassettes back on the shelf before Regina arrived. Phew! The relief was immense – I felt as though I'd been pardoned at the eleventh hour. But like most addicts, once you get away with it you keep going back for more.

That night my bulge was bigger, as I somehow managed to shove *Now 11*, *The Best of Level 42* and U2's *Rattle and Hum* down the front of my pants. Happy days!

I must have taken more than twenty cassettes over the next few nights. As I got braver my bulges got bigger and every morning I expected Regina to stop me and say, 'Have you got cassette tapes down your pants or are you just pleased to see me?' She never did. But life has a cruel way of teaching you a lesson and one evening at closing time she said to me, 'If you ever fancy taking any music home to copy, then just help yourself, I do it all the time.'

I was so mortified, I wanted to drop my pants right in front of her and shout,

'Look at these, Regina.'

I'd been living the life of a sinner for days, pale and emaciated from a lack of sleep, racked with guilt and ready to burn in hell over Level 42 and *Dirty Dancing*.

So the moral of the story is this: either honesty is the best policy, *or* if you're planning to smuggle something down the front of your pants, don't be too hasty because you never know, you might be allowed to already.

Chapter Nine

We Be Jammin'

Ding Dong! Now that was the doorbell, I didn't even have to tip my head to one side this time because I heard it loud and clear. It was my new driving instructor, Marion of Marion Moran's School of Motoring and I was expecting her to call. My driving lessons had come to an abrupt halt after I'd decided to let the inimitable Raymond go, way back at the beginning of the book. I'd been itching to get behind the wheel again ever since and then as fate would have it Marion drove into my life, literally.

I'd got a new part-time job working as a cashier at a local petrol garage and one day Marion came in to fill up her Clio. She looked pleasant enough as she limped towards the counter dragging her orthapaedic shoe, so I plucked up the courage to ask her if she'd take me for some lessons.

I briefly told her about my past history with Raymond and she laughed. Apparently I wasn't the first person to suffer his cigar smoke. We set a date for the following week and then she left owing me a penny, a sign of things to come.

Originally, I'd only taken the job at the garage because I thought it might educate me in the ways of motoring. I'd already had over thirty driving lessons by this point and still I hadn't even been put in for my test. I needed as much help as I could get and surely I'd be able to pick up a few tips working in a garage. But the sad reality was, I remained totally illiterate when it came to cars.

One night I had a drive-off. Some knobhead filled up his car on the forecourt and sped off. It wasn't even busy, but the smart-arse had hung a beach towel out of the boot so I couldn't read the reg. The only thing I did manage to read was '. . . zarote' down the side of the beach towel as he screeched off the forecourt.

We had CCTV cameras installed at the garage but they didn't work. Vernon, the manager, was a tight-arse and he'd just had them wired up to a battery so that the light flashed constantly as a deterrent.

The police eventually rolled up about four hours later (no surprise there). I was still in shock. I remember the policeman asked me,

'What kind of car was it?'

I said, 'It was green and it sloped down at the back like this.' (I motioned with my hands.)

'Oh well,' he said, 'we've as good as got him.' The sarcastic pig.

It wasn't my fault the drive-off had covered up his registration plate with a beach towel! Anyway, even if I'd got his reg I still don't think the police would have done much. They way they saw it was Esso's petrol and a big company like that was guaranteed to be insured against theft, so what was the point of chasing a two-bit chancer over a tenner's worth of unleaded?

I would have pushed the panic button if I'd known we had one but in the fortnight I'd been employed nobody had bothered to mention its existence – it was left up to me to discover that the hard way.

One Saturday afternoon after much soul-searching I decided to help myself to some Juicy Fruit. When I say help myself, I mean steal. I'd seen a few of my co-workers helping themselves to the odd bar of chocolate or the occasional packet of crisps, so I thought I'd have a go, seeing as the coast was clear and it was sat right in front of me on the counter. Well, it was either Juicy Fruit or a magic tree and the latter didn't look very appetising.

The forecourt was dead. The weekly convoy of Saturday shoppers had already passed by, their cars now safely nestled in various NCP car parks around town, while their drivers sat in Debenhams' café eating a cream tea and admiring the purchases they'd got in the Blue Cross sale. Meanwhile, three and a half miles away, I was sat eyeing up a packet of sugar free Juicy Fruit. I was about to drift over to the dark side once again.

My co-worker Steve was round the back vacuuming his Escort, so casually I moved my left hand towards the spearmint rack and reached for a packet of Juicy Fruit. As I innocently gazed out of the window, my right hand was completely unaware of what my left hand was up to. Like a perspiring Dr Strangelove I was just in the middle of peeling back the silver foil when two police squad cars came skidding on to the forecourt and screeched up outside the shop. I jumped out of my skin which sent the evidence hurtling into the air.

'Shit, they're on the ball here,' I thought, 'it's only a packet of Juicy Fruit.'

Two officers came bursting into the shop and ran up to the counter asking me what the emergency was.

'Emergency? What emergency?' I said.

It turned out that unbeknownst to me, I'd leaned back in my swivel chair about half an hour before and accidentally pushed the panic button under the counter.

The coppers weren't happy. I tried explaining to them that I'd no idea that we even had a panic button but they were having none of it. It was only later, after they'd gone, that I realised it'd taken them over half an hour to respond, the bloody cheek! By that time any panic would have been well and truly over. I could have been lying in a pool of blood, riddled with bullets, by the time they'd finished their tea and headed over.

Anyhow, it was a lesson learned and I made damn sure I didn't lean back on my chair the next time I decided to help myself to a bit of Juicy Fruit.

When I first took the job at the garage I was surprisingly shy. I wouldn't have said boo to a goose, which never turned out to be a problem as we never had much poultry buying petrol. But I got so stressed with my new job that I almost quit after the first few shifts. I'd never had to deal with the public before, handling money, swiping credit cards, it was all too much for a seventeen-year-old to cope with. I was used to packing toilet rolls and I'd spent most of my life surrounded by family and friends . . . and nuns.

I didn't have a clue. I remember an Asian lad coming in once and asking for some Rizla papers. I thought he was looking to buy some kind of Asian newspaper. I had no idea what he was on about and immediately informed him that we didn't sell any magazines or newspapers.

Ironically, it was the customers themselves that coaxed me out of my shell. It wasn't the idle banter that we exchanged at the counter or the humorous small talk that we indulged in during

Here I am sat in a farmer's field, ironically the land is just across from where my mum's bungalow now sits thirty years later. It was the middle of August and I was roasting but I didn't have the heart to tell my mum... and I also couldn't speak yet.

Either my dad or the farmer took this. It's a lovely photo and I only rediscovered it again recently when I was searching for photographs for this book. I've since had it transferred on to a set of attractive placemats.

This is my mum and me practicing our ventriloquist act in the back yard. I used to sing *Bridge Over Troubled Water* while she drank it. We had quite a successful club act for years until The Krankies showed up and stole our thunder.

This is my nana and me on a beautiful sunny day in Blackpool. I'm still wearing that same hat and the t-shirt as I type this right now, it's a bit snug under the arms but I'll manage.

This a rarity, me with a football 'Aving it!' on Stanley Park in Blackpool with my dad and grandad. I refused to remove my shirt.

Here I am riding the cable cars at Butlins Filey in 1979. I'd fallen out of one the previous day and knocked my front tooth out… I'm joking of course. Riding the cars was my big birthday treat and we went to a Butlins holiday camp every year until we found earwigs climbing up our bed in Skegness.

This is me dressed as an Indian in my grandparent's front room, Christmas, 1977. My grandad always used to tell me that the reflection shining in the cabinet behind me was the star of Bethlehem, I believed him for years until I realised it was actually just a camera flash. Happy days.

R Julie and me outside Granada Television Studios in Manchester, the Hollywood of the North. My dad only took the picture because he accidentally got off the bus three stops too early. Little did I realise I'd end up writing most of this book in that building twenty-five years later.

This is my dad and me on Christmas day. It was the year Father Christmas brought me the best present ever, a Race & Chase. I was so ecstatic I went blind for several days.

Butter wouldn't melt. This is me and Jesus's mum on the altar at my local church. I got the prestigious honour of being a guard to the May Queen that year. And I also got to wear the same outfit twenty-five years later when I started doing stand-up in the clubs.

My dad sunbathing in Torquay. Although he wasn't doing it for long, I'd got an inflatable dinghy for my birthday the day before and after falling asleep in it I drifted off to sea. Two lifeguards had to swim out and save me half way to France. My dad immediately deflated it and I wasn't allowed to go out to sea in it again. (Incidentally we've still got those bath towels in the airing cupboard).

The cast of TV's
Diff'rent Strokes

This is one of the only photographs I've got of myself in the mid-nineties and even then I had to lean into the frame just to get on it. It was taken by the side of Lake Windermere, there's nothing more to say except I used to love that shirt.

Not content with my part time jobs I often resorted to having sales outside my house with some of the other local kids. Included in this sale was my Millenium Falcon, a *This Life* boxed set and some homemade bottles of Rose perfume. The local Avon lady shit herself when she found out.

Heard about the comic who scooped a top award on his fourth performance?

IT was fourth time lucky for Bolton's rising talent, Peter Kay *(above)*, who burst onto the comedy scene this week when he scooped a top award just 12 months after his first public performance.

Peter, of Croston Street, Daubhill, had performed only three times before wowing audiences and judges at the City Life North -west Comedian of the Year contest, beating nine other comics from across the region.

The former pupil at Mount St Joseph school is still reeling from his incredible achievement and the offers are beginning to pour in.

Anyone wanting to sample Peter's comedy genius can catch him at the Boardwalk in Manchester on Sunday and at the Rubber Chicken Comedy Club at Blakey's In King George's Hall, Blackburn, next Wednesday.
(Pic ref: D2269/10)

This is my graduation photograph and a newspaper article from the *Bolton Evening News*. I had to combine the two when I suddenly realised I'd run out of room in the photo section (I knew I should have left the *Diff'rent Strokes* one out). The graduation photo always makes me laugh as I'm actually holding a piece of a drain pipe with a ribbon tied round it as the scrolls hadn't arrived.

Okay, you've looked at the pictures now buy the book or get out of the shop.

payment, it was the fact that a large percentage of the customers were miserable bastards and I was tired of them treating me like shit.

The customers all had one thing in common: they seemed to hate visiting the garage. I mean, when you think about it nobody really wants to go to a garage. They resent it because garages are a necessity and if it was up to most drivers they'd sooner drive round on fumes all day with their orange fuel lights flashing than pull into a garage for petrol.

As a result I became a target for their frustrations. They seemed to blame me for everything, the hike in fuel prices, traffic congestion, being England out of the World Cup, whatever it was that was pissing them off the buck stopped with me. It got to the point where I'd had enough. It was time for me to shape up or ship out, so I began to give them as much back and in doing so I unleashed a dark sarcastic side to my nature that I'd never seen before.

When filling up most drivers liked to round things up. The cost of their fuel always had to be £10 or £15 and they hated it when they went over by a penny. No matter how meticulously they tried to fill up, that penny always popped up at the very last second. It was the straw that broke the camel's back for one customer and he came charging into the garage like Michael Douglas in *Falling Down*.

'What's going on? That car was at ten pounds exactly when I pulled out that nozzle, now the price has mysteriously jumped up a penny. Did you do that?' he said in a deranged fashion.

'Eh? Why would I want to do that?' I was shocked. I couldn't believe he was actually accusing me of rigging the pumps so I could pocket the extra penny.

'Well, it all adds up, doesn't it, a penny here, a penny there, before you know it thirty customers and –'

'– and what?' I said. 'I've got 30p? Look, get out before I push the panic button.' I looked around – I couldn't believe that it was actually me that had said that. I was shocked. Then he threw a ten-pound note at me and walked out owing the penny. Then he got back into his squad car and sped off.

I was joking about the squad car but it was hardly worth calling the police over a penny. I couldn't have cared less anyway, I was still in shock for standing up for myself. But I'd enjoyed it and so it didn't stop there. It started to happen all of the time.

Vernon, my boss, docked the penny out of my wage. He did it to all staff if a customer refused to pay. We used to get our revenge by pissing in his milk. I'm only joking (or am I?)

I got a customer in one night who'd filled up his car with fuel and before he got to the counter to pay he was distracted by the sweet rack. He got a few bags of chocolate and when I tilled up the amount it came to a total of £12.42.

And then he did what most people do at that point: he fumbled around in his wallet like a tit and said,

'Do you want the 42p?'

I said, 'Yes, I do, otherwise it'd just be twelve quid and that's not enough. Fool.'

I was starting to think maybe I needed to enrol on some kind of anger-management course.

And on one particularly bad shift a bloke leaned round the shop door and asked me if we had a toilet.

'The whole place is a fucking toilet mate,' I replied.

He just nodded and sheepishly shut the door.

We used to make plenty of brews at work and as a result there was always a half-bottle of milk sitting in the shop fridge next to cans of Coke and Diet Lilt (as if normal Lilt doesn't taste bad enough).

A customer approached the counter to pay once and said,

'Do you know you've got half a bottle of milk open in your fridge?

'Yeah, we keep in there to stop it going sour,' I said.

'Crikey, I know what you mean, there's nothing worse than sour milk, is there?' he said.

'Oh, I don't know,' I said. 'Aids is a bit of a pisser.'

Crestfallen, the guy picked up his Tiger Tokens and left. Now that was cruel, I know, but I was starting to hate small talk and what you've got to remember is that a lot of the customers were just as bad. I remember a guy coming in and asking for a vacuum token so he could clean his car out round the back. Five minutes later he barged back into a packed shop, pushed his way to the front of the queue, slammed his vacuum token down on the counter and said, 'You call that a vacuum? The wife sucks harder than that.'

I was truly speechless.

The worst customers were the ones that religiously collected their Tiger Tokens. I don't know if you remember them but a few years ago Esso garages used to give away these things called Tiger Tokens 'free' with every six pounds of petrol. They were an enormous success and the British public went mental for them. They'd hoard the tokens like gold.

I even used to get drivers filling up their cars with an extra bit of fuel, just so they could pick up an extra Tiger Token. Once you'd collected all your tokens you could redeem them against various gifts in the Tiger catalogue, but most customers couldn't wait and with the tokens burning a hole in their shell suits they'd impatiently redeem them for a Tiger frisbee or a God-awful Tiger T-shirt.

Other customers had been collecting their tokens for ever. These people were on an unstoppable mission to redeem their tokens against the biggest and best gifts that the Tiger catalogue would allow, like a deluxe set of family-size leather luggage or a Black & Decker power bench. You could bet they'd be worth about ten thousand tokens and as staff we'd have to count each and every bloody one of them.

That could take an eternity. The manager of the other Esso garage in Bolton had the wisdom to buy a set of Tiger Token scales for his staff. They saved so much time. All you had to do was pop the tokens on the scales and, hey presto, the total amount would appear on screen. The scales were the way forward but Vernon was a tight-arse so there wasn't much chance of us ever having a pair of them.

'Have you seen how much they cost?' he'd complain every time we mentioned them. 'I don't see why should I fork out for scales when all you have to do is count.'

But, as I found, the problem was it could take ages and the arseholes with the most tokens would always want to redeem them at the worst possible time. Like when we were just about to shut or in the middle of my shift with a queue snaking out the door.

I'd really had enough of these people and one night in the middle of the rush hour I saw a fat couple struggling to get out of a Sierra. It was a hot July evening and as the husband heaved himself out of the driver's seat I could see he was clutching a carrier bag full of Tiger Tokens. My heart sank.

'Please GOD, not now,' I said, looking through the window at the gridlocked forecourt.

They waddled into the shop. He was wearing a Tiger bumbag and she was dressed in a colourful XXXXXX-large T-shirt, sporting cartoon images of black children cavorting round a cartoon map of Jamaica and the words 'We Be Jammin' underneath. I hated them both already.

Slapping his carrier bag down on my counter, he said, 'There's nine thousand tokens here, son, and we want to order a set of conservatory furniture.'

'The deluxe set in Nigerian bamboo,' his fat wife added, standing on tiptoes because her head only came up to the screen-wash display.

'I stand corrected,' said the husband. 'There's actually nine thousand and fifteen. We want one of those fancy Tiger T-shirts an' all.'

A queue of impatient drivers was already forming behind them and before I could tell them to FUCK OFF! the husband tipped his carrier bag upside down and emptied the tokens on to my counter. I was livid.

I wanted to slap them and shout, 'Why are you doing this now, can't you see we're busy?', but I didn't; instead, I calmly leaned over my shoulder, lifted a pad of Tiger Token order forms off the shelf and said, 'I'm really sorry but we haven't got any of those left.'

Totally flummoxed, the couple looked at each other in shock, scooped up their nine thousand (and fifteen) tokens and left. I couldn't believe that the gormless sods had fallen for it. I had the order forms right there in my hand. Spurred on by my success, I started to do it all the time with any other customers who attempted to cash in their zillion Tiger Tokens at the most inappropriate moments.

Nine out of ten times it worked, but occasionally I'd get a smart one who'd just look at me and say,

'Aren't those the order forms in your hand?'

That's when I'd have to reply awkwardly, 'Oh yeah, so they are.'

Thwarted, I devised another technique that would take the 'no order forms' scam to the next level, literally. One night I had a woman stroll up to the counter just as we were cashing up. She was pulling a tartan shopping trolley that was piled so high with Tiger Tokens that they were spilling on to the floor as she walked.

Before she even had chance to open her mouth, I went over to a side door behind the counter and, tilting my head upwards I shouted,

'Kev, have we got any of those Tiger Token order forms up there?' (Then I paused for effect.) 'Next week you say. OK, I'll tell her.'

Disgruntled, the woman left the garage leaving a trail of paper tokens fluttering behind her.

As she got back into her car I could see her looking at the one-storey garage with confusion on her face. There was no upstairs, there was no member of staff called Kev and the side door behind the counter only led to a dusty store cupboard where we kept out-of-date Fruit Pastilles and melted Twixes.

The garage was the longest job I had. (Obviously that's if you don't count the one I do now.) The only reason I stayed so long was because I had such a good laugh. Lord knows, it couldn't have been for the money, because the wage Vernon gave me was a pittance. I got £1.80 an hour until I was eighteen and then it went up to £2.40. Downright disgraceful. But there was always plenty of overtime and any shitty part-time job had to be better than signing on. Plus I got to nick my own body weight in Duracell batteries and I never had to buy a blank video or cassette for the next five years.

Every year in August Vern and his wife Pam would go on a golfing holiday to Florida, and before they went Pam would make up our wages and leave them in the safe. I opened mine one week and realised it was a couple of quid short. I was furious as I hardly got much as it was. Luckily Vernon had left the telephone number of the hotel in case of an emergency so I took the liberty of calling him – well, it was an emergency to me.

After much palaver and a few foreign dialling tones, I got through to a camp concierge called Brad who informed me that Mr Vernon Papworth and his wife were unavailable.

'That's OK, I'll hold,' I told him.

'But they may be some time, sir,' he said, slightly concerned.

'That's OK, I don't mind.'

'OK, sir, I shall do my best to locate them,' and with that he put me on hold.

I didn't mind – I had time to kill, and it was Vernon's phone bill at the end of the day.

After ten minutes of listening to Enya, I heard Brad come back to the phone.

'Hello, Mr Kerr,' he said wearily. 'We've managed to locate Mr Papworth and his wife. They're at the fourteenth hole on the golf course, so I've sent my junior concierge Mandarin out to meet them with our portable cellphone. I'll put you through momentarily.'

The next voice I heard was Vernon's.

'Hello, Peter, it's Vernon, is everything all right?' He wasn't even trying to disguise the panic in his voice.

'Yes,' I said, 'everything's fine.'

'The garage, is everything all right at the garage?'

'Yes, it's all OK.'

'Thank fuck for that,' he said. 'I thought the place had burnt down or summat. Well, what do you want then?'

'Well, it's just I that got my wage that Pam did before she left and it's a couple of pounds short. I just wondered whether I should take the money straight out of the till or wait till you get back?'

I literally had to hold the phone at arm's length, Vernon was shouting so much.

When he got home he gave me a bollocking but I didn't get the sack. Vernon knew he'd never be able to find anybody else to work for the wages he paid. We knew our jobs were secure. Perhaps that's why we pissed about so much.

After Vernon left the building at six o'clock we basically had the place to ourselves and we came up with plenty of ways to pass the time.

We started an occasional sweepstake just to see how long it would take for the police to arrive when we pushed the panic button deliberately. I won twenty quid once when it took the police over an hour to arrive. When they did turn up we just blamed it on faulty electrics or the Red Arrows appearing at a local air show.

Sometimes when it was quiet we'd play baseball in the shop, using a tennis racket from the Tiger collection and packets of crisps as balls. We only played that occasionally because none of us could be arsed cleaning the crisps off the wall afterwards. In summer we used to have the most amazing water fights, with hoses and jet sprays. This was always great fun, especially when we took it in turns to ride through the car wash on a bike while it was switched on.

At Christmas we liked to make a bit of an effort with the punters.

We used to jam ten-pence coins under the keys of the tannoy system in order to keep the microphone constantly turned on. Then we'd play a selection of Christmas music for all the customers to hear. And it worked a treat until Steve forgot that everybody on the forecourt could hear everything he was saying. In particular an attractive girl on pump four who clearly heard Steve say, 'Jesus, I wouldn't mind hanging out of that,' as she stepped out of her Renault. She just gave us the Vs and drove off.

Vernon decided to sell greetings cards and helium balloons for a while and after working a particularly arduous bank holiday weekend we thought it would be amusing to let these balloons go. That was only after we'd attached cards to the bottom of them informing any persons who happened to find a balloon that they were entitled to an all-expenses paid holiday to the Maldives if they rang the following number. Obviously the number we put on was Vernon's private home number. Needless to say, he hit the roof when his phone started to ring. Apparently he got calls from 'winners' as far away as Llandudno. We just denied all knowledge.

Sometimes it was more like a youth club than a place of work. In fact, if it wasn't for the customers continually interrupting us I swear we'd have gotten a couple of snooker tables fitted into the car wash.

Of all the lads I worked with at the garage, Steve was my favourite. He was a drifter, a traveller, much older than me, and during our long unsociable shifts together he'd enjoy nothing more than regaling me with stories of his female conquests around the globe. He also used to bring his TV to work. He'd wait until Vernon left the building and then he'd get it out of the boot of his car. I remember an occasion one Saturday evening watching *The Return of the Incredible Hulk* with him on ITV. It was one of those piss-poor TV movies that they made in the eighties. The forecourt was quite quiet when Steve's ex-girlfriend screeched up in her Peugeot sparring for a fight. It was the same routine paranoia she had every weekend after his Friday night out with the lads.

He went outside to talk to her and the next thing I could see they were nose to nose screaming obscenities at each other. Then Dr David Banner started to change into the Hulk. We'd been waiting over an hour to see this and I didn't want Steve to miss it. So without thinking I shouted to him over the garage tannoy: 'Steve, get in here quick, the Hulk's changing.'

Steve just ran off mid-row and came back inside to watch the Hulk. This sent his ex over the edge. She got back into her Peugeot and melodramatically drove straight into a wall at the other end of the forecourt. I casually I mentioned it to Steve but he didn't even look up, as he was engrossed in Lou Ferrigno.

'She's always doing it,' he said. 'She's just attention-seeking.' The next thing I knew the fire brigade arrived and they had to cut her out of the wreckage. Lord, did I feel guilty, she couldn't walk for a month.

The only time I never had any fun was during my Friday-night shift, when I worked with Wayne Paxton. The word fun wasn't in his vocabulary. I realised that when I overheard him trying to recite the whole of the phonetic alphabet with an off-duty fireman on the forecourt. 'It's alpha, bravo, charlie, delta, echo, foxtrot . . .' I think you get the picture.

Wayne liked to think of himself as the deputy manager simply because he was the longest-serving member of staff. He'd started at the garage as a Saturday lad when he was just fourteen but now he was thirty-eight and it'd gone beyond a joke.

I hated working with him – he'd make my Friday nights hell. I couldn't have the radio on too loud, as he'd continually come behind the counter and turn it down or, worse still, stand at the other end of the shop with his hands over his ears, motioning at the speakers. The only time he used to turn it up was for the news or to listen to the shipping forecast on Radio 4.

We had a nickname for him – it was Champagne because of the champagne lifestyle that we imagined he led outside work. He was passionate about animals and drove around for six months with a sticker that we doctored in the back window informing people that 'A Dog Is For Christmas and Not Just For Life'.

Some nights Champagne wouldn't even speak to me, he'd be too busy with his hobby. He used to collect the plastic centres from empty till rolls. He would make us save them for him and he would lose his mind if saw one of us throwing them in the bin. He liked to glue them together into the shape of a Christmas tree or a sailing boat. How do you think I felt? – I had to work with him.

I used to go outside and sweep the forecourt, wash the pumps and empty the bins, anything to get away from Champagne. The back of the garage was just spare land, there was loads of it – so much that we actually contemplated holding a car boot on it when Vernon went on holiday.

There was also a section where the rubbish was burned. For some reason Champagne liked to call this area the 'Pit' and every Friday he'd make me tip all the week's rubbish into and burn it. I was supposed to check through the bins for items unsuitable for burning but I never bothered. It never really mattered until the night I chucked three empty WD-40 canisters into the fire without knowing and almost blew up the garage.

The fire brigade came and Champagne was so embarrassed, especially when one of the fire officers turned out to be the same one he'd had the phonetic alphabet discussion with a few months earlier.

Like most things in my life, the garage was demolished after I left. It's wasteland now. All that remains is the 'Pit' at the back, no doubt with a can of WD-40 still smouldering somewhere beneath the earth.

One Saturday afternoon I was sat behind the counter reading *Viz* when I happened to glance up and see an elephant walking down the road. I froze. Now it's not something that you see every day of the week and I literally had to rub my eyes, but it really was there. An elephant strolling down the road.

I began to fear I had lost my mind. Was I hallucinating? Had I inhaled too many car fumes? I grabbed the tannoy and hollered for one of the other lads in the workshop 'Steve, Mick, anybody, come quick, there's an elephant . . .' It turned out I must have missed the two coppers at the front who were stopping traffic when I was reading, and the elephant was leading a parade that was celebrating the end of Ramadan.

Of all the garage regulars there were only a handful of customers I actually liked and Leonard De Tompkinson was one of them. To say he was an eccentric would be putting it mildly. He was a walking ray of sunshine. I smiled the first time I ever clapped eyes on him as he pulled on to the forecourt in a pink Reliant Robin he named Hercules. I later found out he used to call into the garage on his way to the Church of the Nazarene round the corner. We got to know each other and after a while he'd come in for a brew and sit behind the counter with me, chatting for hours about his remarkable life.

What I liked most about Leonard was the fact that he was such a positive person. He loved every minute of life and he was always telling jokes and singing, which I found all the more humbling when I discovered that he was registered as disabled and suffered from an acute heart condition.

'Hey, I've never let it hold me back, cocker, and many a good tune can still be played on an old fiddle providing your strings don't break.'

He was always coming out with daft sayings like that.

Unable to work, Leonard used to deliver free newspapers every week and he also used to help out at the old people's home on Lever Edge Lane. He'd serve food to the pensioners, make them laugh, and in return the staff would give him a few free meals. Sadly a lot of people in the area thought he was a weirdo just because he used to say hello to everybody and dressed eccentrically.

He loved charity shops and in fact seemed to spend his life in them, buying all kinds of shite for tuppence. He was forever calling into the garage to show us what he'd bought.

'Here, look what I got today,' he'd say as he excitedly pulled items out of a British Heart Foundation carrier bag. 'I got a fancy sailor's hat, a rainbow-coloured sarong, a couple of novelty salt and pepper mills in the shape of Cagney and Lacey, oh and a gym body eight.' (You know, one of those things you attach to your chest and it's supposed to work your muscles while you're watching *Emmanuelle*. I'm guessing probably not the best thing for an acute angina sufferer.)

Once when we were sitting behind the counter I asked him if he ever got lonely. He just shook his head.

'No, I haven't got time to be lonely, I'm always busy and I've too many friends and I love life. Sometimes people say that they get bored with life but how can you get bored when you don't know what's coming next?'

Leonard was a devoted Christian and he was always quoting the Bible to anybody who'd listen. He used to stand in the town hall square in Bolton and preach to people. Now that takes some guts. I remember some lads walking once past shouting 'Hello, JC' to him and Leonard shouted back, 'He's coming soon, lads, and he'll save us all.'

'I've always been a believer,' Leonard once said 'God's been good to me but not just to me, to all of us. Every day is a blessing, every day is a gift and that's why I spread His good news.'

We lost touch for a while after his faithful Hercules failed its MOT. I didn't see him for ages until one night I was walking home from a friend's and there he was up a tree trying to coax a cat down. He didn't even know whose cat it was but he'd heard it crying and climbed up to get it down. Now he was stuck too. I helped him down and we had a chat. He looked much older and, sporting a big white bushy beard, he looked like a cross between God and Captain Birds Eye. Not that I've ever met Captain Birds Eye, you understand. It was so good to see him again. We hugged, we said our goodbyes and a few days later I found out that he'd died later that night.

I went to the funeral the following week and only three of us showed up, including the vicar. It broke my heart, especially because Leonard always used to go on about how many friends he'd got. But I think at the end of the day Leonard was everybody's friend and yet he never had any real friends. Maybe he was right when he said,

'Live your life because you're a long time dead.'

Leonard certainly did.

As well as having the garage Vernon also had a sideline in car hire and sometimes after work on a Saturday night Steve, myself and some of the other lads would take one of his brand-new cars out for a test drive. Looking back, we would have been frigged if we'd crashed, as we were only on third-party insurance and that would have probably been invalid, with six of us crammed into the back of a Vauxhall Astra.

We used to go all over – Blackpool Illuminations, the multiplex in Preston for a late-night screening or sometimes we'd just head up on to the hills and park up. I loved those Saturday-night road trips. We'd just sit and talk for hours. Listen to music and laugh so much. We'd stay until the sun came up and then go straight back into work and do a full shift. I could do that when I was young. Nowadays I get a blinding migraine if I stay up until the end of *News At Ten* and I have to have a siesta the following day.

Getting my own car insurance was one thing that I certainly didn't have to worry about, because I made less progress with Marion Moran than I had with Raymond. In fact she made him look like Stirling Moss she was that atrocious. As a result I'd failed my driving test twice in the last six months. I was at breaking point and genuinely considering giving up. But the only problem with giving up was that it would've meant that all those other lessons I'd had would have been in vain.

Marion was a good person. It's just that she wasn't really good at teaching me how to drive. She was more bothered about running errands during my lesson. I'd be driving down a busy main road and suddenly she'd shout, 'Carrots. Pull over.'

Then I'd be sat outside the greengrocer's with my hazards on while she was queuing up for veg. I felt like Morgan Freeman in *Driving Miss Daisy* every time I had a lesson.

She'd stop for food, magazines, clothes. Once she made me pull up outside a TV-repair shop and the next thing you know I was staggering through the door with a thirty-two-inch Hitachi in my arms. She said she couldn't carry because of her back. More like her fat arse . . . and fat foot.

I felt like a complete mug and when I tackled her about it she said it was all part of learning to drive. Why couldn't I just find a normal instructor?

I was also turning into her marriage guidance counsellor. She had one or two problems with her hubby Graham and I got a running commentary every week. She'd ask me questions like 'I came home the other night and there were two empty wine glasses on the kitchen drainer. What do you think? Is he seeing someone else?' All I wanted to know was whether I should turn right at the next roundabout and whether I should change to third gear now I was over 25mph.

She rang me at home one night supposedly to firm up on the time of our next lesson but an hour later she was still on the phone in tears, confessing her suspicions. She told me that her cocker spaniel Tara had puked up a condom in the middle of *Crimewatch* and now she definitely suspected her Graham of having an affair, what should she do? What the hell did I know? I was eighteen.

I reckoned it was extreme paranoia fuelled by HRT and too much Lambrusco. But Marion was no angel and she loved to flirt. I'd seen her as I sat outside the butcher's, running her false nails up and down his brisket. She also liked to wear the shortest of short skirts, very unflattering especially with that club foot in tow. She'd bought them in bulk after watching *Basic Instinct* and they made my stomach turn. It was like sitting next to a meerkat every time we went over a speed bump.

The final straw came when she started to turn her attention

towards me. I told her a story about the time my dad had taken me to Blackpool Pleasure Beach. I was only a boy and when I saw the ride called 'Grand Prix' I pronounced it as it was spelt – 'Grand Pricks'. Just then she brushed her hand against mine on the gearstick and said,

'I've had some grand pricks in my time and I could do with one right now.'

Enough was enough, I'd seen *The Graduate*. I pulled the car over and got out. The next thing you know I was walking up the ring road in the rain. What was wrong with the world? All I wanted to do was drive.

Chapter Ten

4pm till Raid

I was still on the performing arts course, and at the start of the year I collected my grant cheque. But as it only stretched to a new parka from Primark and a Terry's Chocolate Orange, I decided to take on a second part-time job. I'd heard through a friend of a friend that there were jobs going down at a local cash and carry situated on an industrial park behind the abattoir. And so I got a job working there a couple of evenings and at weekends. The hours fitted nicely around my shifts at the garage and I really needed the money if I was at least going to continue with my driving lessons.

I settled in straight away. My job title was Shop Floor Assistant, which basically meant I dragged food pallets out of the warehouse on a forklift, then I unpacked them and stacked the produce on to shelves. It was the height of glamour.

There were a few female members of staff working on checkout and in the office doing admin but the majority of staff at the cash and carry were male. Most of the lads I worked with were older than me and as it was the early 1990s many of them spent their weekends attending illicit raves in farmers' fields and most of their wages on drugs. I was trying to grow my hair long as I was going through a bit of a Jim Morrison phase at the time, but instead of getting beautiful flowing locks it just grew straight up like Marge Simpson's.

We used to work in pairs and one lad I frequently ended up with was Rob Grundy. Rob liked to work hard and play hard. He was always popping pills at the weekend and Sunday mornings could be a nightmare working alongside him. He'd either be miserable as sin because he was still coming down from the night before or he'd still be high as a kite and hugging me every five minutes. Some days he just wouldn't show up for work at all, like the time he spent the night in the police cells after throwing a litter bin through a McDonald's drive-thru window, just because they'd run out of ketchup.

The cash and carry wasn't open to lay members of the public like you or me. It was the card-carrying shopkeepers of Bolton that were our main clientele. And if I thought the customers at the garage were miserable then it was only because I hadn't met this set of grumpy tight-fisted bastards. It was like watching Van Morrison do his big shop. They used to moan about everything, the price of this, the price of that, there wasn't enough of this, there wasn't enough of that. There used to be a stampede every Saturday morning for the fresh bread. Grown men would elbow each other in the ribs over a Toasty loaf. I remember one Asian shopkeeper losing his rag because there was no thick-sliced bread left.

'I vanted tick,' he shouted in his heavy accent.

'You wanted what?' I said.

'I vanted tick, tick, tick, tick, tick, tick,' he said repeatedly.

'Everybody take cover,' I shouted, 'he's going to explode.'

He wasn't amused.

The other thing that I didn't enjoy about the cash and carry was the amount of managers that they had floating about. On a good day there could be more managers in the store than customers. They'd follow us around shouting orders and hurling abuse at us in a feeble attempt to justify their jobs. But after working at the garage for so long I now knew how to give them just as much back.

I was pulling a pallet of Lucozade across the shop floor once. It was a heavy load and I was having to struggle quite a bit with it. It was on special offer that month and that meant it had to be positioned directly opposite the managers' office. A few of the managers were gathered outside chatting. I could see them elbowing each other out of the corner of my eye as I approached them. Mr Tickle was a smart-arse from Dundee and a real big mouth. When he saw me coming he shouted,

'That's it, Kay, keep going, we'll soon get a bit of that weight off you, boy.'

Then they all laughed. I stopped dead in my tracks, turned to him and said,

'I'll have you know I do over a hundred sit-ups a day'

'A hundred sit-ups a day? That's nothing, the bloody dog at home does more than that,' said Mr Tickle.

'Why?' I said. 'Does she not work?'

The other managers tried hard not to laugh and I could see Mr Tickle turning a violent shade of purple. I'd made myself an enemy and he had it in for me from that day onwards.

Mr Tickle saw that I was transferred over to the fruit and veg department to cover for another member of staff who was absent due to a death in the family. The bloke in question eventually returned to work only to discover that he no longer had a job. Mr Tickle had taken it upon himself to fire the bloke after deciding that he was taking too long to grieve. We advised our co-worker to take the matter further but nobody gave a shit. Part-time members of staff like us were ten a penny.

So now I was stuck in the fruit and veg department. It could be a tough job, having to lug big bags of potatoes and carrots around all day, but I just kept my head down and got on with it. Mr Tickle would stroll past occasionally and I remember he leaned over once and whispered right into my ear:

'You'll be gone by the end of the month, Mr Kay, because nobody fucks with me.'

'I know, I've heard,' I shouted after him as he walked off.

My incompetence at the job proved to be a blessing when I mistakenly mispriced the iceberg lettuce as cabbage. Well, they looked exactly the same to me. How was I supposed to know the difference? Apparently there was a big difference in price, but none of the hard-faced shopkeepers bothered to tell me. Instead they just took advantage of the situation. I had visions of them high-fiving each other as they loaded their transits.

It went on for four days and nobody discovered the cock-up until they did a weekly stocktake. This all reflected badly on Mr Tickle who apparently shouldn't have left me in charge of a department without having had me obtain the correct health and hygiene certificate first.

Totally humiliated, he hit the roof.

'You made me look a right tit, how could you not tell the difference a lettuce and a cabbage?'

'They look exactly the same.'

'You see this? This is a banana, this is a tomato, recognise them?' he said sarcastically waving the fruit in my face. 'You've just lost this company a fortune in produce, my boy.'

I hardly think it was a fortune but he gave me my first verbal warning as a result nonetheless. Apparently that incident became known in the trade as Green Wednesday.

Surprisingly, I remained on the produce department for the remainder of the week until I stabbed myself and ended up at the hospital. One day, due to sheer boredom, I decided to re-enact a scene from the film *Aliens* featuring the knife-wielding android called Bishop. I laid the palm of my hand flat out on the counter face down and with my fingers spread I proceeded to stab in between each of them with a sharp knife. Only somebody shouted my name and, looking up, I stabbed the knife right into the back of my hand. Ow! With blood spurting all over my nectarines I wobbled off to A&E.

Head office had a management overhaul later that month, and in an effort to make the store appear more consumer-friendly, the managers were forced to have their photographs taken and put on display in the entrance area for all to see, with their job titles emblazoned underneath. We thought the photographs were hysterical, all of them posing uncomfortably with stiff, forced smiles on their faces. And as Mr Tickle's photograph was particularly terrible we decided the time had come for us to take our revenge.

One night, at the end of our shift, we discreetly removed Mr Tickle's photograph from the display case in the entrance. Later that night we all piled round to Mark Berry's house. He was a computer wiz who worked in the non-foods department. There was nothing that boy couldn't do with a flatbed scanner. We spent the next few hours designing a fictitious poster featuring Mr Tickle's photograph, next to a headline that read: 'Urgent Police Warning: Have You Seen This Man?', with some more bogus text underneath, including the lines 'do not approach him' and 'mentally ill'. I think you get the picture.

Mark did a convincing job, but it was Mr Tickle's leering smile on the photograph in its new context that made the hairs stand up on the back of my neck. One final touch was a contact telephone number at the bottom of the poster that came courtesy of the miserable Asian shopkeeper who had a penchant for impersonating exploding thick bread.

We printed out about two hundred posters and spent the weekend fly-posting them up around town and beyond. I'll never forget Mr Tickle's reaction when he left the building to find an A5 flyer jammed under the wiper blade of his Ford Capri Ghia. We were watching him out of the canteen window. He did a fabulous comedy double take, his jaw dropped and then he started to twitch.

The news filtered fast and within a week Mr Tickle was mysteriously transferred to the Isle of Man. As he left I took the greatest of pleasure in handing him a gift-wrapped iceberg lettuce.

The big boss of the depot was Mr Husbands Bosworth or, as everybody called him, HB. He was a bit of a silver fox in his fifties and ready for retirement.

'I've forgotten more than you lot know,' he'd proudly shout to us over his precious speaker system.

I'll give him his due, HB could be as sour as all the other managers but he knew his onions when it came to running a cash and carry. The first time I ever met him he gave me a lecture on shelf-stacking.

'Whoa, whoa, whoa, what are you doing?! Don't put that down there!' he said as he single-handedly lifted a case of baked beans off the bottom shelf and placed it on to the middle one. 'Eye level is buy level, Mr Kay, that's golden rule number one. If the customer can't see it, then the customer can't buy it, now think on.'

I always thought that 'Eye Level' was the theme tune to *Van der Valk*, but as it was only my second day I didn't think it was an appropriate time to set him straight.

HB was also a huge fan of *Hill Street Blues* and in a tribute to the series he'd subject us all to an early-morning roll call. Barbara, his assistant, would pull out her specially made flip chart on castors and he'd proceed to bore us to death with the depot's sales figures and targets. He was obsessed with beating a rival cash and carry up the road.

What used to make me laugh was the way HB always used to end the roll call by saying, 'Let's go and do it to them before they do it to us,' and then for some reason he'd fire an air horn at us. He loved his air horn, he'd carry it around with him all the time in a specially upholstered leather pouch that Barbara had made for him. He could pounce with this air horn at any time. You'd be leaning up against a shelving unit casually having a chat and he'd suddenly fire it down the microphone of the speaker system. You'd jump right out of your skin. 'If you've got time to lean then you've got time to clean,' he'd shout down the microphone – that was another favourite catchphrase of his.

He loved that microphone, he was never off it. He'd spend hours dictating and creating scripts with Barbara. I remember when we had a new line of product from Cadbury's once called Secret. It was a soft-centred chocolate bar covered in milk chocolate sprinkles, and on the day it arrived in store HB crafted a very special script.

'Do you want to know a secret, ladies and gentleman?' he said in a stage whisper. ' It's the biggest thing to hit the confectionary market since the Walnut Whip and we have it in store for you today, it's not a secret any more, it's Cadbury's Secret and in a special opening promotion if you purchase two cases or more we'll throw in a complimentary case of Strawberry Push Pops.'

He must have read out the announcement every fifteen minutes that day. We heard it so many times that by two o'clock we were mouthing the words along with him.

Another problem with working at a cash and carry was that everything was in bulk. This proved to be a nightmare if you fancied something to eat on your break. If you wanted a can of Coke, for example, you had to buy a case of twenty-four; if you fancied a packet of Quavers, you had to buy the whole bloody box. The only alternative was to 'accidentally' drop a case of your choice from the top of a shelf, then take it back into the warehouse and stuff your fat face. There were always a lot of damaged items on our shift. Especially when Ramadan came around. The sun had barely set and the warehouse would already be full of Muslim lads pigging out on Mr Kipling's apple and bramble slices.

I don't think I've ever witnessed as much pilfering as I did at the cash and carry. Loads of us were at it. So much so that I'm surprised there was enough stock left to go out on the shelves. As we unpacked and stacked the shelves we'd accumulate a lot of waste, cardboard, polythene. What we used to do was (well, when I say 'we' I'm obviously referring to the royal we – the last thing I want to do is incriminate myself) shove the rubbish into a big box and then we'd take it round to the back of the building and tip it into a skip. But not before we'd hidden a few stolen items underneath the rubbish at the bottom of the box. Then we'd finish our shift and go home.

If it was a Sunday I'd usually have a bath and watch *Highway to Heaven* before enjoying one of my mum's sumptuous roast dinners. I'd then retire to the front room for a nap in front of *The Clothes Show* and a slice of a dairy cream sponge. Then I'd wake up during the Top 40 countdown, grab my rucksack and cycle back down to the cash and carry in order to collect my winnings.

What always made me laugh was the sight that I'd frequently witness when I cycled round the corner. Half the lads from the shift would already be wading into the rubbish skip round the back in an effort to retrieve their stolen goods.

Cigarettes and booze were always a popular pilfer, though I always preferred the more obscure items like a pack of fifteen TDK three-hour blank videotapes or an Alabama Chocolate Fudge Cake with pecan nuts. And, Mum, if you're reading this I can only apologise for my actions and I hope this goes some way to explaining why we always had so many bottles of fabric softener by the side of the fridge.

Retribution came calling in January 1991 when I was involved in an armed raid at the cash and carry. Quite a frightening experience and one that quickly made me realise the error of my thieving ways. Catholic guilt kicked in, plus with CID scrutinising the building after the robbery I didn't relish the idea of them catching me climbing out the back of a skip with four boxes of Black Forest gateau under my arm.

It was a Thursday night just like any other when the robbery took place. I was pricing up tuna fish with Kevin Broughton and suddenly we heard Simone in the cash office screaming over the sound system, 'MR HUSBANDS BOSWORTH!!' Now print obviously doesn't do Simone's panic-stricken squeal justice but suffice to say Kevin and I both knew that something wasn't right.

Quickly, we both ran round into the pop aisle to be confronted by three armed gunmen wearing masks and waving sawn-off shotguns (well, I don't honestly know if they were sawn off but it doesn't half sound exciting). Everybody at the checkout was lying face down on the floor except Bill Sands, a disabled shopkeeper. He just sat in his wheelchair with his head bowed.

What I couldn't comprehend was why the raiders' masks didn't match. We had Pluto, Mickey Mouse and . . . Colonel Gaddafi. Certainly not a well-known trio

It's funny how you react in that type of situation, but I remember that it took me a great deal of self-control to stop myself from asking them why one of their masks was an odd one out. I knew no fear. Nick Ross says that it's common in those situations, especially with so much adrenalin pumping through around your body (and he'd know, wildcat that he is).

One of the gunmen must have heard me and Kevin charge round the corner, because he turned to us and shouted,

'YOU TWO, GET DOWN!'

And with that I dropped to my knees and shouted back at him, 'What? You mean dance?'

I think my reply must have thrown the gunman for a second or two because he didn't reply.

It was surreal, it wasn't happening and I started to giggle as the assailants legged it out of the building. We were both lying on the floor and Kevin was kicking me as I couldn't stop laughing. Once I got home things were completely different though, and I burst into tears in the middle of *Tomorrow's World*. Delayed reaction, you see. Nick Ross says that's also a common occurrence. The man is an oracle when it comes to crime and its effects.

We seemed to be lying on the floor for ages, shell-shocked, after the robbers had fled. The silence was eventually broken by the sound of HB's speaker system as it bing-bonged back in to life.

'Surely to God he's not written a script for this?' I said to Kevin as I rolled around the shop floor in hysterics.

'Ladies and gentlemen,' said HB in a shaky voice, 'I don't know if you've noticed but we've just been robbed. I'd like to ask all customers to calmly make their way towards the main exit. The police are on their way and don't forget we've still got Cadbury's Secrets on special promotion . . .' I'm only joking, he didn't really didn't mention Cadbury's Secrets, but it would have been very funny if he had.

In the swell of the approaching sirens I ran to the wine and spirits department at the back of the building. Rob Grundy and Matt Lennard were busy stacking cases of Heineken Export underneath the cooling fans and they hadn't heard a thing.

'Quick, we've been robbed,' I shouted to them.

'What are you on about?' said Matt.

'There's just been an armed raid on the building – masks, shotguns, the lot. Come on,' I said, beckoning them.

'Fuck off,' said Rob, but then his attention was caught by the sight of Paula Nolan, who was being led to the canteen by two members of staff. She was in a right old state, sobbing and shaking.

Matt waded straight in. He'd been trying to make a move on Paula for some time and he saw this as the perfect opportunity to be her knight in shining armour. For some reason – maybe it was nosiness – I followed them into the canteen.

A few other shell-shocked members of staff from the cash office joined us. They looked like zombies, staring into the distance and shaking. Simone, the wages clerk, had been sick down the front of her tabard and it stunk to high heaven. The kettle was already on the boil when Matt ordered Rob Grundy and me to make some brews.

'I want you to make strong brews and make sure you put plenty of sugar in them for shock,' he shouted.

Rob and I really had the giggles now and we couldn't help but crack up when I tipped practically a whole bag of sugar into each of the brews. The froth was pouring over the top of the cups and on to the worktop. I passed a cup of tea to Matt and slowly he raised it up to Paula's tear-stained lips.

'Here, girl, drink this, it'll do you good,' he whispered in his Essex accent.

He tipped the cup forward into her mouth, she took a gulp and then spat it out all over his face. Rob and I both collapsed with laughter.

'Will you two just fuck off out of it?' Matt shouted with his face covered in froth.

Meanwhile, HB was at the front of the store being interviewed by a couple of CID blokes. Word had spread quickly throughout the building that it was probably an inside job. Well, that hardly came as a shock to anybody. Graham and Colin from the local security firm had been delivering the same wages at exactly the same time every Thursday for as long as I'd been working there. One of them was an asthma sufferer in his late sixties and the other had an orthopaedic shoe. They were hardly Crockett and Tubbs. Even though everybody referred to them as that once they were out of earshot.

When it came to the suspects there were more ex-members of staff with a grudge than there was money missing. Some said twenty grand had been taken, others said forty. I walked past one office to hear a manager telling an insurance claims officer that somehow the gunmen had not only found time to take the wages but also steal his brand new set of golf clubs out of the boot of his car before they drove off. Bollocks.

'Bing-bong' went the speaker system as HB gave us an update over the microphone.

'I know you're all very keen to get home and the store will be closing just as soon as the police have conducted all of their interviews. In the meantime please help yourself to tea, coffee and biscuits.'

I turned to Rob.

'Hang on, did he just say biscuits?' and before Rob had a chance to nod a response I was in the confectionery aisle ripping the lids off as many biscuit selection tins as I could get my hands on. I opened that many that they remained in the canteen for the next six months. You have to seize chances like these when they come up in life.

I was excited because I thought the BBC *Crimewatch* team might turn up and film one of those God-awful reconstructions that they do, but alas they didn't. I thought it might be my big break into show business, because they always use the real people in those reconstructions and I would have loved to have played myself. It's very cruel when you think about it, taking a pensioner back to the scene of the crime and subjecting her to the same atrocity all over again. As if the poor cow hasn't already been through enough.

The other thing that makes me laugh about those reconstructions is that they never swear. No matter how violent or excited the villains get, they never use foul language. They say things like 'Get down on the floor, you sponge' and 'Don't you flippin' move you melon'. I thought the whole point of showing a reconstruction was that it's supposed to replicate exactly what happened in order to jog people's memories, not water down the events to appease the Television Complaints commission.

That reminds me of a friend of mine who got a job working as an engineer at a television transmitter high above Bolton on the moors. It was a desolate, lonely job and he told me that occasionally he used to get people driving up to the transmitter in the middle of the night in order to complain. They'd get out of their cars furious and bang on the door to his hut.

'Have you seen that filth on Channel 4? *Queer As Folk*? You got a damn cheek putting that on.'

'It's got nothing to do with me,' he'd say. 'It's just an aerial transmitter. Look, I can't even get a decent picture on my portable, mate.'

Anyhow, back to the night of the raid.

Eventually we got our coats on and made our way to the main entrance at the front of the store. HB was there to meet us and he thanked us for dealing with the situation so maturely (it's a pity he didn't know what was about to happen). There were about twelve lads in total from the shift and we all stood in front of HB waiting in awkward and uncomfortable silence. HB thanked us all a second time.

'Like I said, boys, thanks very much, sorry we've got to shut early but I'm sure you understand, given the circumstances.'

Another awkward silence followed as we all stood in front of him waiting.

'Is there anything else I can help you with, boys?' said HB. 'Because I really want to get this place locked up and get home myself.'

There were a few nudges and mumbles from the group and then Paul Higgins said,

'The thing is, Mr Husbands Bosworth, it's a Thursday night and we usually get our wages on a Thursday night.'

'Come on, boys, you've seen the stress and trauma that we've all had to go through this evening,' he replied, a bit incredulously.

'Yeah, I know,' said Paul Higgins, 'but my mum does her big shop on a Friday and she'll lose her mind if I come home empty-handed.'

'But you must be able to appreciate the predicament we're in. Surely you could hang on until the weekend for your wages?' Nobody moved.

Ten minutes later, Simone (who was still in no fit state to do anything) was in the cash office making our wages up out of petty cash, sobbing with a blanket round her and still stinking of vomit. Thinking about it all these years later I can't believe that we stooped so low as to actually make her do that. She handed us our wage packets one by one. They were damp from her tears and, hanging our heads in shame, we left the building. We then had to stop Rob Grundy from going back because he'd opened his wage packet and noticed it was 26p short.

'For fuck's sake, Rob, you're pushing your luck now. Here, I'll give you the money myself,' I said as I dragged him through the car park home.

I got my second verbal warning as a result of that robbery. We used to have a staff signing-in/out book at the front of the store and I got a bollocking off HB after I filled in my hours on the night of the robbery and wrote '4pm till Raid'. The week after, HB assigned Rob Grundy and myself to our new positions: security duty.

This basically meant that we both had to take it in turns to patrol the car park until the clocks went forward in March. Talk about locking the barn door after the horse had bolted. I don't know what they expected us to do if we saw an armed gang approaching the store. I mean, I was hardly going to wrestle them to the ground.

It was freezing. I had to wear three layers of thermals some nights just to keep myself warm and I still got a chill on my kidneys. It was also a very boring job, so much so that I secretly began listening to a Walkman, hidden inside my coat. If HB had found out he'd have hit the roof.

'You're wearing a Walkman, you crafty bastard,' Rob Grundy said when he found out.

The next thing I knew, Rob had decided to wear a Walkman too. At least my headphones were discreet ones; black and in the ear, you could hardly notice them under my balaclava. Rob's Walkman was out of the Ark and his bright orange-coloured foam headphones were as subtle as a brick. And he played his music so loud that everybody else could hear it in the car park and so loud one night that he failed to see or hear the security van as it reversed over him. HB caught him red-handed, lying under the wheels of the vehicle listening to Adamski.

A few weeks after the robbery I was on a bus heading into town when a lad called Simon Halliwell got on. I'd taken over from him on the fruit and veg department just before Mr Short had sacked him for grieving too long.

'All right, Si, how's it going?' I said as he sat down next to me.

'Can't complain. Hey, I saw you the other week,' he said.

'When?'

'That Thursday night during the robbery,' he whispered. 'I would have said hello but I didn't like letting on. I was the one who told you to "get down" when you ran round the corner. I almost pissed myself when you shouted "What? You mean dance?" Have you ever thought of becoming a comedian?'

But all I wanted to know was why he was wearing a Colonel Gaddafi mask.

Chapter Eleven

Dettol and Marijuana

With two part-time jobs on the go I hardly had time to concentrate on my performing arts course, which was maybe just as well, as things had really started to fall apart at the college. Attendance figures were dropping – in fact, we were now down to a pitiful six students. I'd completely expected a new course to suffer from teething troubles but this was shaping up like the dentist scene from *Marathon Man*.

I was now into my second year and we'd only just been allocated a classroom. We'd spent the previous eighteen months alternating between the changing rooms in a gymnasium and a gazebo in the middle of a car park. Neither was any place to learn jazz tap and as a result I had become totally disenchanted with the business of show.

In an effort to boost morale (and get rid of us), our course leader, Freda, sent us all on work placements for a month. I was placed in a secondary school on the outskirts of town to teach drama! Me teach drama? What did I know? I hadn't been taught drama myself. Yet here I was about to teach it to kids only a few years younger than me. Talk about the blind leading the blind.

But every morning I'd get up, put on a shirt and tie and travel on the bus to school with the kids. They found it hysterical, as I'd forgotten to put on my pants on . . . (That was a joke by the way – surely I shouldn't have to be pointing them out in Chapter 11.) I felt like a proper adult – well, a student teacher at the very least. I found the whole experience both exciting and rewarding and it certainly beat trying to find a space in the gazebo back at college.

And when it came to the drama lessons, the pupils at Westhoughton High School really didn't need any encouragement. They were truly fantastic. In fact, if truth be told, I probably ended up learning a lot more from them than they ever did from me.

For my first few days at the school I was an observer in the classroom. And I was totally blown away by their confidence. Even the first-year pupils were remarkable. The drama teacher, Mr Banyard, would spilt a class up into small groups to devise short sketches based on a series of themes. 'I'd like you to include the following in your sketches: a wheelie bin, the Taj Mahal and a left-handed screwdriver,' he'd say before sending them off.

Five minutes later they'd return with these brilliant little sketches. The pupils would be incredibly funny and they'd all have a go at doing accents and characterisation. They had enormous self-belief and seemed to relish the opportunity to perform. And if I thought the first-years were good at drama then the fifth-year pupils were in a different league altogether. They were astonishingly good actors, mature beyond their years.

I actually found myself getting quite jealous and longed to join in with them. I regretted having missed out on all of this when I was at school. Mind you, if the nuns had sent us off to devise sketches nobody would have ever come back. Pity really, because if we'd done more constructive things like drama, then maybe the pupils wouldn't have resorted to shoving lighted rags through the convent letter box of an evening.

I've always believed drama to be an important subject. It's not just about play-acting, it's about giving children confidence and ironing out their inhibitions. I realise most of them may never go near a stage again once they've left school, but I guarantee that they'll exude a charisma and confidence for the rest of their lives as a result of being taught drama.

I thoroughly enjoyed my month at the secondary school and I met some really talented people. Perhaps that's why I was so reluctant to return to my performing arts course. Talk about a comedown. I arrived back in time to start work on our big final-year production. Our dance teacher, Jo Jo, was keen to premiere her musical version of *Highlander*, but seeing as there were only three girls and two lads plus me left we opted for the aptly titled *Little Shop of Horrors* instead.

It was a disaster waiting to happen. Due to the lack of male students I ended up playing a total of six parts including Seymour, the dentist, and the voice of the man-eating plant. The plant itself was played by Troy who was from Ghana. He was a disabled exchange student with a spine defect. He spoke very little English and rumour had it he'd originally come to the college to learn joinery but got out of the lift on the wrong floor.

Due to a lack of funds we had to hire the man-eating plant costume from a local amateur dramatics society. Their costume was ten foot tall and we lost our £50 deposit after we had to 'adapt' their costume to fit Troy's motorised wheelchair. The image of Troy inside that costume wheeling around the stage to 'I'm a Mean Green Mother from Outer Space' will stay with me for ever.

We wasted so much rehearsal time adapting costumes that we never actually got round to having a proper run-though. Then the night before the show I went on a coach trip to watch Sting in Newcastle (it was a belated Christmas present – don't ask). Sting was crap; I nodded off during 'Roxanne' and I later read a review that described Sting as sounding 'like a drunk in a broom cupboard. He'd lost his mojo and was apparently spending too much time knocking about with blokes with CDs in their mouths.' (But I think you're great, Sting, just in case you're reading this.)

Our driver got pulled over for speeding at Scotch Corner and we didn't get home until half six in the morning. I was shattered and I overslept, missed the dress rehearsal and ended up getting to college just in time for the first (and last) performance of the show. The gymnasium was packed out with parents, friends and anybody else we could drag in off the street.

Francis was chaotically working both sound and lights and it was just one cock-up after another. Wrong lights, wrong sound cues, and when the tape snapped on the reel-to-reel player I had to resort to an impromptu singalong with the audience. I did a medley of hits from *Joseph and the Amazing Technicolor Dreamcoat* and a heartfelt version of 'My Name is Tallulah' from *Bugsy Malone*.

With the technical hitch rectified, we soldiered onwards towards the finale. Out of the corner of my eye I could see Troy positioning himself in the wings and having a last-minute spray with WD-40. And as the music kicked in he came speeding onstage in all his man-eating-plant regalia. The audience applauded the costume but then Troy came to a juddering halt.

In all the excitement he'd neglected to recharge himself during the tea break. So there I was on stage pretending to be chased by a stationary disabled man dressed as a man-eating plant.

The song was supposed to climax with the plant exploding. I reached for the pyrotechnic charge hidden underneath Troy's back wheel and pushed the button. Nothing happened. The way things had been going I wasn't surprised in the slightest. I tried it again. Nothing. Shocked and confused, the audience stared at me in silence. Time stood still.

Then as the rest of cast reluctantly joined me onstage to painfully take their bows, the charge ignited and Troy exploded into a shower of sparks and smoke. Too much smoke as it happened, because the next thing we heard were the fire alarms and we all had to evacuate out on to the front street. What a balls-up!

I've no idea what passing motorists must have thought they saw on the pavement that rainy night in June. Seeing a group of people huddled around a charred man-eating plant on wheels. Who knows? What I do know is that whenever I have a nightmare you can bet Troy rolls through at some point in that man-eating plant costume.

Because the course was drawing to a close, I'd taken it upon myself to start applying for proper work several months earlier. I went to the library every Monday and browsed for jobs in the *Guardian* media section. I also wrote to every television company in the IBA guide. Yorkshire, Carlton, Grampian, etc. They would have all got a letter and CV from Peter Kay at one time or another.

Then one day I actually got a reply. A lady from Granada Television in Manchester rang me up. She was secretary to some bigwig called Grant Spencer and they were looking for a new runner to work in the editing department. I realised it wasn't acting but after the *Little Shop of Horrors* fiasco I'd decided perhaps my future lay behind the scenes. It seemed safer all round.

Anyway, at least I'd had a reply. I was excited enough just to get a call from Granada Television, the Hollywood of the North and home to *Coronation Street, Brideshead Revisited* and *Albion Market.*

So I went for the interview. I was very nervous.

'What an amazing view,' I said to his secretary as we travelled up to the seventh floor in the lift.

Well, I had to say something to disguise the fact that I'd just farted and thought that any form of conversation might eliminate her sense of smell.

'Oh look, you can almost see our house,' I said and farted again.

I shook hands with Grant Spencer over a bottle of Perrier that sat on his desk. Then I pumped once more before I settled myself back in a chair. What was wrong with me? I had been nervous before but this had gone beyond a joke.

'Right,' he said, startling me into another breakage of wind, 'I'm going to cut to the chase. I'm not going to bullshit you, Paul (I was far too nervous to correct him), it's not a glamorous job. Basically you'll be working six days a week making tea for the editing staff downstairs and you'll get £58 for the privilege. It's a crap job for shit money but it's a foot in the door and the last runner we had is now working in Spain on *El CID* with Alfred Molina so, hey, there's potential.'

I nodded, shook his hand, farted and left. The secretary didn't come back down in the lift with me and frankly I didn't blame her.

Travelling home on the bus I found myself sinking into depression. I had a very tough decision to make. I'd arrived at a career-changing crossroads in my life. Finally there was an opportunity to work in television, to get a foot in the door as Grant had suggested, but financially I just couldn't afford it.

Fifty-eight pounds a week? I know that money isn't everything but it's a start. The weekly bus fares to Granada would cost me half of that alone and what did that leave me for my driving lessons? Not enough. I truly believed that passing my driving test would open just as many doors in the long term. I was bringing in three times as much as that with my other dead-end jobs, but that's all they were, a dead end. What a dilemma.

Later that day back at home I got a call from Grant Spencer's secretary. For a second I thought she might have been calling to have a word with me about the state of my bowels, but she wasn't. She rang to say that after interviewing several candidates she was pleased to offer me the job.

Both elated and devastated, I declined the job there and then and regretted it as soon as I put the phone down. I felt like I'd thrown away my one chance, a decision I let haunt me, and I punished myself with 'what ifs' and 'maybes' for a very long time. I began putting any thoughts of my ever being in show business to the back of my mind. Anyway, who was I trying to kid? I had to be realistic. I was just an ordinary working-class lad from Bolton who made people laugh on their lunch breaks. I could never compete in the big leagues. It was time for me to face facts: I had no business in show business.

Despondent, I threw myself into work and took on a third part-time job.

I don't know if you're familiar with Netto. They're a chain of cheap supermarkets that have been popping up all over Britain for a number of years now. And when I say cheap, I mean cheap. A friend of mine won a trolley dash around a Netto store once and when he got to the checkouts and the woman tilled it up the total came to £11.20. Now that is cheap!

Working for Netto wasn't the end of the world, but I could certainly see it. My badge said 'Shop Floor Assistant' and on the opening day I assisted the shoppers through the automatic doors of Bolton's first Netto superstore. What a shithole.

No matter how much I tried to make a go of this job it really was the pits. I think what made it worse was the whole Granada TV thing still echoing round my head. I continued to torture myself about it, particularly on busy Saturday afternoons, surrounded by kids up the freezer aisle, screaming for Mini Milks. You'll never know how close I came to tipping them head first into the freezer and sitting on the lid.

Occasionally I'd get the added excitement of shelf stacking or rotating the fresh milk in the fridges, but other than that my designated job was working the cardboard crushing machine in the back of the warehouse. Now that was a monotonous job, it was crush, crush, crush all day long.

I did it so much that I used to dream about it in my sleep. So now I was crushing practically twenty-four/seven. Only I didn't get a paid for the night shift.

I had friends who worked in the cake factory over the road and they'd told me how they dreamed about work. They put cherries on top of Bakewells as they went by on a conveyor belt and when they shut their eyes at night all they could see were cherries floating past. I never thought I'd end up the same.

My dreams were slipping further away from me. I now had money for driving lessons – in fact, I had more money than I really needed – but absolutely no time to spend it. Between the garage, the cash and carry and Netto I had one afternoon off every fortnight on a Tuesday. On an average day I started at 6 a.m. and finished at 10 p.m. The work was relentless and I'd like to tell you I was happy but I wasn't.

The wages at Netto matched the food – cheap. I only stayed because the store was near home. We had a lot of managers too and in the four months I worked there we had seven. They'd arrive from other branches with a head full of fancy ideas and then leave when they realised the budget constraints. But they also knew they could get labour for a lot less than they were paying me.

Due to a clerical error at head office I'd been on £3 an hour since the day I signed my contract. That's why the managers attempted to make it their mission to get me to leave. Luckily they all left before me.

The other shop-floor assistants were on the disgraceful wage of £2 an hour. They were mainly students with debts up to their eyeballs. Then Tony Billingham arrived. He was a nasty piece of work in my opinion – wore Paco Rabanne and kept ferrets. He found out about my clerical wage error and offered me a deal. He said I could either work seven hours a day at £2 an hour or four hours a day for £3 an hour. Reluctantly, I took less hours at the £3 an hour. I think he really wanted me to tell him to stick the job up his arse, but I didn't give him the satisfaction.

The following week I turned up for work with the flu, and when I say the flu I mean proper flu, not just man flu. I could hardly breathe, my eyes and my nose were streaming, but I soldiered on regardless. I had a sworn cardboard-crushing oath to uphold. At the end of the day I was called into the manager's office.

'I'm afraid we're going to have to let you go, Peter,' he said all formal like.

'We?' I said looking around. 'Are you schizophrenic?'

Then his mood suddenly changed.

'Look, I don't like a smart mouth, you're sacked, all right?'

'Why? What have I done?'

'You've not done anything and that's the problem. Your work isn't up to the standard we require here at Netto.'

'I crush card. What do you want, orgasms?'

He ignored my comment and asked me to hand over my Netto jumper and knife. Now just so you know, when I say knife I am referring to my standard issue Netto Stanley knife that every shop-floor assistant was required to carry on his/her personage at work. Just in case you thought I'd turned into a knife-wielding psychopath.

Furious, I handed them over to him, but then I did something that I'd never done before. I threw him into the lockers and threatened to bite his nose off. Now I'm not a violent person. I'd like to blame my actions on a number of things: the flu, blind rage and the half-bottle of Night Nurse that I'd knocked back on my tea break.

I went home and waited half expecting the police to come battering down my front door at any moment. But it was just his word against mine and thankfully nothing ever came of the incident. Well, not unless he reads this book and I get sent down for common assault.

Out of one shit job and into another. I got a job up the road at Hollywood Nights, a video shop situated in the back of the Spar supermarket next to a small subpost office. When I was growing up I'd always imagined working in a video shop would be my dream job. I seemed to have spent half my life in them, hiring the latest video releases or badgering the store owner for the cardboard stands

I'd seen in the shop window of *Police Academy 5* or *Cannonball Run II*. But now I was on the other side of the counter and, disappointingly, I found the job to be quite boring and rather lonely.

I spent most of my shift reading magazines that I'd managed to smuggle out of the Spar on my way into the building, or eating out-of-date Monster Munch from the back of the stockroom (not that I could ever taste the difference). The customers in the Spar and the post office could hear the TV in the video shop, so as a result I was only ever allowed to watch family films. Consequently I must have seen *The Love Bug* and *Lassie* about seventy times.

Bored on pension days, I'd deliberately play *Bonnie and Clyde* on the video and turn the volume up during the robbery scenes – 'Stick 'em up, get down on the floor.' Then I'd close my eyes and wait for the pensioners' screams from behind the partition. It worked like a charm, but the Spar manager never saw the funny side. Some people have no sense of humour.

Occasionally the area manager would show up and make me justify my wages. He'd force me to hoover the shop and polish the video covers on the shelves. Can you believe I actually had to polish the video covers?

Sometimes I'd put a few adult-film cases in the Kiddies' Castle but even that backfired. One night I had a bloke lingering in the shop. I could tell from his fingerless gloves that he wanted soft porn. He deliberately waited until I was about to close and then he slammed an adult-video case down on the counter. Then without making eye contact he hastily snatched the tape out of my hand, scooped up his loose change and bolted.

About ten minutes later, as I was just about to padlock the

serving hatch, I saw the same bloke charging down the aisle in the Spar towards me. He thrust the rental case into my hand and whispered, 'Are you taking the piss?' I opened the box and read the tape, but instead of *Free My Willy 2* it was *Rosie and Jim*.

I don't know if you're familiar with *Rosie and Jim*, but basically it's a kids' show about two puppets and an old man who sail around on a canal barge. Not really the kind of thing you want when you've got the big light dimmed and your pants around your ankles.

The only time we ever had a rush on was on Saturday nights and then it was usually couples arguing over what video to get. They used to drive me mental. They'd pick a Top Title from the latest releases section no problem, but it was when they came to the counter and I told them they were now entitled to a 'free pound video' that things went tits up.

They'd spend ages choosing a second film because the bloke always wanted something violent and trashy about 'ninjas settling old scores' while his girlfriend wanted something slushy and trashy like a mother fighting to get her kids back from her estranged husband who's taken them to Iraq.

But in the end it didn't matter which video they decided upon because it would never get watched anyway and I guarantee you they'd both be asleep before the end of the Top Title.

Getting a 'free pound video' from Hollywood Nights was a false economy, a bit like trying to chose three DVDs for £15 in HMV. You can only ever find one you like, maybe two at a push but try for a third and you'll be in there for hours. Then when you get home you look in the TV guide and the third film is on Channel 5 the following night.

The only perk I had working at Hollywood Nights was that occasionally I got to take home a Top Title at the end of the shift. I'd type my staff password into the computer and put the video hire through the till. Big mistake. I only did it a few times and then I got a call at home from the area manager Gavin.

'I have reason to believe you've been stealing from Hollywood Nights.'

He said he'd found confirmation on his hard drive that I'd made numerous transactions over the last few months and the Top Title he shopped me on was *What's Love Got to Do With It*.

He accused me of hiring videos out to customers and pocketing the money, the cheeky bastard. I confessed to occasionally borrowing a few videos at the end of my shift but I said I'd never once profited from my actions in any way. Gavin said he'd no choice but to 'let me go' and sacked me over the phone. I was gutted and couldn't believe I'd been sacked for taking Tina Turner home.

So what do you do when you lose a job? Well most people would go to the pub and get drunk. But I went to the pub, or in this case the Wine Lodge, and got another job. It was to be my first and hopefully last time working behind a bar.

I've never had a taste for alcohol, except for Baileys, but then again that's more of a dessert than a drink. Being teetotal, pub culture was completely alien to me and I hadn't a clue what some of the customers were asking for half the time.

'Can I have a Blastaway?'

What the hell is a Blastaway? I mean, how was I to know that it was a bottle of Diamond White and Castaway mixed together? Who thought these concoctions up, for God's sake?

A Snake Bite, a Black Russian, I was beginning to get paranoid and thought that customers were just making these names up in order to take the piss out of me. The final straw came when one bloke asked me for 'a pint of Golden'. I had half a mind to take his pint glass into the Gents and urinate into it. Why couldn't somebody just order a pint of beer and be done with it?

And as it was the Wine Lodge there were all the names of the wines to contend with as well. I'd have customers asking me for 'Ozzie Whites' and 'Blobs'. For the first few weeks I thought everybody was speaking jive.

I was also incapable of getting a head on a pint of beer. There must be some special kind of magic involved because I could never master it. I'd watch the other members of staff and try to copy them but it was useless. I just couldn't get any head (story of my life). The drip tray would be overflowing, the floor would be sopping wet, and I'd be trying everything, shaking the glass, waggling my finger around in the drink when the customer wasn't looking. Apart from actually spitting into the beer I just couldn't get a head on any of the pints. I even considered coming in early and squirting fairy liquid into all the pint glasses.

I was quickly turning into a bit of a joke at the Wine Lodge, but I wasn't laughing. After two weeks the manager decided to 'let me go'. And even though it was just another dead-end job I was gutted again. I seemed to be being 'let go' all over Bolton. I could see a pattern emerging.

Why couldn't I just settle down into a job and work like a normal person? Because I was living a lie. Deep down, no matter how hard I tried to deny it, I knew that my destiny lay elsewhere.

Secretly I still fantasised about being a comedian and was tired of being told what 'a funny fucker' I was by other staff at work. But funny at work wasn't enough. I had to be funny enough to work. (Did you see what I did there?)

So after much deliberation I decided to go back into further education, or in my case forward to university. The only problem was I had no qualifications but, hey, I wasn't about to let a trivial thing like that get in the way. I decided to bluff my way in. I realised that there might be consequences to my actions but what did I have to lose? Nothing.

The first thing I had to do was get the proper application forms. When they came I filled them in at the garage. I bought a thesaurus and the other lads chipped in by helping me write fictitious references and forging lecturers' signatures. Then I popped the forms in the post recorded delivery and waited. Within a week I had a reply and was called for an interview at Liverpool University.

I'd deliberately applied to universities close to home. Some people don't have a problem with distance, they're able to fly the nest with ease, but home is where my heart has always been. People sometimes make you feel ashamed of admitting that, but I've always loved being around my family.

Astonishingly, following my interview, I was given an unconditional offer at Liverpool University for a place on a combined honours degree. I chose Drama and Theatre Studies, American Studies and Information Technology, or IT as it's called in the business (what business?). Now all I had to do was make it past the education board with no qualifications.

The Sunday night I left home was heartbreaking. I had all of my worldly goods crammed into the back of my Uncle Tony's trusty Sierra including a 12-tog duvet, six bottles of Vimto and my black-

and-white portable telly. I felt like a contestant on *The Generation Game*.

My Uncle Tony couldn't see out of his back window, the car was packed that tight. I still felt sick to my stomach as we headed down the East Lancs in silence. I was about to pass a point of no return for the first time in my life and everybody in that silent car knew it. Except my Uncle Tony, who just kept slagging off all the tracks they were playing on the Top 40 countdown: 'There's no melody anymore, it's just drumming'.

I carried my gear up the stairs to my halls of residence and was immediately overwhelmed by the smell of Dettol and marijuana. I was paying fifty-two quid a week and I'd still got to design my own nameplate for my door in felt tip. Quietly we said our goodbyes and I remember bursting into tears as the Sierra turned the corner and drove off into the night.

I must have sobbed myself to sleep and then a few hours later I was woken up by the sound of an electric guitar reverberating through the paper-thin ceiling above me. I stared at my official 'Gladiators' alarm clock. it was twenty past two in the morning.

Slowly I staggered up a staircase with my 12-tog draped round me and hammered on the door of the culprit. The noise subsided and the door was opened by a tall blond lad wearing a bandanna.

'Rock 'n' roll, dude,' he roared into my face. 'My name's Brad, I'm from Salisbury, come into my crib and smoke some blow.'

I scanned his room. He had a lava lamp and a poster on his wall with the lyrics from 'Stairway to Heaven'.

'I can't, *dude*,' I said, 'and unless you fancy going up the stairway to heaven tonight I suggest you unplug your guitar and go to sleep before I wrap it round your neck.' I really didn't want to be there. Who was I trying to kid? This student life wasn't for me.

Shattered, the next morning I made my way over to the main hall for enrolment. It was make or break time. I had correspondence from my local education authority and my passport as proof of ID. The only thing I didn't have was any proof of my qualifications (which I obviously didn't have as they only existed in my fabricated world of lies and deceit). I reached the enrolment clerk. Pleasantly, she took all my details and that was it, she never asked to see any proof of anything. I was so completely thrown for a second that I almost offered to show them to her like a fool. I didn't though. I might be dumb but I'm not stupid.

I approached a lecturer and asked him what time lessons started, to which he replied 'next week'.

'Next week?' I said. 'What are we supposed to do until then?'

'Get to know your fellow students,' he said, 'settle in and enjoy Freshers' Week, familiarise yourself with your Student Union rep . . .'

I left him jabbering on because I was off. I ran straight out to the main road, got a bus to Lime Street station and caught the first train back home.

I rang my mum up from the payphone at the top of the street.

'Hello,' she said. 'Hello,' I said. The silence was painful and stilted.

'So, are you settling in?'

'Yeah, not so bad. I miss home. What are you having for tea?'

'It's Monday, your favourite: chicken Kiev, chips, beans and a fried egg. What are you having?'

'Oh, I might have a walk round to the university refectory, see if there's anything left and see if I can make some friends, you know. Anyway I'll give you another call tomorrow.'

I hung up and then I legged it two hundred yards round the corner to our house and banged on the front door – she must of thought it was the bailiffs again. Opening the door she saw me stood on the front street beaming like an idiot. We hugged for what seemed liked for ever. It was good to be back and we both had to laugh when we realised I'd only been gone for twenty-four hours.

Chapter Twelve

Let's Tickle Those Balls

What's got ninety balls and screws old women? 'Bingo.' That was without a doubt the worst job I ever had – working at the Top Rank bingo hall in Bolton. There didn't seem to be a cloud in the sky during that summer of '94 but maybe it just felt like that to me because I was stuck in a building with no windows.

Surely you must remember that summer? It was the hottest one we'd had for a hundred years – well, that's what Wincy Willis said on *Good Morning Britain.*

Wet Wet Wet were number one for what seemed like for ever with 'Love is All Around' from the hit film of that year, *Four Weddings and a Funeral.* I didn't mind the film but couldn't really relate to it, having never been to a wedding in a castle. I also didn't know anybody who'd set foot in a marquee, except for my dad going in the beer tent at the Bolton marathon, but that doesn't count really.

Every wedding I ever went to was either in the function room of a working men's club or in a tatty room over a pub with dads playing air guitar and grandmas leaving early. But I'll save all that for another book.

The Top Rank used to be the Odeon cinema and I'd considered it to be an absolute sacrilege when the cinema had been shut and turned into a bingo hall ten years earlier. I never imagined that I'd be working there one day as a part-time customer-care assistant. Not that any of the customers needed any care or assistance. What they needed was dropping into a vat of boiling oil, as far as I was concerned.

When I first started working at Top Rank I used to try to be nice to the customers but it was short-lived. Because as soon as they set foot through the front doors they'd turn into a pack of vicious wolves. They just seemed to change, as if they'd been brainwashed in one of those religious cults you see on CNN. Sweet grey-haired old ladies would turn into the devil and eat their young if it meant getting a win on the bingo.

They'd pour in week in and week out, the same faces in the same seats – their lucky seats – and heaven help you if you ever sat in one by accident. They'd break your arms. And believe me, I've seen it happen. I've witnessed the violence of bingo first-hand. The swearing, the lying, the fighting – I even saw two grown women dragging each other around by the hair in the foyer over a 10p slot token.

I don't mean to appear sexist but bingo was and is very much a ladies' sport. You didn't get a lot of men in, apart from the odd gay bloke in a shell suit or occasionally a woman daring to show up with her husband in tow. Then, I swear, the other women would boo and hiss the couple as they took their seats in the hall. Women reckoned it was their only safe haven of pleasure and that the blokes should be back at home looking after the kids.

The other thing that amazed me was their concentration during the game. They would be so focused on what they were doing, they wouldn't budge or even flinch when they were playing, they'd hardly even breathe. I remember one woman collapsing halfway through a game. The paramedics were called to the scene, they took her to hospital, ran some tests, she woke up, discharged herself and was back playing bingo the same night. Now that's what I call dedication . . . 65. (That was just a crap gag on those compilation albums. No? OK, forget it.)

The women couldn't spend their money quick enough. I'd see old people with pension books burning a hole in their shoulder bags, loose change, life savings. They didn't even have enough left for a still orange from behind the bar. That's why most of them brought their own drinks in. I'm not kidding. They used to come up to the bar and ask for water with ice because it was free, then they'd take it back to their table and sneakily top it up with a bottle of orange cordial they had hidden under the table in their handbag.

Janice, the supervisor, used to do a stocktake on the bar once a week and bemoan the fact the profits were always down because nobody bought a bloody drink. But the Top Rank water bill was massive. It was a pity they weren't able to charge for 'Corporation Pop', they would have made a fortune.

My job was mainly washing cups and plates in the back. Occasionally I'd have to venture out into the hall during a game of bingo and do a bit of glass collecting. The women could be very fussy about that too. I'd attempt to pick a glass up off the table during a game only to have my hand slapped away by some misery. 'It's not finished,' she'd shout when all I could see was the tiniest speck of fluid at the bottom of the glass. Sometimes they'd shout at me with such ferocity that the caller would construe their cries as a 'house call' and the whole game would be thrown in to disrepute.

I remember one woman called Martha who was always false-calling and causing chaos, but she couldn't really help it as she was numerically dyslexic, the poor cow. The other women hated her for it. She was forever shouting out 'House' and stopping the game. The caller would read out her numbers and they'd all be completely wrong. The management had no choice but to ban her in the end because the regulars were threatening to firebomb her flat. That reminds me of a joke. How do you get a room full of women to shout bollocks? Shout 'Bingo'!

When I wasn't collecting glasses I'd be out collecting plates, dirty plates of half-eaten fish and chips left rotting underneath the table. I hated that with a passion, especially in hot weather. Some of the women could be dirty bitches when the weather turned clement. They'd sit dabbing their bingo cards with one of those huge coloured felt tips in one hand and a battery-powered pocket fan in the other; they'd also like to take their shoes off and rest their stinking bare feet either side of the tray of food. Then I'd have to crawl on my knees like a dog in an effort to try to rescue the tray of crockery from underneath their table. I'm retching just writing about it.

One night when I was out glass collecting, a woman down at the front of the hall had some kind of fit. I've no idea what was wrong with her. All I saw was her topple out of her seat and the next thing she was jigging about on her back.

But what freaked me out was that everybody just carried on playing. Nobody even glanced over to see what was happening because bingo was so important to them. Eventually a supervisor came over and put her in the recovery position while another member of staff called for an ambulance.

Similarly, Roy, the bingo caller (I'll get on to him in a minute), just continued reading out the numbers as if nothing had happened – 'Five and one, fifty-one, Six and two, sixty-two' – but finally he had to shout for another member of staff to go over and help the woman's husband because he was struggling with two bingo cards. He was doing his own and his wife's and he couldn't manage! Unbelievable!

The Top Rank had managers and assistant managers, but it was Roy Diamond who really ran the bingo. He was the self-proclaimed King of the Callers and what he said went, staff included. He was a tall wispy man who put me in mind of a black Bruce Forsyth. He always wore a rainbow-coloured cummerbund and he'd force Janice the supervisor to iron it every night before he went on stage for 'a session', as he liked to call it. He used to play 'Let's Get Ready to Rumble' before he went onstage too and as soon as we heard it everything had to stop at Roy's insistence. He called the shots. Bloody bingo mafia!

Roy used to have a little room underneath the stage where the organ had been when it used to be the Odeon. He'd converted it into a dressing room complete with a minibar, a fan and one of those mirrors with bulbs around the edges. An ex-supervisor once told me that it was her job to push 'play' on his midi hi-fi before he went onstage. She said he took it all very seriously. Apparently he'd knock back energy drinks and do a bit of a workout, stretching and all that, before he went onstage. Christ knows why because when he went got up there he just stood still for twenty minutes and called out the numbers. I mean he was hardly Daley Thompson.

But for some reason the women loved him. They idolised him

and Roy Diamond knew it. They'd try and touch him as he walked past their tables on his way to the stage. It was quite sickening to watch. Especially when he used to snog the pensioners full on the lips. It would turn my stomach because everybody knew Roy was gay. He'd been an item with Jason off the slot machines for years.

Even my Auntie Phyllis knew that Roy Diamond was gay. I remember her telling me on her deathbed down the ICU.

'He's as bent as a figure eight, everybody knows that,' she said under her oxygen mask. 'You know there only used to be two queers in Bolton at one time, everybody knew who they were and everybody stayed AWAY!! And if you ever saw them coming down the street towards you, you crossed over.'

Mind you, she was delirious on morphine at the time and went on to tell me she'd just seen a forty-foot Chris de Burgh in the car park kicking Minis over for charity. Bless her!

My nana belongs to the generation that is totally oblivious to the ever-changing world of political correctness. I could have died the other week when we were in Primark and she asked the young shop assistant if the blouse that she'd seen in the sale was available in nigger brown?

'What? It's a colour,' she said as I dragged her out of the shop.

Some people thought that Roy had his favourites among the women. He'd kiss them one night and then they'd win the next. I'm not saying it was rigged or anything but God help you if you won too often, the other women could get so vicious and jealous. I'd overhear them when I was glass collecting making comments about the winners under their breath.

'Look at her, the dirty slut, giving Roy the glad eye. I'll break her legs and then she won't be able to spread them so easily.'

I know that Jason would occasionally get fed up with Roy's

flirtations with the female punters. And if he ever dared linger too long on the lips of certain women Jason would leg them up as they left the bingo hall at the end of the night. He ended up getting suspended for breaking a woman's teeth with a plastic tennis racket.

I don't know if Roy drank out of both taps or not but what I do know is that, love him or loathe him, the Top Rank bingo would have been empty without him. He had a fortnight in Fuengirola the summer before I worked there and attendance figures dropped by 64 per cent. The managers didn't know what to do, they crapped themselves because they actually had to come in and do a bit of work.

After charming the ladies Roy would eventually climb up into his pulpit and start the game. He used to begin each night by reading out dedications and birthday wishes.

'Hello, everybody, welcome to the Top Rank. My name's Roy Diamond and it's great to see so many of you here this evening . . . was the cemetery shut? Ha, ha, ha, ha, only kidding. Just a couple of hellos before we begin. It's birthday wishes for Elsie Jackson at the back somewhere tonight. Hello, Elsie love, seventy-eight years young today. Many happy returns, my love, that's from your sister-in-law Andrea and your daughter-in-law Cherise, and I'm telling you, Elsie, if I was ten years older . . . you'd be dead.'

The women used to find these insults hysterical but I couldn't figure out why. Perhaps it was because Roy was giving them some attention.

'. . . and speaking of death,' he continued, 'I'm sorry to have to tell you that the lady who collapsed at the back of hall last night sadly died this morning at Bolton Royal Infirmary, but we sent her a wreath of flowers from the Top Rank. OK, let's tickle those balls and it's eyes down for a full house,' and he'd start the game without missing a beat.

Top Rank used to have a monthly staff magazine and in one issue they featured an interview with Roy. The article was entitled 'Bingo's From Strength to Strength,' and I remember reading it in the staff canteen. I was shocked at just how much he considered himself to be the saviour of modern-day bingo.

He said that the secret to the success of any bingo hall was giving the 'Billy Bunters' what they wanted. In his case it was class.

'That's what they get at my club every time. That's why I'm guaranteed bums on seats for ever and a day. I'm full of ideas. For example, I organised a Christmas party a couple of years back and it was so successful that we've started having it annually. We were also the first club in the region to bring major acts to the club on a Saturday night.' That was something that Roy was particularly proud of ever since he'd booked Greengrass (the actor Bill Maynard) from *Heartbeat* for a Halloween party.

The acts read like a *Who's Who* of shite.

'We've had all the top artists including Johnny Logan, Dr Hook and the Wee Papa Girl Rappers. I even put in an offer for Shirley Bassey last Easter but her manager said she wouldn't get changed in the toilets. It was her loss.' Roy came across as a right bloody bighead.

Roy also used to organise coach trips to other Top Rank bingo halls. That amazed me. I mean, why would anybody want to visit another Top Rank bingo hall that was practically the same as the one you've just come from? But they did in their droves.

It reminded me of a mate of my dad's who worked on Bolton Fish Market. He went on holiday to Blackpool for a fortnight once and while he was there he decided to go on one of those 'Mystery

Tours'. He got on the coach and had absolutely no idea where it was going until it pulled up outside Bolton Fish Market. So there he was, back at work.

'I thought you were away?' his co-workers said when he turned up at work.

'I am,' he said. 'I'm on a bloody Mystery Tour.' He ended up working a shift and selling some fish while he was there. True story.

One thing Roy didn't like was people like me, or 'the new blood' as he called us in the article.

'They've got no enthusiasm, no passion and if they don't buck up they'll be the poison that rots bingo for ever.' I thought that was a bit strong. He ended the article by mentioning that he'd never had a day off sick in twenty-eight years, not even when the doctor suspected meningitis.

He was obsessed with part-timers like me progressing up the bingo ladder and eventually becoming callers ourselves. I remember one of the lads that I worked in the kitchens with getting a right lecture from Roy one night.

'Is there nothing you want to do with your life?' he said.

'I'm only here for the summer to earn a bit of cash before I go back to university,' the lad said.

Roy hated students.

'And what are you studying?'

'Politics, European Law and Advanced Semantics,' he replied.

'That's all very well and good but where's that going to get you?' said Roy.

I worked a lot of hours that summer. I had to, just to feed my expensive habit – learning to drive. After two tests I was now on to my third instructor, Norris. I got him out of the free paper *Loot*. And what a big girl's blouse he turned out to be. He was a nervous wreck with a sweepover and a tank top. Like Frank Spencer on steroids. And he had absolutely no confidence in my inability to drive. I remember he once said, 'The road is the classroom and you are the pupil.' To say we didn't get on would be putting it mildly.

Impatient and stubborn (well, so would you be after 146 lessons), I demanded that he put me in for the test, which he did. I failed miserably on both attempts. Once, for arguing with the examiner before we'd even left the examination centre car park. He wanted to go left and I wanted to go right. The second time I failed because I had to swerve to avoid hitting a bread van on Bury Road. Surely that couldn't be deemed as my fault? The feckless arsehole never indicated.

But when I got back to the test centre the examiner told me what I already knew.

'I'm sorry to tell you, Mr Kay, but you've failed your test. Can I ask you what you plan to do now?'

'Find the driver of that bread van and kick his fucking head in,' I said.

The examiner got out of the car leaving me slumped over the wheel in a deep depression.

The closest I'd got to owning my own vehicle was buying a knock-off mountain bike. I loved that bike and used to cycle to work on it all the time. It frightens me now when I think that I never used to wear a cycling helmet. The bike didn't have any lights either and I always used to listen to my Walkman when I was cycling too. How I wasn't knocked down and killed I'll never know.

Like I said, I worked a lot of hours, but Sunday was my worst shift. I used to do fifteen hours straight through with a twenty-minute tea break. I'd usually grab some food and sit out the back on some bread trays admiring the baking sun. Wincey Willis was right, it truly was a glorious summer and I was bitter to be missing it. The stifling heat made the Top Rank even more unbearable. And every Sunday would culminate with the mother of all bingo games, the National.

The National was when all the bingo clubs in the region linked up to play live for a jackpot prize of half a million pounds. It was a very prestigious game, so much so that Roy changed the colour of his bow tie when the club switched to a live link-up. Lord knows why as the other clubs couldn't see him. He used to call it 'PP', 'Professional Presentation'. God, he was a knob.

In order to comply with the national gaming federation rules nobody was allowed to make a noise during the national. The bar shutter went down and food was no longer available. The staff had to stand like mannequins. No one could glass collect, no one could move, no one could breathe because there was so much 'big money' at stake. And if there was any kind of disruption the bingo hall responsible could find themselves landed with a hefty fine.

One night during the National, I was busy in the kitchen washing cups and plates. I was knackered and hot. It had been an incredibly hectic night and the floor in the kitchen was wet through. I'd forgotten to put the 'Caution: Slippery Floor' sign up as the health and safety act requires, but I don't think even that would have helped my supervisor Janice as she came charging through the door to tell me that 'the National has just started'. But before I had the chance to warn her, her feet hit a wet spot on the floor which sent her skidding across the floor on her arse.

I got a verbal warning. Apparently Roy was furious but he never said anything to me. Still, things started to go downhill after that.

I got a second verbal warning a week later for putting the wrong fluid in the dishwasher. That was a genuine mistake but the kitchen supervisor wasn't happy when three hundred teacups came out of the dishwasher dirtier than they went in.

The following Saturday night it was my twenty-first birthday. I'd booked a meal for the family at a pub restaurant that had been highly recommended. I was all set for a lovely night out until I found out they'd double booked the table. The place was chock-a-block, so all we could do was wait . . . and wait . . . and wait some more. We finally decided to throw in the towel at half past nine. We were all hungry, fed up and my nephew was about to have one of his tantrums. He was tired after having spent all day pounding the streets as a traffic warden. That was a shit joke, sorry.

We ended up calling into a Chinese chippie on the way back. Then when I got home I threw up all over the vestibule. I thought the sausage had tasted a bit funny. So there I was, twenty-one years old and my head stuck down the toilet. Happy Birthday!

The next morning I felt rotten but got up and cycled to work regardless. When I got to the Top Rank, Beryl, one of the kitchen staff, took one look at me and told me to go home. 'You can't make three hundred sandwiches when you've got the shits.' She always had a way with words did Beryl.

The next day I was hauled into the manager's office and he sacked me. I asked him why and he accused me of neglecting my work due to having a birthday hangover. I tried to tell them about the dodgy food but he wasn't having any of it. Bloody bingo mafia. I'm convinced to this day that Roy was yanking his chain.

'Plus you were seen on the CCTV footage cycling your bike through the main hall,' he said.

I had to admit that was true but I'd always done it. It was half seven on a Sunday morning for God's sake, I was hardly going to knock down any pensioners. And anyway, how was I to know I was being filmed?

'I have no choice but to terminate your employment,' he said.

'When you say terminate my employment, what do you mean?'

'I mean as from today you are no longer an employee of Top Rank bingo.'

But still I quizzed him. 'When you say terminate does that mean I can't even come into the building for game of bingo? Are my family terminated? Or are they allowed to play bingo?'

We discussed the word terminate in great detail for over twenty minutes and then he eventually lost his cool.

'Look,' he said, 'we've been over and over this, I have nothing more to say, you are finished working for Top Rank bingo, your employment is no more and still you persist in discussing it. Why?'

'Because I've not clocked off yet and I've just got another twenty-five minutes out of you.'

'Get him out of my office,' he said through gritted teeth.

I ended up being escorted off the premises like a common criminal. I never went back there ever again. It's shut down now and boarded up. Good riddance.

Chapter Thirteen

With Bert by Torchlight

Last night I went to the cinema and watched *Superman Returns*. And as the opening titles came on the screen I found myself filling up. Before I knew it I was unable to control myself and had tears streaming down my cheeks. I must admit that I like a good cry occasionally – I'm sure you'll agree it does you good to shed a few tears – but at *Superman*? I mean it's hardly *The Champ* or *Who Will Love My Children?*

I think it touched me so deeply because Bryan Singer, the director, has gone to great lengths to recreate the feel of the original *Superman* movie from 1978 and for a few minutes I was completely transported back to my childhood, to the Lido cinema in Bolton, to when I was five. I know it sounds freaky but I can even remember exactly where my Dad and I sat when we first watched the film.

Superman was a big deal when it was released in 1978 and the tag line for the film was: 'You'll believe a man can fly.' I was so overwhelmed and fired up after seeing it that as we left the cinema that afternoon in December I immediately removed my arms from

my parka and I flew off down Newport Street. Skidding through
sleet and snow thinking I was Superman, humming the tune over
and over while my dad bought some new steel toecap boots from
the World-Famous Army & Navy Store.

Those feelings of excitement came back last night as soon as I
heard that powerful John Williams score again and I found myself
a blubbering mess.

I've talked before about memories being relived through music,
but this was the first time I'd ever experienced a similar feeling on
a visit to the cinema. That's why I still love cinema so much,
because even after all these years no matter where you are, when
you go or what you're watching you completely escape from the
real world for a couple of hours.

Superman was one of the first times I ever felt completely
removed from the world outside. Then it happened again when I
saw *Close Encounters of the Third Kind – Special Edition* (that's the
one where they show Richard Dreyfuss going into the spaceship at
the end). I remember my amazement when I saw the colossal
mother ship landing. I just gawped at it with my eyes out on stalks.

But if there's one film that succeeded in transporting a whole
generation it must be *Star Wars*. That was the big one, no doubt
about it. I'm not even a huge *Star Wars* fan. I can't rattle off the
make and model of Han Solo's screwdriver and I can't tell you the
name of Luke Skywalker's mother's cousin, but I do have total
admiration for George Lucas and what he's achieved (excluding
Howard the Duck). Is it me or does George Lucas look as though
he's slowly turning into Chewbacca the older he gets?

When I saw outer space on the big screen for the first time it had
me hook, line and sinker – by the end of the film I was bouncing
up and down in my seat, shooting pretend rayguns at the other

baddy spaceships and Darth Vader. I genuinely felt as though I was in the final battle scene at the end. I too should have got a medal for blowing up *Death Star*.

The reason I'm telling you all of this is because after leaving Top Rank bingo my next part-time job was to be a cinema usher at the very same cinema where I first saw *Superman* and *Star Wars*.

Still furious from the Top Rank fiasco, I found myself down the jobcentre yet again. I was still working at the garage but my hours were down to just one morning a week. If truth be told, I was only keeping my hand in order to feed my ongoing dependency on blank tapes and batteries.

I'd also left the cash and carry job a few months earlier after they decided to close the branch behind the abattoir and move to a new state-of-the-art store eight miles away. The new depot was enormous, so big that HB and the other managers had to drive around in golfing buggies just to get from one end of the store to the other. But all the fun was at the old building. I found the new store very corporate and clinical. HB wasn't allowed to use his air horn any more and we were no longer able to nick ourselves a fortune. The new depot was like Alcatraz the security was that tight. It was time to leave.

'Customer Care Assistant at a busy town-centre cinema' – that's what the card said in the jobcentre. Fourteen hours a week, £3 an hour.

'The wage is crap,' I thought to myself, 'but imagine all the films I'll get to watch for free.' It would hardly be like work at all.

It must have been the fastest job I ever got. I took the job card out of the stand over to Mandy behind the desk (we were on first-name terms as I'd become one of her regulars). She rang the cinema and they told her to send me straight round. So I walked the two hundred yards to the Lido on Bradshawgate. It was there I first met the manager, Mrs Hayworth. She looked me up and down and said, 'Right, you can start Saturday, wear a white shirt and black trousers, we supply the bow tie.' And that was that. Within fifteen minutes I was officially a cinema usher.

It felt strange at first being on the 'other side', I mean to be *working* in a cinema, especially one I'd been going to as a customer my entire life.

There used to be two cinemas in Bolton when I was growing up. The Lido and the Odeon on the other side of town opposite the bus station. I have to say that my favourite (and most people my age in Bolton will probably agree) was the Odeon. Sadly it was shut in the mid-eighties and turned into the Top Rank bingo hall. Which was an absolute abomination in my opinion (and so was my job there).

I thought the Odeon was a magnificent cinema, with striking chandeliers and two giant staircases that wound up either side of the beautiful art deco foyer. I used to love that walk to the screen. It was so exciting, shuffling into the darkness, having to adjust your eyes to the light so you could find the aisle and choose a seat for yourself.

The Odeon's was one of the grandest foyers I've ever seen in a cinema. It was huge, with two cashier desks to cope with the demand during the school holidays. There were always a plethora of exciting and colourful cardboard stands in the foyer, advertising the new film releases. I loved those and the posters too – 'James Bond is Back', or a tenth *Police Academy*. God, it was exciting. It never leaves you.

I also love watching the trailers before the film starts. In fact, you could forget all about the main feature as far as I'm concerned. I'd be happy just sitting watching trailers for two hours. I'm gutted if I ever get there late and miss them. Because that for me is what going to the cinema is all about, watching trailers and seeing just how much food you can stuff into your mouth before the film starts and then spending the rest of the film craving a Kiora to quench your thirst.

The other thing I always loved about the Odeon was the smell of it, that sumptuous aroma of warm popcorn and Westlers hot dogs. I know all cinemas have that smell but for some reason it always smelt better at the Odeon.

Not that we ever bought popcorn or hot dogs at the cinema, oh God no, we used to smuggle all our own treats in with us. Well, I say we, it was my mum who used to do all the smuggling. We'd visit the paper shop across the road from the cinema and stock up on eats and treats. Pop, crisps, lollies, chocolate, the lot. Then nonchalantly my mum would stagger into the foyer, scrunching as she walked over to the counter with a bottle of Rola Cola down each sleeve of her anorak and her pockets stuffed full of Twister crisps and Sherbet Dib Dabs.

'Can I have three for *Pete's Dragon* please?' she'd say as casually as she could muster.

Smuggling treats into the cinema has been a hard habit to break, much to the disgust of my wife. Even today I can't stop myself from visiting the Texaco garage on the way to the multiplex in order to stock up on Evian water and a family bag of Revels. Some people may consider me to be a tight arse but it's hard to fight tradition. It's been bred into me not to 'pay those cinema prices'.

Once every twelve months I'll treat myself to a pick 'n' mix selection but even then I try and stick to the light stuff like marshmallows and flumps. Stick three pieces of fudge in the bag and you can be paying over a fiver. I'm surprised they don't wear a mask and a striped jumper at the tills, the robbing swines.

Another thing I liked about the Odeon was the Saturday-morning kids club. We used to watch old Norman Wisdom films and serials like *The Double Deckers, Banana Splits* and *Big John, Little John.* We also watched one with Charlie Drake where he played a professor who shrunk to the size of a telephone after drinking some kind of potion. I can't remember what it was called but it wasn't much good.

They also used to play games at the kids club, have competitions and occasionally they'd have publicity stunts. Like the time three hundred of us turned up to watch Spiderman scale the walls of the Odeon at half nine in the morning. Well, it obviously wasn't the real Spiderman, just some fella in a fancy dress costume. A bit like Fathers for Justice.

It was chucking it down with rain but we all let out a joyous cheer when Spiderman turned the corner in a Hillman Avenger. But our happiness was to be short-lived when some council workers turned up with the local health and safety officer and told Spiderman he wasn't allowed to climb the Odeon. They said it was too much of a risk and blamed adverse weather conditions.

We were gutted and vented our anger by pelting the council workers with pop bottles out of a skip at the back of the building. As a result the kids club was closed for two weeks and we missed the regional premiere of *Digby – the Biggest Dog in the World.*

Bloody jobsworth council. It's a pity they weren't on the ball as much when I played the town hall on my last tour and my bloody dressing room got robbed. Unbelievable. I played almost every theatre in Britain and then got robbed in my home town. Charming!

One thing you don't get at the cinema any more these days is double bills. They were all the rage in the seventies and eighties. I can remember my grandad sneaking me off school and taking me to watch *The Pink Panther Strikes Again* and *The Spy Who Loved Me*. I thought double bills were great because you could be in the cinema for up to four hours at a time.

My arse was numb watching double bills such as *The Black Hole* and *Condorman, Hooper* and *Airplane!, My Little Pony* and *The Killing Fields*. I made the last one up but it wouldn't have been out of place back in the day when the double bill was king. They really had some bizarre combinations of films thrown together. Regardless of genre, cast or certification. Like *Sweeney 2* and *Convoy, The French Connection* and *Bugsy Malone*, and I swear I once saw a listing in our local paper for *Mary Poppins* and *Deep Throat*.

That would have been at the Lido. They went slightly pornographic for a few years after the cinema industry slipped into a decline due to the arrival of home video. They resorted to showing soft porn in their 'adult lounge' as they called it. It was actually an upstairs café they had turned into a seventy-seat cinema screen.

Meanwhile, on the other side of town the Odeon struggled on, managing to hold its head up high as one of the last bastions of traditional family entertainment. And while they were screening children's classics such as *Dumbo, Bambi* and *Snow White and the Seven Dwarfs*, the Lido had resorted to showing filth like *I am a Nymphomiac, Sandra is Anybody's* and *Snow White Does the Seven Dwarfs*.

Cinema came out of its decline in the mid-eighties thanks to box-office smashes like *Ghostbusters* and *Gremlins*. Not to mention the *Rocky* and *Rambo* films. The latter was banned by the local council after being considered too violent for public consumption. Bloody council killjoys again. I noticed they weren't so quick to stop the Lido having a late night screening of *Titty Titty Gang Bang.*

I was at the cinema every week during my teenage years and continued to be just as totally consumed with it as I was when I first saw *Superman* and *Star Wars.* I'd run out of the cinema each week believing I was a character from the film I'd just watched. I remember thinking I was Marty McFly on my pretend skateboard, sliding through the snow to the bus station after watching *Back to the Future.* Or sweeping the leg all the way to the 582 bus with Paddy after watching *The Karate Kid.* Both of us waxing on and waxing off as we climbed the stairs to the top deck.

Another film I went to watch with Paddy was *Rocky IV,* the one where he fights the Russian. It was a huge success when it was first released and everybody wanted to see it. We sneaked out of school early and caught a bus into town so we could catch the teatime showing at half four. The plan worked. The place was only a third full but as we exited through the fire doors at the end of the film we walked into pandemonium. People were queuing twice round the block and down to the red-light district. Anyway, a scuffle had broken out after the cinema staff informed the customers that they were now full. In the bedlam that ensued someone smashed the glass casing on the poster for *Death Wish 3* and the police had to be called to restore peace. It made it on to the headlines of the *Bolton Evening News* the next day: 'ROCKY RIOTS CINEMA STAFF ON THE ROPES'.

Eventually the Lido shed its soft-porn image and was rejuvenated as a Cannon cinema with a Monday-night film club.

You could watch any film you desired for a pound. My mum and dad used to take me every week and we had a great time watching films such as *The Jewel of the Nile*, *Remo – Unarmed and Dangerous* and *Clockwise* with John Cleese, to name but a few.

We also went to see *Crocodile Dundee*, an experience I'll never forget as that was the time my dad decided to take a flask of coffee into the cinema with him. They sold it in the foyer but of course my dad refused point-blank to 'pay those cinema prices'.

Anyway, in the middle of the trailers my dad attempted to pass my mum a cup of coffee (you know, the screwtop lid that doubles as a cup), only he caught his elbow midway and tipped the scalding hot contents all over my legs and my brand new fawn-coloured chinos.

I let out a yelp. My dad shouted 'Bloody hell' and an usher shouted 'Shush'. But my parents refused to leave and so I had to sit through the whole of *Crocodile Dundee*, cold, damp and stinking of Kenco. My chinos were ruined and the coffee stains were so bad that my mum ended up throwing them out after soaking them for three nights in Omo (and that was a washing powder, not a place).

The only consolation I got after watching *Crocodile Dundee* was that on the walk back to the bus station we bumped into Alan Bennett and Kenneth Brannagh having a brew on the benches outside Mothercare. They were filming an episode of *Fortunes of War* for the BBC and our local town hall was doubling for the Kremlin. Bit of irony there for the jobsworth staff.

Bolton has been used for many film locations over the years, including *The Family Way*, *Spring and Port Wine* and the *Die Hard* trilogy.

My mum remembers *The Family Way* having its premiere in Bolton and some of the cast including John and Hayley Mills and

Hywel Bennett actually came onstage at the end to take a bow. If you haven't seen *The Family Way* then I highly recommend it. It's a brilliant film with a wonderful score by Paul McCartney. Only you won't catch it on telly in the afternoon before *Channel 4 Racing*, as the storyline is a little racy. It was actually considered quite contentious at the time of its release in 1966 and it was almost banned in the US as a result of its controversial subject matter. The plot, in a nutshell, is that Hywel Bennett can't get an erection. I think that may have been the tag line for the film, which probably explains why the Yanks frowned upon it.

Even today I get a small thrill reading the weekly cinema listings in the paper. It's another habit I formed as a boy and something that became particularly important to me when I worked as an usher, as the cinema listings governed the quality of shifts you'd be getting at work.

If we had a Disney or kids' film on, the cinema would be full of little brats and custody dads. Mrs Hayworth loved custody dads because they always spent a shitload of money on eats and treats out of guilt. Or if we had an adult action-type film on with Steven Seagal or Jean-Claude Van Damme then the cinema would be empty in the afternoon but full of solvent-abusing knobheads at night, so it was swings and roundabouts really.

I liked it when the films changed every week – we always got different ones each Friday during term time. But during the school holidays you could forget it. Then we'd have the same big blockbusters on for weeks at a time. Personally I'd be happy if I never saw *Batman Forever* ever again, having watched it over forty times during the summer of '95. The same goes for *Independence Day* and *Judge Dredd* (or *Judge Dreadful* as I prefer to call it). In fact, the only film I enjoyed watching time and time again was

Babe. You know, the one with the talking pig? It broke my bloody heart every time I saw it and put me off bacon for months.

My main job as an usher was ripping tickets. It was a skilful job – I used to have to tear the tickets into two and then thread the stubs on to a needle attached to a piece of string with a knot in the bottom. It was all very high-tech. Connie Parlow, another usher, showed me the ropes (or should I say string?). She'd been at the Lido since *Teen Wolf Too* and knew every trick in the book, which I found slightly ironic as I don't think she could read.

We had other duties as well as ripping tickets. Like sweeping out the auditorium after three hundred kids had trashed it during *Casper.* Scraping chewed sweets and bubbly off the back of seats was always a favourite duty of mine, especially on baking hot Saturday afternoons in August. And yes, I am being sarcastic.

It was also an usher's job to be responsible for the upkeep of the toilets. Topping up toilet rolls, towels and soap. The flushing of many a buoyant turd and the mopping up of piss from leaky urinals. Funny they neglected to mention any of that in the job description.

I remember we were short-staffed once during the big summer holidays and Jackie who worked on the kiosk had to both issue customers with tickets and rip them at the same time.

'I'm sorry,' she said, 'I don't normally do this, I've usually got a lady at the top of the stairs ripping but she's in the toilets changing a towel.'

I had to laugh when she told me later what she'd said, as that was just a bit too much information for the customers.

The downside of being an usher was that I got to see behind the scenes of a cinema, which took away some of the magic. Most people don't get to see the other side (apart from Derek Acorah, but we won't go there). I had a similar experience when I did the *My Mum Wants a Bungalow* tour. People would come backstage expecting to see me living a rock 'n' roll lifestyle, with expensive caterers and big coaches. It came as a bit of a shock when they discovered that I just rolled up in a Peugeot at the last minute with twelve balloons in the glovebox and a meal deal from Boots.

That's what it was like at the cinema. Behind the scenes it was just an empty shell. I'd always imagined the cinema to be a lot bigger on the inside but it was more like the Tardis in reverse. And once I got to see behind the façade I was shocked. Because the Lido was also in an extremely bad state of repair and they were losing business to state-of-the-art multiplexes in the neighbouring towns. Perhaps that's why there seemed no financial sense in pouring money into a dated, crumbling cinema like ours. In fact, if it wasn't for weekend custom, the place would have been shut down long ago, as we were more or less empty during the week.

Mrs Hayworth and the staff all knew deep down that their days were numbered and that it would only be a matter of time before a fancy new twenty-screen multiplex would be springing up on a retail park on the outskirts of town.* But like the band on the *Titanic* we still played on and continued to tread water. Quite literally in fact when it came to the Gents upstairs.

When head office stopped sending money for development things fell apart very quickly. We ran out of letter 'M's for the front canopy and had to make do with capital 'E's turned on their sides. The curtains in Screen 1 were so thick and heavy after

---

*Ironically, Bolton jumped up dramatically from having three screens to thirty six when two multiplexes opened in the space of six months.

accumulating sixty years' worth of dust that they slid off their tracks one day before *Evita* had even started.

Mortified, Mrs Hayworth had been to apologise to the customer and give him a refund because he couldn't see the screen. That's right, 'the customer', and even he wasn't really bothered. Old Billy the bearded tramp couldn't have cared less about seeing Eva Peron and had just come in for a warm out of the cold. Head office refused to pay for the curtain to be fixed and so as a result it stayed open permanently. Mind you, nobody ever commented on the curtain in Screen 2 and that had been broke since *My Fair Lady*.

Then we got rats. It must have been a combination of dodgy drains and hot weather. One showed up in the bowl while a female customer was sat on the bog. She nearly screamed the place down and I didn't blame her. It's one of my worst fears is that, which is why I always put some toilet roll down the bowl first so I can hear the little bastards coming. Mrs Hayworth had to bribe the traumatised lady into accepting a year's cinema pass and a large popcorn so that she wouldn't blab to the local papers.

We didn't have enough money to call environmental health out to deal with the rats so Bert, the projectionist, put down some illegal rat poison his brother had brought back from the Falklands. I think Bert was the only partially sighted dwarf projectionist in the country. He used to have a pair of binoculars and a stool so he could see the films through his little porthole at the back. There was almost a riot once when he accidentally played the trailer for *Striptease* before the start of *Pocahontas*. I had to put the cleaning lights on and apologise individually to each and every parent.

I always found Bert to be a tad eccentric. Mind you, I think I'd be eccentric too if I'd been cooped up in a projectionist booth since before we went decimal. He lived in that booth morning, noon and night. He'd had so much time to kill over the years that he'd crafted an exact replica of the Paramount Mountain out of used chewing gum. Now that's a level of dedication that I can't relate to.

I'd often go up and visit him during my tea breaks. It looked more like a flat than a projectionist booth. He had a hammock, a slow cooker and photographs of his family on the walls. Occasionally I'd sit out on his roof terrace sipping tea out of an official *Species II* cup and watching the sun set over Bolton. It was truly beautiful.

He'd tell me incredible stories about all the mishaps he'd had over the years, like celluloid stock igniting and almost burning down the cinema, and how he used to have to cycle across town from one cinema to the other in order to swap reels. Hold on, that's a scene from *Cinema Paradiso*, the lying little swine.

He once took me on a tour of the cinema but it wasn't the cinema I knew. We climbed up through a serving hatch at the back of Screen 3 where the notorious 'adult lounge' used to be. We scrambled onwards into the rafters and over the asbestos. Then he swung his huge rechargeable torch round to reveal something I never expected to see. It was the remains of a cinema screen.

'This is how it used to be before the arseholes destroyed it,' he said angrily.

I could just make out the top half of a cinema screen and it was straddled on either side by two huge gold columns. Over the top of the screen was a perfectly painted mural of a gold-coloured gondola surrounded by leafy green vines. It took my breath away and for a few minutes I felt like Indiana Jones uncovering a piece of hidden treasure.

'What happened to it?' I said.

He told me that the Lido used to be one enormous screen but after video arrived in the late seventies they were bought out by a local property developer, Den Perry. He took a chainsaw to the stunning art deco framework and cut the entire building into two storeys. Then Bert shone his torch lower and revealed where the columns had been mercilessly hacked in half. Fibreglass insulation had been strewn all over the chipboard floor.

'He turned downstairs into a nightclub,' said Bert, 'and Perry did quite well for himself until someone found a dead body in the cellar. Then he turned it into a Laser Quest and buggered off to Marbella.'

Finally Bert took me round to the back of the building and, unlocking a padlocked fire door, he led me up an old staircase into some half-flooded dressing rooms. It was eerie – they still had the costume rails standing in the room and some torn variety bill posters on the wall from years ago. They were left over from the days when the cinema doubled as a theatre.

'They've all played here at one time or other,' he said proudly, with the water almost up to his waist. 'Laurel and Hardy, The Beatles, Depeche Mode.' I was astonished that I'd been working with so much history around me and had never realised.

Funnily enough, the cinema was demolished just a few weeks ago (another bloody building demolished behind me; I must be jinxed). *The Bolton Evening News* did a story about the demolition company uncovering this hidden screen in the back of the building, with a hand-painted mural of a gondola and two gold columns on either side of it. I felt honoured to have seen it years before with Bert by torchlight.

To mark the hundredth anniversary of cinema in Britain, the

powers that be held a National Cinema Day in May 1995, which again basically meant everybody could see any film they desired all day for one English pound. As a result we were packed out.

I remember being stood at the bottom of the stairs watching *Twelve Monkeys* and keeping an eye out for crafty smokers sneaking a fag on the back row. That's when I saw a rat. I wasn't sure what it was at first but then when I focused my eyes during the bright scenes and I could see it really was a rat slowly making its way down the steps of the far aisle.

'Oh my God, if anybody sees it there'll be a stampede,' I thought. 'They'll shut us down and I've got a lot of overtime coming up.'

The rat seemed to be swaying from side to side as if it was drunk. Then I realised that it must have swallowed some of Bert's poison and was about to croak it. I made a split-second decision and, casually walking over to the far aisle, I booted it straight under a radiator. Everybody was too busy watching the film to notice and thank God because it was a big fat frigger. It was also the closest I'd been to a rat since I brushed passed Jeffrey Archer at the Southport Flower Show.

You know, behind the scenes the cinema may have been held together by Sellotape and string, but once you'd swept the last few remaining pieces of popcorn under the seats, turned on the red gel mood lighting at the front of the stage and given Bert the thumbs up to stick on his eight track of the *Hits of Richard Clayderman*, nobody could ever see the join at the Lido.

It must have been hard for Mrs Hayworth though. She was a nice lady who'd been working in cinema most of her life. And we actually used to get on quite well, which was a first for me when it came to a manager. She must have felt as though she was banging her head against a wall sometimes, in fact I actually caught her doing it once in the storeroom but I never let on.

She used to get really upset if she ever overheard any of us talking about visiting the multiplexes.

'They've not got anything we haven't got,' she'd say, but they had and she knew it. They had curtains that closed for a kick off, toilets that didn't leak and they also didn't have drunken rats staggering down the aisles. She was just fooling herself.

I used to go to the multiplexes all the time on my nights off. But it turned into a bit of busman's holiday, especially as I'd already seen most of the films at work, several times. The main draw for me was that they had a decent sound system and the Lido didn't. Instead of having Pro Dolby Logic surround sound Bert just used to turn it up full blast and deafen the punters into thinking it was good.

One thing I did enjoy was building the huge cardboard stands that advertised the new releases just like the ones they used to have in the foyer of the Odeon. We also used to position them in the entrance and at the top of the stairs.

They'd come in very handy, especially in summer when the heat was unbearable. I'd sometimes remove a piece of card from the stand and use it as a makeshift fan. I never once realised how odd it must have looked to the customers, turning the corner to find me stood at the top of the stairs fanning myself with Gene Hackman's head.

That reminds me of the time we had a bloke come into the foyer who suffered from epilepsy. It was a Saturday afternoon, the place was packed out, we had over four hundred kids spread between two screens when this guy came in off the street. He looked pale and emaciated. He also had some spit in the corner of his mouth and was wearing denim. I thought he'd come to give us a quick rendition of 'This Ole House' but instead he just handed me a scrap of paper and said, 'I wonder if you can help me. I suffer from epilepsy and this is the number of my care –' and before he could say 'worker' he fell on top of me like a dead body in a film.

It took me all my strength to prop him up. Struggling, I shouted over to Jackie, 'Go and get Bert,' as he was the only qualified first-aider in the building. The only problem was he was four flights up and was just about to start showing *Jumanji*.

'Hurry up, where's Bert?' I said. The guy was beginning to get heavy and, God forgive me, I dropped him. Well, what did you expect me to do? He was starting to jerk around in my arms. Anyway, the carpet was a thick shag so I don't think he hurt himself.

Bert arrived on the scene mid-fit and put the guy into the recovery position. Jackie called for an ambulance and his care worker. Luckily for us the foyer was empty but then I realised the time.

'Oh no! *Toy Story*'s coming out in a minute. This foyer's going to be full of kids. What are we going to do?'

'Quick, get that thing,' Bert shouted, and before you could say 'Green Door' we were both carrying a ten-foot cardboard cut-out of Flipper across the foyer. We stood it upright in front of the fella and thankfully it almost covered him.

We were just in the nick of time. All the kids started pouring out of *Toy Story* and luckily they never noticed a thing. The paramedics turned up a few minutes later with the bloke's care worker.

'Where is he?' she said.

Guiltily, I just nodded towards the Flipper in the corner. All you could see was the guy's head sticking out at the end, next to 'coming this summer'. She must have thought we were sick.

We used to get some really thick customers at the cinema. They'd lean around the door in the foyer and say, 'Have you any idea what time the films start?' or 'Do you know what films you're showing tonight?' I wanted to drag them outside by their hair and show them the huge twenty-foot canopy displaying the film titles that you could see for miles around.

I remember someone coming up to the kiosk once. He looked at the admission prices, studied them for a second, then turned to me and said, 'Can you tell me if that's any good, that Senior Citizens?'

I said, 'It's like a Mexican version of *Cocoon*, now get out.'

I used to really enjoy telling people the endings of the films as they came in. Like the time when we were showing *Seven*. As I was ripping their tickets I'd turn to Connie and say, 'Hey, I didn't expect Gwyneth Paltrow's head in a box at the end, enjoy the film.' Or, when we were showing *The Sixth Sense*, 'I was surprised when Bruce Willis turned out to be a ghost.' I know it was cruel but it helped pass the time.

I started to bring plays to work with me to read when it was quiet. I had joined the American Literature Section at the Central Library in Manchester so I could borrow plays. I've always loved plays because I find them concise and to the point. They also tell you which characters are in the room. Novels confuse the hell out of me. I always have to go back a few pages just to find out who's where. I also never know who's speaking but with plays it's written there on the page, enter/exit, it's straightforward and you know where you are.

I must have read over twenty plays that summer and they taught me a lot about writing. Especially the plays of Neil Simon. I'd fallen in love with his writing after reading *The Odd Couple*, *Brighton Beach Memoirs* and *Last of the Red Hot Lovers*. I enjoyed the sarcastic humour and the wit. Plus I liked them because they were very thin books and I could easily conceal them from Mrs Hayworth in my trouser pocket.

Not that she ever said anything when she caught me sat at the top of the stairs reading. We'd come to an understanding, you see.

A few weeks earlier I'd been to the Warner multiplex in Bury and who should I see strolling out of *James and the Giant Peach?* Mrs Hayworth. Her face was a picture when she saw me standing outside the Gents mouthing the word 'Judas'. After all she'd said to us, preaching about the evils of multiplexes, making us all feel guilty about going to the cinema and all the while she goes her-bloody-self. So I continued to read my plays that summer and Mrs Hayworth never once said a word.

Chapter Fourteen

The Magic Thumb Trick

How sad was I? Every few weeks I'd visit other jobcentres just to see what work was available. I'd go to Bury, Wigan and Manchester a couple of times a month and I'd always have a quick browse in the jobcentre while I was there. I was quite content working at the cinema but there's never any harm in looking, is there? In fact, if I hadn't bobbed into the jobcentre in Manchester when I did I wouldn't have got my last ever part-time job, working as a steward at the newly constructed Manchester Arena.

Being a steward, now that would be a crackin' job because basically I'd be getting paid to watch concerts. It'd also be good to be indoors. I'd started to hate going to outdoor gigs mainly because I was sick to death of being treated like shit.

The last one I'd gone to was U2 at Roundhay Park in Leeds and it was joke. The tickets cost a fortune and then there was the booking fee. We paid ten pounds to park in a primary school car park four miles from the gig and to make matters worse I'd had all my wisdom teeth taken out three days before and my cheeks were still severely swollen. I looked like Gail Tilsley bouncing about in the crowd. I really shouldn't have gone by rights but I didn't want to miss it.

We brought a load of food and drink with us but then some bollocks at the gate said we couldn't bring any of it in. We tried to argue the toss but it was pointless. They do that so you have no choice but to spend a fortune on their grub once you're inside.

I couldn't believe what I was seeing. People were tipping their untouched food and drink into wheelie bins outside the gig. I thought, sod that, I'm not going to let the system beat me and so stubbornly I stood in front of the security blokes and downed all my food and drink in one. I felt like Paul Newman in *Cool Hand Luke*. And eighteen ham sandwiches and six litres of Tizer later I defiantly handed them my ticket, entered the grounds and threw up behind a tree.

Then once inside you're just herded like cattle. If you want to get close to the stage you've got to turn up to the gig a week before they've built it. You daren't go for a piss because the Portaloos look like something out of *Tenko*. I ended up spending three quid and forty minutes queuing up for a warm can of Panda Cola and then by the time I found the others in the crowd I'd missed the support act. U2 eventually came onstage five hours later. We were so far away that I just ended up watching them on the enormous video screen. I'd have been better off sticking a portable telly at the bottom of the garden and watching a video of them live in concert, while sipping a warm glass of cola.

Toby Foster is a very good friend of mine and fantastic stand-up comedian. I remember him telling the story of how he took his girlfriend to that very same concert.

'I don't even like U2,' he said, 'but the girlfriend did and the whole day cost me a packet – tickets, merchandise, food and drink. The final insult came when Bono sang the only song I like, "Where the Streets Have No Name", and when he got to the chorus the cheeky bastard stuck his microphone in the air and shouted to the crowd, "You sing!" I shouted, "No, No, No, Bono, you've just cost me over a hundred quid . . . you fucking sing." "*

And then when U2 finished we couldn't see anything. It was pitch black and we had to slide about in mud for ten minutes as we tried to find something that resembled an exit. Then to cap it all, as we wearily traipsed the four miles back to the car, I noticed hordes of scally kids sitting in backstreets feasting on confiscated food and drink out of upturned wheelie bins.

It was getting light when I fell into bed feeling as if I had been trampled on by a herd of African elephants. I quickly nodded off to sleep mumbling the words 'never again'.

I filled out my application to be a steward while I was in the jobcentre and within a week I was called to the Free Trade Hall in Manchester for an 'Inaugural Recruitment Campaign'. The place was packed. I'd never seen such a cross-section of people in one room at the same time. Every race, creed and colour that you could imagine was in the Free Trade Hall that day. Black, white, old, young, smackheads, hippies, ginger – it was like the enrolment day from *Police Academy.* And I quickly came to the conclusion that everybody who had completed an application form had been offered a job.

Marshall Entertainment were the Canadian company that had built the arena and their name was emblazoned everywhere.

*Toby, I apologise if I ruined your material but that's just how I remembered it.

Banners, flyers, they even had specially designed lighting gobos projecting the words 'Marshall Entertainment' on to the back of the stage. We took our seats and were each given an itinerary booklet the size of a small Argos catalogue. I thought, 'Jesus how long is this going to take? I was hoping to be home for *Countdown.*' The lights slowly dimmed and dry ice drifted across the stage.

Then I heard the opening bars of 'Ride Like the Wind' by Christopher Cross (for what reason I'm still not sure). And as the music built from behind the curtain I saw the silhouette of a tall stocky man making his way towards a podium in the centre of the stage. The lights came up and the music faded clumsily. The man beamed a confident smile and hesitated as if anticipating applause – none came. Then there were a few embarrassing claps from other Marshall Entertainment employees at the back but they soon ceased when they realised they were on their own.

'Welcome, one and all, to this inaugural recruitment campaign for the new Manchester Arena.' He had a deep Canadian accent – I found it quite attractive, in a Paul Gambaccini meets James Earl Jones kind of way. I glanced down at page 1 of the bulky itinerary. It said, 'Opening Introduction with Marshall Entertainment's Director of Operations, Mike Gunner IV.'

'Manchester,' he continued, 'famous for many things around the globe, like Manchester United.' There was a bit of a mixed reaction to that mainly from the Manchester City supporters.

'Famous for its weather, in particular its rain,' he laughed – alone.

He was starting to struggle a bit with this crowd and from where I was sat I could just make out the beads of perspiration as they began to roll down his forehead.

'And Manchester – famous for Boddington's Bitter'.

There was a huge cheer and you could see the relief in his smile, finally having made a positive connection.

'Yes, that's right Boddington's Bitter and just like Boddington's it's my belief that you too are the cream of Manchester.' Nice pun. 'You have all been individually chosen, hand-picked from thousands of prospective employees.' I could have sworn I heard someone cough out the word 'bollocks' on the row behind me.

We were in there for what seemed like for ever. And they could have condensed all the information contained in their itinerary booklet on to the back of a fag packet for all the good it was. I even nodded off at one point. They ended by subjecting us to an excruciating training video from Canada – 'How to Give Customers a Solid Gold Service'. It was corny and clichéd, with all the 'dos' in colour and all the 'don'ts' in black and white. Every time one of the 'don't' scenarios came up all the wannabe stewards laughed. I could see Mike Gunner IV and his associates looking increasingly worried at our responses. Why were we laughing at all the bad scenarios? The cream of Manchester my arse.

We were told to reconvene a week later for an initial training course at a secondary school in the centre of Manchester. We had the place to ourselves as the kids were off on their big summer holidays. The weather was glorious outside and I found it quite claustrophobic being cooped up inside a classroom for three days listening to a couple of clowns from a specialist security company called Live Sec.

Their names were Sean Bannon and Chris Choi and they'd been brought in to teach us the basic skills required for being a steward. Both in their late thirties, Sean was a completely bald Geordie, with no eyebrows or nasal hair, nothing. Chris, on the other hand, was hair personified. He had it draping down over his muscular shoulders. He spoke in a deep South Yorkshire accent and could have passed for an ageing rocker himself if it hadn't been for a very gay-looking handlebar moustache that sat perched on his top lip.

The way they delivered their spiel I could tell they'd done it a million times before. They had it completely off pat, even the bad jokes. It was slick and polished to perfection and I particularly liked it when they handed back and forth between each other, like so:

'Now, what do you do if a member of the public alerts you to a suspicious package in the arena? Sean?'

'Thanks, Chris. Well, if a member of the public does alert you to a suspicious package the first thing you should do is tell your supervisor straight away because time saves lives, isn't that right, Chris?'

'That's right, Sean. Get your supervisor on the scene and please, whatever you do, don't try and handle the situation on your own. Sean?'

'Chris is right and one thing you must never do is run out on to the concourse shouting, "I think I've found a bomb." It'll cause just one thing: instant panic. Isn't that right, Sean?'

'That's right, Chris.'

Our heads were twisting from left to right and back again. It was like watching the men's semi-finals at Wimbledon listening to them talk.

Sean continued: 'I knew a young lad who tried to be the hero and he's currently now dead. You won't get any medals from the Grim Reaper. So don't be a hero, right, Chris?'

'Correct, Sean. Nobody's holding out for a hero apart from Miss Bonnie Tyler. Do the right thing and tell your supervisor straight away and they'll QQC the situation – Quickly, Calmly, Quietly.'

Quickly, calmly, quietly wasn't QQC but they were in mid-flow and I didn't have the balls to stop them. What they were saying was comedy gold and I couldn't write it down quick enough. My hand was aching. They even commended me at one point for my eagerness at taking notes.

'You've been warned,' Sean continued. 'Don't come running to us when you've had your legs blown off. Chris?'

We covered the lot over those three long days – evacuations, first aid, frisking. We spent a considerable amount of time learning how to conduct a complete and thorough body search.

'When we frisk the public what primarily are we looking for? Any ideas?'

An oldish bloke in front of me stuck his hand up and said, 'Knives? CS gas?'

Sean and Chris exchanged worried looks.

'Er . . . not really, mate, we're going to be hosting a lot of family events at the arena, *Disney on Ice*, *Postman Pat*, that type of affair,' said Sean.

I had to admit that I was still dubious about some of the other potential stewards. There were some right oddballs in the room, including a bloke who was sat by the side of me. He was very sinister-looking with dark straggly hair and a long black overcoat. I mean, what was the crack wearing that? It was over seventy degrees in the shade and here he was looking like a cross between Edward Scissorhands and the Child Catcher from *Chitty Chitty Bang Bang*. I think he was just getting a kick out of being around a school, albeit an empty one.

We broke for an hour and then continued with frisking the public after lunch.

'There's one thing you've got to be vigilant for when frisking the public. One thing that has become the arch-enemy of every steward and performer in the world. Tell them what it is, Chris.'

And before Sean had finished his sentence Chris had already written two words on a blackboard behind him: 'Flash Fotography' (and yes, he did spell it like that).

'People might think we are being over the top when we talk about the dangers of flash photography but we've seen the dangers first-hand, haven't we, Sean?'

'We have indeed, Chris, many times. I'll give you a scenario. Somebody tries to take a photograph at a live event, a husband, a lover, whatever, and "bang", one flash, in all innocence. But what they fail to understand are the repercussions that single flash can cause. Because now the floodgates have been opened. Isn't that right, Chris?'

'All hell has broken loose, because once one does it, they all do it. We did a concert in Stockholm recently with one major artist, I'll not give his name away but let's just say, "Wake up, Maggie". He was onstage parading an assortment of his classic hits when a member of the public who'd smuggled a camera into the arena let rip with a flash, and before you could say "Hot Legs" all hell had broken loose. It went flash, flash, flash, flash, flash, flash, flash, flash . . .'

He carried on chanting the words aggressively as if reliving the whole experience, with his eyes glazed over. Like veterans do in those films when they get flashbacks to Vietnam. Then just as things were becoming uncomfortable, Sean continued in an effort to snap Chris out of his trance.

'The whole concert hung by a thread and all for what? A selfish snapshot, Chris.'

'Luckily the band carried on and saved the day by playing a medley of his greatest hits. So please do be vigilant for photographic equipment at all times, it's your biggest enemy,' Chris said as Sean chalked the letters 'NME' on the blackboard behind him.

God only knows how they must be coping with all these camera phones today. Perhaps the inevitable tsunami of camera phones has caused Sean and Chris to leave the business altogether. Who knows?

'Now, when the public are entering the arena, men search the men and the women search the women. I know there's probably a few of you who'd like it the other way round, but hey, hands off.' Then they both laughed. It was a bit of humour that they'd obviously banked on in the past but it fell on deaf ears that day and the tumbleweed that blew through the room was excruciating.

Sean quickly tried to pick things up. 'But seriously . . . when the public enters the arena always ask them politely to open their handbags and for God's sake never, I repeat never, put your own hands inside. Isn't that right, Chris?'

'That's correct, Sean. Always get the public to search their own bags because for all you know there could be a hypodermic needle or anything in there.'

I thought, Jesus, that's cheery. All I wanted to do was watch some free concerts and now there's a risk of HIV.

'What we're asking for is 110 per cent, eight days a week, twenty-four/seven. It's not an easy job by any stretch of the imagination but it'll probably be the most rewarding job you'll ever have. Isn't that right, Chris?'

'Sean's right and I know if we work together we can build a great future. Now, has anybody got any questions?' said Chris.

At that point the child catcher by the side of me stuck his hand up in the air.

'Yes, my friend,' said Chris.

'Can we frisk children?'

My darkest fears were confirmed.

The next stage of the training saw us being taken into the actual arena itself for the first time. I'm sure I would have been impressed had it not been seven o'clock on a Sunday morning and my birthday to boot. Nevertheless, it was a colossal structure and I'd never seen anything like it in my life.

'This place is gonna rock,' I said to the steward next to me.

'Do you reckon? We open next Saturday with Torvill and Dean.'

'Maybe not straight away then,' I said.

We'd been called so early because we were about to take part in a huge evacuation drill with the emergency services . . . oh, and several hundred construction workers who were desperately trying to complete the building around us.

Each steward was placed at the bottom of a stairwell or fire exit, then we had to usher a pretend crowd out to safety through the fire exits. For added authenticity the management played a CD of *Dire Straits Live* over the PA system, while Sean and Chris shouted encouragement to us through megaphones.

'Quickly, Kay, help that woman, she's got a baby, help the baby.'

'Where? What baby?' I shouted, looking round.

'Row H, seat 12 . . . and don't climb over the seats,' shouted Sean.

They were taking it all a bit too seriously for my liking.

'Hurry up,' he shouted. 'Those people are burning to death'.

Five hours it took. My arms were knackered from gesturing to a pretend public. We had to do it over and over again. I was sick to death of hearing 'Money for Nothing'.

Halfway through the evacuation drill Mike Gunner IV walked down my stairwell with some other execs in suits. He stopped for a breather at the bottom and said to me, 'So, son, is everything A-OK?'

'No,' I said, 'not really, it's Sunday morning, it's my birthday and I've just let a coach full of pensioners burn to death in Row Q.'

Mike Gunner IV just grinned at me with his gold teeth, said, 'That's swell, kid,' and walked off.

I was missing *Little House on the Prairie* and wanted to go home.

A week later it was the official opening night with Torvill and Dean. Suited and booted, all the stewards arrived early to pick up their name badges. I was gutted because for some reason they didn't have one for me. I had to take the last badge left in the box, which was 'Mohammed'. So for the first night and from then on I was known as Mohammed Kay.

All three hundred of us made our way up to the concourse for a final debriefing with Sean and Chris.

'OK. Tonight's the night, people. You should all know what to do. Those stewards on the doors, don't forget to ask the public to open their own handbags and show you what's inside. Sean?'

'Thanks, Chris, and don't forget to keep an eye out for the sworn enemy of every steward, which is . . . Mohammed?'

Why did he have to pick on me? Unenthusiastically I mumbled, 'Flash Photography.'

'That's correct. And last but not least, don't forget to have fun tonight. Isn't that right, Sean?'

'Affirmative, Chris. Enjoy yourself and remember: you're never fully dressed without a smile.'

I couldn't believe he just quoted a song from *Annie*.

'You've hit the nail on the head, Sean, and whatever you do, don't be frightened of building up a relationship with Joe Public. We're not the bad guys . . . or gals.' They both laughed but it quickly tailed off into silence again.

'Here's a tip for you. If you see any little children coming into the arena tonight, why not show them the magic thumb trick?' said Chris, and then simultaneously they both demonstrated the trick. You must have seen it. You tuck your thumb under your finger, then you lean it up against the thumb on your opposite hand and by manoeuvring it back and forth it appears as if you're pulling your thumb on and off.

'I guarantee you, the kids might not remember who they came to see tonight,' said Sean, 'but they'll remember that thumb trick for the rest of their lives.'

And so shall I, dear reader.

Over the next few months I learned how to buck the system. It was relatively easy because the arena was so big and there were so many members of staff you practically went unnoticed – well, as much as a white steward called Mohammed could possibly go unnoticed. One trick was to walk around the arena looking serious as if you were on some life-or-death mission. If you walked quickly enough the other supervisors and management would leave you alone to roam anywhere you liked. In my case it was always near to the stage so I could watch the show. After all, that was the reason I became a steward.

Another tactic I devised was relieving stewards (and I obviously don't mean that in the biblical sense). I'd find them in a prime position overlooking the stage, at the bottom of a stairwell or a fire exit, and walking over to them, I'd say, 'I've been told to relieve you, you can go on your break.' They'd gladly bugger off for ten minutes leaving me to enjoy the show.

And I managed to watch some absolute corkers during my time at the arena: Pulp, the Eagles, Eric Clapton, Wet Wet Wet, Simply Red (well, they couldn't all be winners). I remember enjoying Simply Red that much at the time that I failed to notice St John's Ambulance rushing past me with a lady on a stretcher who'd collapsed. I got a bollocking for that off Sean and Chris because I don't know if you are aware of this but one of the golden rules of being a steward is that when you're working in the auditorium you're not supposed to enjoy yourself.

'That's the audience's job,' said Sean. 'Your job is to keep them safe while they're doing it. Chris?' (Sorry, force of habit.) When you're a steward you're just supposed to watch the audience. You're not supposed to clap your hands, you're not supposed to tap your feet and you're certainly not supposed to dance. But all that was about to change when Take That came to town.

Their live show in 1995 was without a doubt the best show I ever worked on. They did ten nights in total at the arena and I worked nine of them (I would have done the tenth but I was best man at a wedding). Now I'd never really liked Take That before I saw them live. To me they were just one of many teenage boy bands that had totally passed me by. But after working on nine nights of that tour I was completely hooked.

They blew me away when they opened (every night) with 'Relight My Fire'. The lights went down, the lads came on and the audience went berserk. The hairs would go up on the back of my neck the screams were that loud. They were that deafening Sean and Chris issued all the stewards with earplugs. I fell in love with the show, I got to know it inside out and I absolutely adored it. So much so that when the shows were over I found I had withdrawal symptoms and had to buy two of their live videos just to get my fix.

Without a doubt the best part of the show was when they ended the night with their last song, 'Never Forget'. The whole audience used to raise their hands up in the air and do a slow overarm clap when they got to the chorus. A bit similar to Queen in the video to 'Radio Ga-Ga'. It was quite emotional. I was determined to get to the front of the stage on the last night just to see the audience in all their glory.

That last night I went on a mission to relieve every steward on the aisle leading directly to the front of the stage. And I managed to get to the front just in time for 'Never Forget'. The view was truly breathtaking as I stood with my back to the stage watching thousands of people waving their hands in the air. I'm getting tingles just remembering the moment. I also got a verbal warning for joining in. But I couldn't help it, it would have been a sin not to.

I still find it incredible to think that ten years later I was stood on a stage in the same arena watching crowds waving their hands at the end of my show. That's got to be the biggest 'unbelievable' of them all.

The funny thing, is I never officially left my job at the arena and have since been told by the management that I'm still on the books. So you never know, if things go tits up you may find yourself being escorted to your seat one day by a steward called Mohammed who looks remarkably like me.

Chapter Fifteen

Nobody Puts Peter in a Corner

Things weren't really working out for me over in Liverpool on the combined honours degree. To say I'd bitten off more than I could chew would be an understatement. I was struggling, desperately so, and considered it divine retribution for lying about my qualifications in the first place.

What was it? Why couldn't I settle? I think part of it was all the written work that was required of me. All those essays and dissertations, they really did my head in. I couldn't see the point in reading something and regurgitating it back onto paper in five thousand words. I've always loathed written work. In fact this book is probably the most writing I've ever done in my entire life.

In my Information Technology lectures I pushed my lecturer, Mr Tibbs, to the verge of a nervous breakdown, due to the fact that I was computer illiterate and kept flicking mine off at the wall every time I spelt a word wrong. Well, it's what my parents did every time something electrical went on the blink at home. 'Flick it off and count to ten' seemed to be the golden rule in our house. As a result I spent most of my IT time re-booting my computer, whilst counting aloud with my fingers crossed.

American Studies turned out to be a complete waste of time altogether. I'd only picked it because the prospectus stated, and I quote, 'you will be covering all aspects of modern American media'. I thought that sounded right up my street and quite fancied a few weighty discussions about JFK's assassination and *The Godfather* trilogy. But in the six months since I'd been attending the lectures all we'd ever talked about was O J Simpson's film career and two of the Latino actors out of *Sesame Street*.

On Thursdays we did the only part of the degree I enjoyed – practical workshops in drama and theatre studies. That was more my cup of tea and I quickly came to the conclusion that I needed to be doing a more practically-based course, and so in my spare time I started to look at other universities. Bit cheeky when you think that I shouldn't even have been doing the degree in the first place. Ah well, God loves a trier.

After lengthy research I came across an HND in Media Performance at Salford University. It was a two-year course that seemed to cover all the areas I was interested in – drama, singing, script writing. But the one subject that attracted me most was stand-up comedy. I couldn't believe they actually did a course in stand-up comedy. I was hooked and decided to call them.

After chatting to a very high-pitched admissions tutor (he sounded like Joe Pasquale on helium) I was pleased to discover that the course was mostly practical. The students were assessed and graded on performance skills rather than dissertations and course-work and there were no exams. It sounded perfect for me, a kind of showbiz Mode II with jazz tap instead of car maintenance.

Another bit of good news was that, because I would be transferring from a combined honours degree onto an HND, and would therefore seem to be academically taking a step backwards, the high-pitched admissions tutor said they'd 'welcome a higher-level student like me, with open arms'. (His voice actually went a little bit higher when he said that – in fact there was only me and a few dogs that heard him.) I was thrilled and delighted, so much so that I failed to mention that I only actually had one legitimate qualification and that was in art.

They wrote to me with an unconditional offer that I, of course, immediately accepted. So in September 1994 I started my new course at Salford University. The next two years were a complete blast for me. I acted in plays, wrote scripts, recorded radio dramas. For the first time in a long time I was completely in my element.

I no longer felt thick, I no longer felt academically inferior. I started to excel like I never had before. I was enjoying what I was doing and rose to every challenge they put before me. Even my dance lessons every Tuesday afternoon. They were actually more hi–energy aerobics than Royal Ballet, but I gave it my best shot, regardless of the fact that I was no Patrick Swayze. Nobody puts Peter in a corner.

The other thing I loved about the course was that I was able to go home every night. I could separate myself from the course and switch off at the weekends. It also meant I could go back to my part time jobs at the cinema and the arena. Even though it was work, it gave me peace.

Don't get me wrong, I genuinely loved the course, but I just didn't subscribe to student life. I was three years older than most of the other students and when you're twenty one, three years feels like a lifetime.

Thankfully most of the students on my course were normal (well as normal as you can get for a bunch of 'showbiz wannabes'). They came from industrial towns throughout the north of England – Sheffield, Leeds, Liverpool – and the Midlands (we even had one from Wales).

I also liked the fact that they didn't fall into the archetypal student bracket. You know the ones I mean. They turn up on Freshers' Week searching for a new identity, dye their hair purple and pierce themselves in an assortment of places because it's their first time away from home and they want to rebel against their parents. They blow their grant money on a pair of thigh-length leather boots and a donkey jacket from a local charity shop. Then, completely broke, they refuse to get any kind of part time job to support themselves and choose instead to spend the rest of the term living off handouts from Mummy and Daddy, whilst sending their dirty washing home once a fortnight. Not that I'm generalizing or anything.

One of the subjects I enjoyed the most was my characterization classes, which we had on Friday mornings with our lecturer Bob Steen. He was quite a character. Tall and permanently tanned, he paraded himself around campus in a denim shirt unbuttoned to his navel, like Barry Gibb on stilts. As the dark nights drew in Bob chose to wear a cloak and now resembled something out of a Seventies prog rock band like Yes or Emerson, Lake and Palmer (the latter has always sounded like a firm of solicitors to me). Bob wouldn't have looked out of place playing synthesizer in the middle of the desert, silhouetted against a setting sun. He loved himself and, bizarrely, so did most of the female students. They hung on his every word, buzzing round him like flies round shit.

We did a few productions over the two years, the first of which was a Greek tragedy, *Electra* by Sophocles and it was directed by Bob Steen. He came up with the idea of setting our production against a backdrop of Sixties gangland London after watching *The Krays* on ITV one Saturday night. The lads wore long black cashmere coats and the girls had to wear mini skirts (which he loved) and we all talked in bad cockney accents – like Sophocles had written an episode of *Eldorado*.

Bob could be a moody swine sometimes, especially if he hadn't had his daily fix of six black coffees and some marijuana. I remember one weekend myself and the rest of the cast had come in to help paint the set for *Electra*. It was November and some of us had walked leaves into the theatre on the bottom of our shoes. Hardly a hanging offence, but when Bob saw them on the stage, he stopped dead in his tracks and bellowed 'Who has walked leaves onto my set?'

We all just looked at each other and shrugged. We all had. It was autumn outside – what did he expect us to do, levitate into the building? I shut my eyes, expecting him to explode with rage, but instead he just pulled a joint out of his back pocket the size of a roll of wallpaper and, lighting it, said 'I like it, I like it. Let's bring the outside inside. Let's bring the outside inside!' The next thing I knew, he had us all outside in the car park filling up carrier bags with leaves and then he made us throw them all over the set.

Electra was very intense and bleak (well, it is a Greek tragedy) but our next production was even bleaker. It was *The Crucible* by Arthur Miller. In case you're not familiar with *The Crucible*, it's basically the story of the witch-hunt trials that took place in Salem, Massachusetts in 1692, when local villagers burnt each other at the stake after accusations of heresy. It wasn't *Grease*, let's put it that way.

I found it slightly frustrating, as it was the second serious production that we'd done since I'd arrived and I really wanted to have a stab at doing something comical. Bob Steen gave me the lead, John Proctor, because he reckoned it would be a good discipline for me. I strongly disagreed and so, on the last night, I thought I'd inject a little bit of humour into the production. Unbeknownst to Bob, I decided to end the show with a big band number and with a karaoke backing tape behind me, I belted out Frank Sinatra's 'Witchcraft' as I burned at the stake. Even Bob managed to see the funny side and it went down a treat with the audience. A few of them even woke up and sang along during the chorus. It reminded me of *The Wizard of Oz* all over again, but without the lion costume obviously.

After that the staff looked favourably on my pleas for comedy and chose an ageless Russian farce called *The Government Inspector* as out next production. I've mentioned to you before that I'm not very keen on farces, but it was the closest we'd come to doing a comedy so far and beggars can't be choosers etc, etc, etc.

The story is based on a classic case of mistaken identity. In fact John Cleese and Connie Booth paid homage to the play and adapted the same storyline for an episode of *Fawlty Towers* that they entitled 'The Hotel Inspector'.

I was given the role of Mayor. It was a comic tour de force and I relished the opportunity. Bob Steen even allowed me to improvise my lines, a process I found truly liberating.

The University of Salford had many patrons, Robert Powell, Ben Kingsley, Ice T (I'm joking) and the wonderful writer Jack Rosenthal, who sadly passed away a few years ago. He was married to the actress Maureen Lipman and one day, totally unannounced, she popped into the theatre to watch us rehearse *The Government*

Inspector and then gave us a fascinating talk on theatre and comedy. She even singled me out as being a naturally gifted comedian at one point. I was genuinely thrilled to receive such an accolade from someone I admired so much. But I wasn't half as thrilled as I was three months later when Maureen Lipman phoned our house and invited me to audition for a part in a West End show.

My mum was speechless and dropped the phone in shock. It turned out that Maureen (I think I can safely use her first name), had gotten my number off Bob Steen, after contacting him at the university. Apparently a director friend of hers was casting a farce in the West End and for some reason she had mentioned me to him.

My stomach churned at the enormity of the proposition that lay before me. It was a huge opportunity, to be plucked from obscurity and offered a chance to appear in a West End comedy. Okay another farce, I grant you, but hey beggars can't . . . Oh, I've just said all that, well you know what I mean.

A week later I was travelling down to London town on the train with my dad sat beside me. He insisted on coming with me. In fact his exact words were 'it'll be a nice ride out'. It was a difficult time for him, as he'd been made redundant from his engineering job a few weeks before. But I had no idea how bad things had got until he pulled out a notepad on the platform in Bolton and proceeded to write down the numbers of the passing trains.

'Oh my God, what are you doing?' I said, mortified.

'I've decided to do a bit of trainspotting' he said, as he flicked through his notepad, revealing page upon page of names and numbers. The Conservative government had a lot to answer for.

'A bit?' I said, 'it looks like you've seen half the trains in Britain already'. No wonder he was so keen to come with me. This journey to London clearly ticked a lot of boxes for him.

'Put it away' I said 'Christ, we're in the middle of the rush hour man'. The platform was choc-a-bloc with morning commuters and I hardly had any credibility left in Bolton as it was.

Personally, I could never see the point of trainspotting. You write down the name and number of a train in the hope that one day you'll see it again and then, when you do, you write it down again. When does the fun ever end?

I arrived at the Criterion Theatre in Piccadilly Circus two hours too early – just to be on the safe side. It was the first time I'd been to London since a school trip in 1984 and that turned out to be a complete waste of time. After a four-hour train ride we got put into groups and assigned a group leader. Sadly I got saddled with a Polish nun who was terrified of traffic. So while the other kids went to Buckingham Palace and Big Ben, we sat on Euston station waiting for our train home. The most I saw of London was a map of the underground fastened to the wall outside WH Smith's.

Nervously I sat backstage at the Criterion Theatre, waiting to be called through. There was nobody else there, except for an elderly man who was working the stage door. He sat in his booth reading the *Daily Star* and dipping his Kit Kat. I don't think he was up for an audition.

I was terrified. It was like the whole Granada interview thing all over again. The next thing I knew my bowels kicked in and I must have pumped about forty times in a row before a pretty girl leaned round the door and called my name. I could tell by the look on her face that the smell that greeted her wasn't very friendly. I naughtily gestured over my shoulder to the old bloke working the stage door as I followed her into the theatre, shaking my head.

She handed me some photocopied lines as I walked towards the stage. 'Here's your script' she said. 'Sorry, I didn't get it to you earlier, the copier was out of ink'. Jesus, I'd been here almost two hours. I would have been word perfect by now. I'd always been crap at sight reading, especially at school. I hated it when the nuns made us read out loud from a book in class. We had to read a paragraph each, and so I used to have to count how many people there would be before it was my turn, and then count the same number of paragraphs down the page. It gave me a little time to scan the text for any big words. But sometimes the nun would say 'Continue' after I'd confidently read my paragraph. 'Eh? What does she mean continue? That was a paragraph, she said a paragraph'. I'd turn to the others around me, but it was useless. I had no choice and in a blind panic I went from Laurence Olivier to Joey Deacon in two lines. So I don't know what this girl was expecting me to do with the script that she'd handed me at the eleventh hour. Out of ink indeed. It was the West End not a public library.

Desperately trying to read the script in the darkness, I followed her to the stage and casually glanced up. Oh my God! The place was huge. Mesmerized, I stumbled towards the spotlight in the centre of the stage like a big fat moth. The light was blinding and I couldn't see anything except the enormous black void of the auditorium and a couple of green exit signs.

'It's Peter, am I right?' said a voice in the darkness.

'Yes, I think so, unless my parents are playing a big elaborate joke.'

There was a laugh. Southerners, they find anything funny. Mind you, so would I after twenty five years of Jim Davidson and Jethro. (Now come on southerners, that was just a bleedin' joke, me old cock sparras.)

'Maureen speaks very highly of you' said the voice in the darkness.

Good old Maureen, I thought to myself. I must write a part for her one day and return the favour.

'You're reading the part of Derek,' said the voice 'he's a bit of a cockney wide boy.'

'Right' I said, clearing my throat several times in a desperate attempt to stall for more time. I then proceeded to read the lines badly and quickly. I sounded like Dick Van Dyke on speed.

There was a pause. A very long pause. So long I could have bobbed out to Greggs and bought myself a meal deal in the time it took them. I had paranoid visions of the director turning to the producer and saying 'Maureen raved on about this?'

Eventually the voice spoke and asked me to read out the lines again, only this time much slower and in my own accent. I obliged and actually managed to get quite a few laughs. More silence followed and then the voice said the inevitable. I was told that I wasn't really what they were looking for and they thanked me for travelling so far to the audition.

I should have been crushed by the rejection, but I wasn't. Well I was a little but not that much. It was a beautiful day and I was still made up about being singled out by Maureen and invited to the audition in the first place. I don't want to sound sickeningly humble, but that really was good enough for me. And besides, I'd never be able to stomach being away from home doing a play for six months. I'd slit my wrists with depression.

I met back up with my dad at Euston station. He was on platform fourteen, scribbling into his notebook like a madman. 'Look' he said ecstatically 'I've had to buy another pad. I filled the other one up, there've been that many trains.' It was a shame to disturb him as he was as happy as a sand boy, but we had to go home.

'Here, grab this' he said, passing me a half-drunk bottle of Schweppes Lemonade. I had to laugh because, even though the pop was flat and warm, he made me carry it all the way back home.

'Why don't you just throw it away?' I said as we chugged through Rugby.

'Not a chance, it cost me £1.80,' he said, taking the bottle from me. 'I'm gonna enjoy every mouthful if it kills me.'

Every year Granada Television held a directors' training course in an effort to give up-and-coming directors a chance to break into the business. Part of the course was to direct and film short pieces of drama in the studio. Luckily for me, the actors that year came courtesy of Salford University, ten minutes down the road.

Even though the students didn't get paid, it was a great opportunity for the fortunate ones who got chosen. We all got a chance to audition for the trainee directors and Granada executives. Most of the students performed extracts from pieces that already existed, but I decided to write something of my own. That's when I first came up with Leonard.

It was a short monologue loosely based on my old friend Leonard, you know, the bloke from Chapter Eight who used to call into the garage when I worked there and chat to me for hours. I'd occasionally recorded our conversations and it was those tapes I returned to as the source of most of the monologue.

Leonard

(A lady is sat in a bus shelter by the side of a main road, waiting patiently for her bus to arrive. Leonard approaches her whistling 'Young at Heart'. Startled, the lady smiles politely as Leonard attempts to make conversation with her.)

Hyer flower, been waiting long? Hey, you'll stand here for ages and then three'll come all at once. It makes you laugh, doesn't it? I tell you what else makes me laugh, this weather, it can't make its mind up can it? I didn't know what coat to put on. *(Embarrassing silence.)* I don't usually get the bus, I've got a car, a Reliant Robin, hey and they are you know. It's a super little runner, it gets me from A to B. Hey, it blew up last Tuesday, it's in the garage. I've just bought a sticker for it, it says Don't Follow Me, Follow Jesus. *(Leonard chuckles. The lady just smiles politely.)*

Do you believe? I do. I always have. I found God in Fleetwood in 1980 and I became a Christian. Oh I go to The Church of the Nazarene behind Rick Johnson's Swim School *(pointing)*. When I'm not at church I go to work, well I say work, I can't work really because I'm registered disabled. I work with the elderly pensioners at the ol' people's home on Lever Edge Lane. They pay with a meal or a packet of fags. I shouldn't smoke really because I suffer from angina. I've narrow veins like Jack Duckworth. But I haven't let it stop me. A good friend of mine, Jimmy Boydell, he works at Kwik Save collecting the trolleys, do yer know him?

(The lady shakes her head. Leonard misreads her acknowledgement as an invititation and innocently takes a seat next to her on the bench in the bus stop. She immediately stands and begins to nervously move forward towards the kerb.)

Anyway well Jimmy's registered disabled just like me, he got a pacemaker fitted for Christmas but he's always listening for the bleep, you can't live your life like that can you? In fear, it's wrong innit? You've got to get on with things, after all we've only got one crack at the whip. Everyday's a blessing, everyday's a gift. Life's an adventure! Someone once said to me, how can you be bored when you don't know what's comin' next? Isn't that true flower? Live your life. I'm fifty eight flower and I've plenty of life left in me yet. I'm never lonely, I've got plenty of friends and . . . oh, is this one yours love? *(The lady inches herself forward to the edge of the kerb as her bus approaches)* Okay right . . . mine's the next one . . . well take care flower, nice meetin' yer and God Bless.

(The lady boards the bus and it departs. Leonard walks off behind the bus shelter. Another person approaches, stops and waits for a bus. Leonard approaches them from behind)

Hyer cockers, been waitin' long? Hey, you'll stand here for ages and then three'll come all at once.

It was quite a funny piece, but I wanted to give it some underlining pathos. I also wanted the lady's reaction to reflect what I believed most people's initial impressions of Leonard used to be. At first glance, they always mistook his unusual attire and happy demeanour as a threat and, as a result, they never hung around long enough to really get to know the man.

I performed the piece with a friend off the HND called Sian. When we'd finished, the directors, lecturers and Granada executives gave us a spontaneous round of applause. We were delighted. Then they asked if we'd like to perform the piece in front of the cameras over at Granada TV? Of course, we said yes.

So, I found myself back at Granada Television once again. Only this time I wasn't being offered the job of making tea. I was now on the other side of the camera. It's funny how life turns out. I know it wasn't in the same league as *Cracker*, but everybody's got to start somewhere.

I was assigned to an Irish director, called Brendan. He was pleasant enough and seemed quite skilled at his job, which is why I was shocked to see his name on the end of *DIY SOS* the other week. We spent the morning rehearsing in a small studio at Granada and then we went over to the main studios in the afternoon to record the piece to camera.

I really didn't know what to expect, but I was completely gob-smacked when I walked into the studio. The production team had constructed a whole set just for the purpose of my script. Everything was there in amazing detail from the bus shelter scrawled in coloured graffiti to the real life foliage that sat behind some cast iron park railings behind the bus stop. They even had a pavement complete with double yellow lines. It looked incredible.

Both in costume, Sian and I took our places on the set. It was a very strange feeling, but I have to be honest, I wasn't nervous in the slightest. That was mainly because I knew the piece so well and also because there was hardly anybody there, just a couple of lighting blokes occasionally shining lights to signify passing traffic. Brendan, the director, was up in the gallery (TV talk) calling all the technical shots from there.

The whole thing went smoothly and we recorded the scene in just two takes. The first take had to be abandoned due to some sort of technical hiccup (they'd forgotten to press record). I was extremely proud, especially when they gave me a finished VHS copy of my performance to keep forever (well until my mum accidentally taped over it with an episode of *Hornblower*).

Meanwhile back on the HND my first year was coming to an end. I'd thoroughly enjoyed it and couldn't wait to get stuck into my second year options, including my weekly lecture in stand-up comedy.

But as fate would have it, I got a chance at stand-up even earlier than I'd imagined. Returning to the course in September, I decided to assert myself straight away by putting my name forward as compere of a cabaret night the students were holding upstairs in a local pub in Salford.

It was the first time I had ever really stood up in public and performed any of my own material, so you can imagine how nervous I was. I had some rough ideas – observations about Salford, the weather we'd had over the summer, Michael Barrymore coming out of the closet, nothing too ground breaking.

Because I was compere on the night, I decided to take the liberty of using cards as visual aids. Not only was I able to have the name of the next act written on the cards, but I could also write one or two key words referencing my own material.

It should have worked like a charm, but I was so nervous that every time I casually glanced down at the cards, the words made no sense at all. Staring at them, I became completely paralysed with fear. What did they mean? And so the first couple of times I just resorted to gabbling the name of the next act as I fled the stage in terror.

But as the night went on, my nerves began to subside slightly. I started to feel more confident and at ease with the audience. One of the good things about being a compere is that you don't have to be the centre of attention. A lot of the pressure is lifted. And by the end of the night I was flying. It felt so comfortable being up on stage and it also felt different, because for the first time ever I was relying on my own wits and material.

It completely opened my eyes. If I could do that and feel comfortable, who knows what would happen if I went on stage in a real club?

After the show I was approached by a degree student. She was doing a BA in media production and had to make a documentary in her final year and she wondered if I'd be interested in taking part.

'Me? Doing what?' I said.

'Stand-up comedy.'

Her proposition was to film me performing stand-up for the first time at an open mic night in Manchester. At first I said 'no' and nervously laughed off the idea. But I thought about what she'd said as I travelled home on the bus that night, and I discovered that, secretly, I liked the idea. This documentary could be the chance I had been waiting for my whole life.

Chapter Sixteen

A Happy Accident

It's been eleven years since I first performed stand-up at the open mic night in Manchester. I've just watched it back on video and it was odd because, as soon as I saw myself walking towards the club and heard the narration on the documentary, my nerves came flooding back. It seems like only yesterday, and not only am I amazed at how confident I appear to be, but also at how thin I once was.

I had spent a lot of time preparing my material for that night, rehearsing it in front of the full-length mirror on the landing at home and recording the whole of my act into a Dictaphone, so I could listen to it every morning as I travelled into Salford on the bus. But at the last minute I decided to completely change my act. I mean literally as I was walking towards the stage. Perhaps it was a combination of nerves and adrenalin, but suddenly I didn't have confidence in my material anymore. I think I'd rehearsed it to death and sucked all the fun out of it as a result.

I've still no idea where most of my material came from that

night. In fact at one point I even shout to my mate Michael sat in the audience: 'I didn't plan on doing any of this'.

I do some material about a TV programme that had been on the night before. It was all about the convicted mass murderer Fred West. I say 'no matter what people say about him there's no denying he's a grafter' and then I tell the audience that apparently 'he's selling his house on Cromwell Street and it's advertised in the local property guide as a two up, nine down'. I get laughs, but I haven't got a clue what I'm doing.

I then go into a completely bizarre routine about the Yorkshire Ripper being a guest on *This Is Your Life*. I describe Michael Aspel having to wheel Peter Sutcliffe on set in a cage and how later Dave Lee Travis appears as a guest, simply because they resemble each other physically. Again I get laughs, but on the whole I find the material unrefined and tasteless in a few places, which I think is quite out of character for me. One thing that is clear is that my delivery is much stronger than my material.

I leave the stage after about ten minutes to generous applause and, even though I considered my first open mic spot to be a success, I didn't return to stand-up again until the following spring, when it would become part of the HND timetable.

There weren't a lot of universities that could boast having stand-up comedy as part of their curriculum in 1996. In fact, saying that, I don't think there's that many today. Every Tuesday afternoon eight students, including myself, would do our very best to 'stand-up' to our tutor, the uncompromisingly bitter Paul J Russell.

I don't know what experience you need to teach stand-up comedy, but Paul J Russell reckoned he was an expert, after having been a regular performer at the world famous Comedy Store in

London*. With the bright lights of London now faded, Paul had chosen to pass his distorted wisdom on to us – whether we wanted to hear it or not.

We spent the majority of each lecture deconstructing stand-up videos. We'd analyse the different styles of comedians, look at the way they linked their material and study their stage presence. And then, at the end of each lesson, it would be our turn to step up to the mic. Every week we'd have to perform three minutes of our own material, derived from a variety of topics that Paul had set us the previous week. These ranged from holidays to DIY, space travel to the priesthood, golf to anal sex. I think you get the picture.

The idea was to gradually build up a comic portfolio over the duration of the ten-week course and then perform our material live on stage in a packed pub on Salford Crescent. Not only would our fellow students be in the audience, but there'd also be a panel of moderators lurking in the darkness, grading our performances on the night.

I'll not bore you with the material I did on that night because, suffice to say, I'll probably still be trotting it out on my 'If It Ain't Broke, Don't Fix It' tour in a few years time. I didn't do too badly considering it was only my second performance. Saying that, I would have been gutted if I hadn't done well, considering I'd only enrolled on the HND to do stand-up comedy in the first place. With my two-year course drawing to a close, I could feel the cold chill of the real world whistling under my door. I knew that I

*Years later I was lucky enough to discuss Paul J Russell's stand-up career with the comics he used to boast about: Ben Elton and Alexie Sayle. They both separately confirmed my suspicions, that Paul J Russell died on his arse many a night.

couldn't hide in further education any longer – it was time to face reality once again.

I graduated on 14th June 1996 with my mum, my dad, R Julie, my nana and Uncle Tony (he gave them a lift in his Sierra) proudly sat in the audience at Salford University. They were all smiles when my name was announced and I climbed the steps to the stage in my mortarboard hat and graduation gown. I was chuffed to bits. It was a hell of an achievement receiving an HND diploma for a boy with no former qualifications and I'm sure if the nuns from school could have been there they would have been proud too.

After shaking hands with some dignitaries, I exited the stage and immediately handed my diploma back to a woman with a facial hair problem behind the curtain. Apparently they only had six diplomas to go round as there was a 'balls-up at the printers' as she so delicately put it. 'You'll get your real one in the post in a few weeks' time'. Ten years have passed by and I've still not received it.

My mum has a framed picture of my graduation hanging proudly in her bungalow to this day. Can you believe she paid fifteen pounds for a copy of that photo and I'm holding a forged diploma? The photo didn't even come with a frame.

That night my fellow students and I went out into Manchester to celebrate. We had a great time and ended up staying over in a Travel Lodge. The following morning we said our goodbyes and went our separate ways. I boarded the bus outside Marks & Spencer and with a heavy heart headed back to Bolton. I arrived home thirty minutes later to discover that the IRA had detonated a bomb in the centre of Manchester, and a whole area of shops, including almost all of Marks & Spencer, had been demolished after I'd left. Some things never change.

*

The biggest ambition of most of the students on the HND, once they'd left the course, seemed to be the acquisition of an acting agent. I was lucky, as after performing Leonard for the directors' training course at Granada and my West End audition for Maureen Lipman, I was snapped up by a local acting agency in Manchester called Victoria Management. It was a workers co-operative, which basically meant that we all had to chip in for tea and coffee out of our commission*.

I know I should have been happy about getting an agent but I wasn't. With my undying scepticism I just saw them as a bunch of vultures preying on new talent in order to line their own pockets. I wasn't too keen on the other 'actors' in the agency either. They were all a bit stuck-up and they never made me feel very welcome. They were too busy bragging about being a burns victim in *Casualty* or having two lines playing a prostitute in *Band Of Gold*. I had much higher aspirations than that.

The only work Victoria Management ever 'managed' to get me was Theatre In Education work, an area most actors despise. It usually involves you travelling around the country performing educational plays about the inherent dangers of casual sex and drugs to completely un-arsed secondary schools students. So as a result, the only real acting I ever did was when Victoria Management would phone and I pretended to have a throat virus. Then I'd hang up the phone and go back to watching *This Morning* from under my duvet.

* When I eventually left Victoria Management, they threatened to chase me through a small claims court for an outstanding bill of £29.60 for tea and coffee money. It must be thirsty work being an agent.

I knew exactly what I wanted to do. I wanted to work in comedy. But I also realised that being an actor was tough enough without limiting yourself to just playing comic roles. Thankfully I still had money coming in from my jobs at the cinema and the arena, but I also knew I'd have to get out and push for something bigger, otherwise all I had achieved on the HND would be in vain.

I looked to my peers for inspiration. At the time Steve Coogan and John Thompson were breaking through and, as a result of entering the business via stand-up comedy, they were now recognised as comic actors.

So that's what I decided to do. If I could prove myself as a stand-up, then maybe I'd be able to do the same as them and secure some work as a comic actor. It sounded like a good plan. Now all I had to do was establish myself as a stand-up comedian – and a successful one at that.

Do you ever get one of those days when the world seems perfect? You wake up to the sound of tweeting birds, you pull back the curtains to find the sun beating down and blue skies above. Well 15th August 1996 was such a day. I felt as if I could conquer the world and his wife. Inspirational days like that don't come around very often and, totally caught up in the moment, I decided to respond to an advert that I'd seen in a copy of a local entertainment guide called *City Life*.

They were asking for all budding stand-up comedians to step up to the mic and enter a competition called The North West Comedian of the Year, whose previous winners included Caroline Aherne and Dave Spikey. Any other day I'd have read the article, pondered 'what if' and then turned to the TV page, but today was different because today the radio was playing 'Walking On

Sunshine' by Katrina and The Waves and I thought what have I got to lose?

I even surprised myself when I dialled the number at the bottom of the advert. A voice eventually answered:

'Hello this is Agraman – The Human Anagram'.

'Er . . . hello,' I said. 'My name is Peter Kay. I've just read your advert in *City Life* and wondered what do I do if I want to enter the comedy competition?'

'Have you ever done stand-up comedy before?'

'Well I did a bit at college and an open spot last year,' I said.

'Have you ever performed it professionally though?'

'No never, is that a problem?' I could feel my sun floating behind a cloud.

'No, that's exactly what we're looking for. Just fill the application form in, send it to us and we'll be in touch about a place in the heats.'

A date to appear in the heats – bloody hell! I couldn't believe what I'd just done and, as my nerves kicked in, I noticed it was starting to rain outside.

Sure enough, a few days later I got a call from *City Life* telling me the date of my heat. It was to be at a place called The Buzz Comedy Club in Chorlton, Manchester. I'd have to perform five minutes of stand-up for which I'd get £10 expenses. A tenner? I was made up just to get that.

My nerves were so bad I could hardly breathe when I turned up at The Buzz Club that hot September night. I'd travelled there by bus and, not exactly sure of where the place was, I arrived much too early. The front door was opened by a cleaner, holding a mop.

The Buzz was actually a function room situated over a pub. I sat

in that room and waited. Eventually the bar staff and Agraman –
The Human Anagram arrived. He came over and introduced
himself. I recognised his voice from the phone and he turned out
to be an amiable sort of bloke. I wasn't quite sure what all of that
anagram bollocks was about but hey! that's comedy.

Slowly the place started to fill up with a mixture of punters and
other potential stand-up comedians. They were easy to spot, as they
were the ones going in and out of the toilet with terror in their eyes,
mumbling and gesturing their material to themselves.

I managed to strike up a conversation with one of them, well, he
was a stand-up but he wasn't taking part in the heats. He was a
previous winner of the competition.

'So how many gigs have you done before tonight?' he asked.

'I've done a bit, but I've never really performed on a proper
comedy night like this before.'

Then he looked me straight in the eyes and said 'Don't you think
you're a bit out of your depth, son?' reassuringly.

Now if there's one thing that fires me up more then anything
else, it's when somebody tells me that I'm not up to a job. It was all
I needed. I was like a bull to a red rag after that.

The next bit of 'good' news was that I was on first and, as
everybody knows, first is the toughest spot of the night. The place
was almost full. I could feel myself entering a deeper level of
nervousness than I'd ever felt before. The butterflies in my stomach
were doing the Macarena and I suddenly found I couldn't speak as
my throat had dried. I reached into my rucksack and pulled out a
plastic Coke bottle filled with orange cordial. I'd swallowed a few
mouthfuls before I noticed a fierce-looking woman glaring at me
from behind the bar. I hadn't realised what I was doing, but did
now and smiled politely as I screwed the lid back on. I felt like one

of the women from the Top Rank Bingo who used to smuggle their own drinks in.

My mum had made me a packed lunch before I left, as she knew I wouldn't be having my tea. Not only had she stuck the bottle of cordial in my rucksack, but she'd also made a couple of tuna mayonnaise spread sandwiches wrapped in foil left over from Franny Lee's. But what she'd failed to tell me was that she'd written me a good luck note and stuck in between the slices of bread as a surprise. I didn't discover it until it was halfway down my throat. Choking, I ran to the toilets as Agraman – The Human Anagram came on stage and the audience applauded. He's the compère? I thought to myself as I kicked open the bog door.

Kneeling over the urinal I dragged the note out of the back of my throat: '. . . luck my darling boy' was all I could read. I appreciated the sentiment, but did she have to put it in between the bread?

The next thing I heard was Agraman – The Human Anagram shouting my name, and I realised that for a couple of seconds I'd completely forgotten the reason why I was there. I wiped the tears from my eyes and pulled open the toilet door to the sound of applause. This was it.

Everything seemed to be in slow motion as I walked through the applause towards the stage, still carrying my rucksack. It was lucky for me I did, as I was still clearing the remains of my mum's soggy note from the back of my throat and had to reach inside my bag for the bottle of cordial. By the time I'd gotten the bottle out of my bag and unscrewed the lid, the audience had already stopped applauding. I placed the bottle beside my feet and then, as I nervously adjusted the microphone stand, I accidentally knocked the bottle over. The whole room watched in silence as the contents trickled over the edge of the stage and on to the cork dance floor. I could have died and the pause felt like an eternity as I desperately searched for something to say. 'I knew I'd lose my bottle' I said, and the audience laughed. I looked round, where on earth did that come from?

Continuing to think on my feet, I decided to run with it and, picking the bottle up, I began explaining to them why I had a Coke bottle filled up with orange cordial. I told them about my mum making me a packed lunch and about the note that she'd secretly stashed in between my bread.

'I was still choking in the gents when I heard my name being announced,' I said. The sandwich incident had totally thrown me initially but, because I'd talked about it honestly, the audience seemed to warm to me and somehow find it funnier. Encouraged by their response, I decided to dig a little deeper.

'Why do mums always buy crap pop? My mum does her Friday big shop and always comes home with bottles of Rola Cola, three litres for 40p, and it tastes like floor cleaner. What's worse is the bottles are too big to go in the fridge, so now we've got crap pop that's warm.' I was going down a storm. Just like in the open spot the previous year, I didn't do any of the material that I'd prepared. I told it straight from the heart.

I continued by telling the story about the time I caught thrush from the Orangina bottle and had to endure a rectal examination by a female urologist. They loved it. So I told them about our dog Oscar and how he used to like to get his lipstick out in front of female company. They loved that too – perhaps because the stories were rooted in reality and told with conviction. I wasn't sure, but one thing I did know was that the whole thing had been a happy accident. Perhaps it had been fate that my mum had put the note in the middle of the sandwiches, who knows? Clutching my cordial, I left the stage to the sound of laughter and smiled graciously at the previous winner as I walked past him at the bar.

Eight comedians later, the judges made their announcement. I won the heat and was through to the grand final in two weeks' time. I truly couldn't believe it. It was only my third time on stage and my first time in a proper comedy club. Out of my mind with joy and fear I ran to the pay phone to tell my mum the good news – and to tell her she'd almost killed me.

The pessimist inside me made sure that the joy of victory was short lived, as I started to doubt that I'd ever be able to pull it off again. Luckily a friend of mine set me straight as we travelled home on the bus that night: 'You can't see the wood for the trees, can you? What you don't understand is that it doesn't matter if you're making people laugh in a works canteen or sat in the back of a hire car at two o'clock in the morning. And it doesn't matter if it's three people or three hundred people. You've been preparing for this your whole life. You were born to do it'.

I said 'Shit, we've missed our stop' and we had to walk home in the rain.

Three weeks after the heats I got off a bus outside the Levenshulme Palace. Personally I'm still surprised they haven't been sued under the trade descriptions, because one thing it certainly isn't is a palace, not by any stretch of the imagination. I read the large banner that had been pinned across the entrance above the doorman's head. 'Thursday 25th September – The Grand Final Of The North West Comedian Of The Year 1996.'

The first thing I noticed was that the place was packed out, and then I noticed the heat. It was stifling. I'm sure the management had cranked the boiler up in an effort to sell more drink.

Backstage Agraman – The Human Anagram had gathered all the finalists from the heats together. I remember trying to make small talk with the other comedians, but they weren't having any of it. I put this down to nerves at first, but sadly over the next few months I was to discover that a large number of stand-up comedians are vicious, two-faced bastards with egos the size of Belgium and hearts the size of fly shit.

An exception was the compère that night, another comedian from Bolton and previous winner of the competition, Dave Spikey. It turned out he worked in the haematology department at Bolton General Hospital and was just doing stand-up at the weekends. We hit it off straight away. Chatting about living in Bolton and comedy, we quickly discovered that our sense of humour was very similar. Who knew at that point what the future held for us both?

Each of the finalists had to pick a name out of a hat to decide the running order. I have no idea whose hat it was, but as luck would have it, I was to be the last act on the bill.

Now most people, including myself, would consider being last on any bill the best spot of the evening. But when the bill consists of twelve comedians whose acts are of varying lengths and quality, and you're stuck in a room for over four hours with the heat intensity of equatorial Africa, then being last on that particular bill isn't very good at all.

Odds on favourite with the bookies that night was a comedian from St Helens called Johnny Vegas, and he was a powerhouse. The place was in uproar at the very mention of his name, and an aching desperation fell over me as the audience began chanting his name 'Johnny, Johnny'. He leapt from his seat and charged the stage like a rhino in flares. Clutching a copy of *City Life* (who were sponsoring the event), he shouted out '*City Life*? You mean Shitty

Life'. The audience went wild as I leaned over to my friend Michael and said 'If we go now, I think we can catch the last bus'. So far as I was concerned, the verdict was signed, sealed and delivered. Mr Vegas was a comic triumph. I'd never seen anything like it in my life before or since.

I was a total wreck and the night seemed to be taking forever. I swear the brewery clock on the wall was turning backwards when Dave Spikey announced yet another interval. The audience was now more than a little worse for wear. Drunk and overheated, their patience had worn thin and they were merciless with the act that preceded me. Sister Henrietta Boom-Boom, the roller-skating nun, had travelled all the way from the Isle of Man to be in the final and was dying a death.

It was hard for the audience to hit a moving target as she wheeled back and forth around the stage singing songs about the crucifixion and playing the ukulele. I don't think the audience hated her because she was blasphemous, I think it was because they were tired and she was shit.

I wasn't relishing the idea of performing in front of an angry mob. I paced around backstage with the sweat pouring off me, the running order of my material racing through my head. I had been through my set a million times the last three weeks. I'd performed it over and over for anyone and anything that would listen. Even a woman waiting with me at the bus stop got a free performance.

I knew what I had to do, but I was quickly losing all confidence in my material, just like at the open spot when I'd over rehearsed. Suddenly my opening gag seemed stilted and weak. This audience was asleep. They needed grabbing by the balls and shaking, so at the eleventh hour I had an idea: to reverse the running order of my act. I decided to begin with my big finish and worry about the rest later.

I could hear Dave Spikey through the stage curtain: 'Give it up for Sister Henrietta Boom-Boom, ladies and gentleman, all the way from the Isle of Man. Have a safe journey back, Sister. Now let's keep things moving and, don't worry, there's just one more act to go.' I thought, cheers Dave, that'll get them whipped up into a frenzy. 'Please will you welcome all the way from my hometown of Bolton, your last act tonight, Peter Kay.'

Then the weirdest thing happened. Just as I was about to go on, Sister Henrietta Boom-Boom wheeled past me in floods of tears and grabbed my hand. 'Knock 'em dead, my child' she said and skated off. Her hand was cold and, seeing her stood in front of me dressed as a nun, I was transported back to my childhood for a split second. That it should happen just as I was about to walk on stage was even weirder. Maybe it was divine intervention.

I ran on stage, grabbed the microphone off Dave and said 'Why is it every time you go to a wedding reception all you see for the first hour are kids doing this on the dance floor?' And then running across the huge wooden stage, I dropped to my knees and slid the rest of the way on the floor. I was right; it was just what the audience needed. I'd lit the blue touch paper, now all I had to do was stand back (or up, as the case may be).

I hit them with all I'd got in the ten minutes I was allowed. I told them about the robbery at the Cash and Carry. I told them about the time I accidentally pushed the panic button at the garage whilst trying to steal some Juicy Fruit. I told them about the epileptic guy at the cinema and how we hid him from the kids behind a cardboard cut out of Flipper. I told them about growing up, about my family, about my life. I knew it would all come in handy some day.

Other comedians talked about sex, drugs and drink, but I didn't drink, I'd never done drugs and if I had talked about sex my mum would have battered me senseless out of embarrassment. So I talked about what I knew best, myself, and it proved to be a breath of fresh air.

Fifteen minutes later I was stood in the gents waiting for the judges' decision. This was more nerve-wracking than the build up to the performance. Based on the reaction I'd got from the audience, the best I could hope for would be second to Johnny Vegas.

I could hear Dave Spikey reading out the results through the toilet door. I can't remember who was third, but I know for a fact that it wasn't Sister Henrietta Boom-Boom. My heart leapt just before Dave read out the second name, but it was Johnny Vegas. I was disappointed. 'Bloody hell, I didn't even make it into the top three'. Then my mate Michael looked at me and said 'You've won, it's you' and Dave read out my name. I'd won.

That's the last I can remember. I've sat for the past few minutes and thought about what happened, but honestly it's all a total blur. I had quite a bit of support in from Bolton that night, family and friends. One of my friends had an Audi convertible for some illegal reason I can't remember and we drove back to Bolton with the roof down in the moonlight. I sat in the back singing 'Don't Look Back In Anger' as loud as I could, clutching a bottle of champagne and a cheque for £125. Happy days.

I gave the champagne to a local hospice for a raffle and bought *The Beatles Anthology* boxed set on VHS for myself. Well, I think I deserved a treat.

The day after I got a call from Agraman – The Human Anagram. He congratulated me on winning the competition and asked if I'd be interested in doing twenty minutes stand-up at a club called The Boardwalk in Manchester. He said he could offer me £30 and would I be interested? I almost did a back flip for the second time in my life, but I'd put a bit of weight on since we'd bought our first video recorder.

£30 for twenty minutes work? I couldn't get my head around it. I worked four shifts at the cinema every week and I still didn't get that. Things were certainly starting to change.

An Epilogue

Ding Dong! Was that the doorbell again? You can never be too sure. Only this time I was expecting the doorbell to ring. It was my new driving instructor and this one actually seemed to know what he was doing, or perhaps at last I was finally getting the hang of it all. He'd been taking me for lessons over the summer and now said he felt confident about putting me in for my test. Fifth time lucky?

It's bad enough when you fail the first or second time. Family and friends will always try to comfort you by saying things like 'look at your Uncle Tony, he passed third time', but when it gets to your fifth time their references have run out and the silence is unbearable. Nobody knows anybody who's *that* crap at driving.

I'd just become indifferent to the whole 'learning to drive' thing. The excitement had long gone and I'd been round the block, quite literally, so many times that Bolton council had built a completely new contraflow system.

I remember Raymond saying to me on my first lesson that it'd take time for everything to click into place. I just never imagined it would take five tests, six years and a hundred and sixty seven lessons.

The point is, I couldn't have cared less whether I passed or not when the examiner took me out for my test that day. I was still high from winning the competition and maybe that was the reason I passed.

'I've what?'

'You've passed, Mr Kay' he said.

I remember staring at him for a few seconds and then I tried to mount him. The other examiners gave me a round of applause. I knew them all by now and they were no doubt sick of the sight of me. I can't describe to you the feeling of joy I felt when I finally passed my test. It was such a relief, I cried. Nobody deserved to pass more than me that day.

I once sat down and calculated how much I'd spent on learning to drive. I'll not disclose the eventual figure I arrived at but, suffice to say, I could have bought myself an Audi convertible.

That night I went out to celebrate both passing my test and my best friend's birthday. We ended up in a nightclub in town and to say I was in a good mood would be putting it mildly. I was wired to the moon.

Now I've not really talked to you much about the girls in my life. There were a few and I quite literally mean a few. I always ended up falling into the 'just good friends' category, so I finally decided to give up looking for love. I was tired of waiting for the right girl to come along – in fact I was tired of waiting for 'a' girl to come along. So after winning the competition, I made a conscious decision to concentrate on my new career.

They say 'love always hits you when you least expect it' and that happened quite literally to me, as I bounced off the bonnet of her car at the traffic lights. I'm joking of course. I met her in the club that night and on our second date I decided to take her ice-skating in Blackburn and I slipped and broke my arm in two places. Luckily the whole disaster worked out for the best as the girl took pity on my incompetence and eventually she married me (I hasten to add there was a five year gap between the broken arm and the wedding day). And, if I'm right, this is where my story began in Chapter One.

I'd come to the conclusion that Leonard was right, life *is* like waiting for a bus. Nothing happens for ages and then three come all at once. I mean, what a week! I'd finally met the love of my life, passed my driving test and won The North West Comedian Of The Year.

I thought about what Sister Sledge had said to me all those years before, just after I cocked my leg up on the tree during *The Wizard of Oz*. 'Is that what you're going to be when you grow up, a comedian?' Back then what I had really wanted to say was 'Yes, Sister, it is' and now I finally could.